'The EU and NATO are the two "big beasts" of Europe's international relations but the systematic study of their interorganisational relationship has been relatively neglected. This volume provides overdue insight into the puzzle as to why the EU-NATO interrelationship has been troubled. Ewers-Peters, by focusing on the role of states that share membership of both organisations, provides us with an empirically-rich and comprehensive analysis that significantly enhances our understanding of the EU-NATO dynamic'.

– *Richard G. Whitman, University of Kent, UK*

'*Understanding EU-NATO Cooperation: How Member States Matter* offers the reader a systemic account of how member states shape EU-NATO cooperation. It enriches the EU-NATO literature, and the interorganisational cooperation literature more broadly, through its detailed account of an understudied question, namely, the ways in which member states can circumvent legal and institutional barriers to shape EU-NATO cooperation. In showing how member states contribute to the dysfunctionality of EU-NATO relations, Ewers-Peters' book will be of considerable interest to scholars of European security'.

– *Jocelyn Mawdsley, Newcastle University, UK*

'NATO and the EU have many common members and share similar goals, yet they often act as if they are on different planets. Understanding why this is so means knowing more about how member states shape each organization's priorities. Nele Marianne Ewers-Peters breaks new ground with her insights into the crucial role of individual member states in NATO-EU dynamics. A valuable book for practitioners and theorists alike'.

– *Daniel S. Hamilton, Johns Hopkins University, US*

'Most analyses on the troubled relationship between NATO and the EU focus their attention on a few actors whose frozen positions arguably stand in the way of a constructive and cooperative future. In this well-crafted monograph, Nele Marianne Ewers-Peters adds depth and nuance to this well-trodden path by setting up a highly innovative framework for understanding all member states' positions on the relationship. The book elegantly draws on interorganizational theory and identity perspectives to add a much needed conceptual and theoretical perspective for understanding not only the limitations, but also the opportunities in the NATO-EU relationship'.

– *Trine Flockhart, University of Southern Denmark*

'European security has been shaped since the end of the Cold War by two international bodies: the EU and NATO. Despite their seemingly overlapping objectives, an efficient and effective relationship has yet to develop between the two organisations. The reason may seem obvious – that NATO and the EU have overlapping but differentiated memberships. Obvious, it may be, but until now the implications of differentiation have not been fully explored. Nele Marianne Ewers-Peters takes a comprehensive look at the member countries of the EU and NATO – how some states facilitate inter-organisational cooperation and how some block it. The analysis is sustained and forensic. We may bemoan the NATO-EU relationship, but we no longer have the excuse that we don't understand why it remains so dysfunctional'.

– Mark Webber, University of Birmingham, UK

Understanding EU–NATO Cooperation

This book examines the development of cooperation between the EU and NATO, two key non-state actors in the European security architecture.

It also examines the relationship between the EU and NATO by focusing on the perspective of member states. Highlighting the relevance of member states' role in shaping EU–NATO relations, it conceptualises interorganisational cooperation and develops a typology of member states based on four types: advocates, blockers, balancers and neutrals. To apply this typology and analyse member states' specific roles, the analysis considers their foreign and security policy orientations, bilateral relationships with other member states and contributions to both military operations and division of labour between the two organisations. The book also examines states' use of political strategies – such as forum-shopping, hostage-taking and brokering – that influence the design, evolution and practicalities of cooperation between the EU and NATO.

This book will be of much interest to students of European Security and Defence Policy, international organisations and security studies in general.

Nele Marianne Ewers-Peters is a postdoctoral researcher at Johns Hopkins School of Advanced International Studies, USA, and a lecturer at Leuphana University Lüneburg, Germany.

Understanding EU–NATO Cooperation

How Member States Matter

Nele Marianne Ewers-Peters

Routledge
Taylor & Francis Group

LONDON AND NEW YORK

First published 2022
by Routledge
2 Park Square, Milton Park, Abingdon, Oxon OX14 4RN

and by Routledge
605 Third Avenue, New York, NY 10158

Routledge is an imprint of the Taylor & Francis Group, an informa business

© 2022 Nele Marianne Ewers-Peters

British Library Cataloguing-in-Publication Data
A catalogue record for this book is available from the British Library

Library of Congress Cataloging-in-Publication Data
A catalog record has been requested for this book

ISBN: 978-0-367-77159-1 (hbk)
ISBN: 978-0-367-77161-4 (pbk)
ISBN: 978-1-003-17006-8 (ebk)

DOI: 10.4324/9781003170068

Typeset in Times New Roman
by Newgen Publishing UK

Contents

Figures

Tables

Acknowledgements

This book was written and finalised during my DAAD Postdoctoral Research Fellowship at Paul H. Nitze School of Advanced International Studies (SAIS) at Johns Hopkins University, Washington, DC, amidst the unusual time of the Covid-19 pandemic, the US elections in 2020 and the shifts in the European and international security order. The majority of this book was finalised during yet another lockdown in my hometown in Northern Germany and while under quarantine in Washington, DC. Revisiting a book about EU–NATO cooperation during a time when direct interactions are absent, personal exchanges are restricted and where one is confined to limited personal space made me ponder about what international cooperation might look like in the future. What is more, the experience of virtual events and meetings, that are very likely to remain in place at least for the foreseeable future, actually made me wonder how this will contribute to strengthening exchanges and interactions on an international level. In fact, should online formats not facilitate cooperation between states and between organisations? The ease of calling and messaging someone as well as the greater inclusivity of people from across the transatlantic should be much easier than ever before. The Covid-19 pandemic has once again shown how crucial international cooperation is for the wellbeing of people as well as for peace and security. It is thus still surprising to see on a daily basis, how states counteract and pursue their national preferences over the common good. And this is also what drove this research from the very beginning: why certain states do not play by the book and what greater implications result from their behaviour. I am grateful and proud to present my research findings in this book and to make them available for everyone interested in learning more about EU–NATO cooperation.

Special thanks to the civilian and military staff at the EEAS, NATO headquarters and the member states' delegations and missions to the EU and NATO for participating in interviews and allowing me to gain profound insights. Their generosity, time, expertise and interest in my research have made a major contribution and without their participation and sharing of valuable knowledge, this book would have not been possible. I also would like to thank the University of Kent, Addressing Needs in Teaching and Research in EU Foreign Policy (ANTERO) Jean Monnnet Network for European Foreign Policy, the University Association for Contemporary European Studies (UACES) and the German Academic Exchange Service (DAAD) for their generous funding and scholarships that allowed me to conduct the research. In addition, my thanks go to the three anonymous reviewers for their engagement with my manuscript and their valuable comments and feedback.

My sincerest gratitude and appreciation go first and foremost to my supervisors, Prof. Trine Flockhart, Dr. Toni Haastrup and Prof. Richard G. Whitman, for their continuous support, motivation and intellectual debates throughout my PhD journey. Their challenging questions, encouragement and invaluable feedback made this book what it is today. All of you have been – and still are – great mentors and I have been extremely lucky to have you as my supervisory team, who cared for me and ensured that I always stayed on the right track.

For their enduring support, intellectual exchanges and laughter, I am grateful to have been part of the PhD and academic communities at the University of Kent, Katholieke Universiteit Leuven, University College London and SAIS at Johns Hopkins. I would not want to miss the many hours spent together in our little office at Kent, followed by the occasional pint in the pub. I also would like to thank UACES and its Graduate Forum and the BISA European Security Working Group, who all provided great platforms to engage with like-minded and other young researchers across the UK and Europe. They allowed me to be a part of a thriving community and provided invaluable feedback and support at numerous conferences, workshops and beyond. My thanks also go to my supervisors in the research programme 'The United States, Europe, and World Order' at SAIS, Dr. Daniel S. Hamilton and Prof. Andreas Rödder, for their insights, support and wise words.

Finally, very special thanks go to my family – my parents, to my brothers and to my 'auntie' in Germany. Thank you for your unconditional love and faith in me. This also counts for my second family in New Zealand who always check on me and do not shy away from expressing their pride. A huge shout-out goes to my friends from near and far. Without their support, encouragements and urgently needed distractions throughout this journey, I would have not made it this far. *Merci, dass es euch gibt.*

Abbreviations

AFISMA	African-led International Support Mission in Mali
ASEAN	Association of Southeast Asian Nations
AU	African Union
CARD	Coordinated Annual Review on Defence
CDP	Capability Development Plan
CEU	Council of the European Union
CFSP	Common Foreign and Security Policy
CJTF	Combined Joint Task Forces
CMPD	Crisis Management and Planning Directorate
CSDP	Common Security and Defence Policy
DCI	Defence Capability Initiative
DPC	Defence Planning Committee
DRC	Democratic Republic of Congo
DSACEUR	Deputy Supreme Allied Commander Europe
EAPC	Euro-Atlantic Partnership Council
EATC	European Air Transport Command
EATF	European Air Transport Fleet
ECAP	European Capabilities Action Plan
EDA	European Defence Agency
EDF	European Defence Fund
EEAS	European External Action Service
EI2	European Intervention Initiative
EPF	European Peace Facility
ESDI	European Security and Defence Identity
ESDP	European Security and Defence Policy
ESS	European Security Strategy
EU	European Union
EUBG	European Union Battlegroup
EUFOR	European Union Force
EUGS	European Union Global Security Strategy
EUISS	European Union Institute for Security Studies
EUMC	European Union Military Committee
FPA	Framework Participation Agreement

FNC	Framework Nation Concept
FYRoM	Former Yugoslav Republic of Macedonia
GDP	Gross Domestic Product
HR	High Representative of the Union for Foreign and Security Policy of the EU
IEA	International Energy Agency
IMF	International Monetary Fund
ISAF	International Security Assistance Force
MPCC	Military Planning and Conduct Capability
NAC	North Atlantic Council
NATO	North Atlantic Treaty Organisation
NORDAC	Nordic Armaments Cooperation
NORDCAPS	Nordic Coordinated Arrangement for Military Peace Support
NORDEFCO	Nordic Defence Cooperation
NORDSUP	Nordic Supportive Defence Structures
NORTART	Nordic Tactic Air Transport
NRF	NATO Response Force
OPEC	Organisation of the Petrolium Exporting Countries
OSCE	Organisation for Security and Cooperation in Europe
PESCO	Permanent Structured Cooperation
PfP	Partnership for Peace
PSC	Political and Security Committee
SACEUR	Supreme Allied Commander Europe
SFOR	Stabilisation Force
SHAPE	Supreme Headquarters Allied Powers Europe
SIPRI	Stockholm International Peace Research Institute
TEU	Treaty on the European Union
TFEU	Treaty on the Functioning of the European Union
UK	United Kingdom
UN	United Nations
US	United States of America
WEAG	Western European Armaments Group
WEU	Western European Union
WTO	World Trade Organisation

1 Introduction

Since the end of the Cold War, Europe has found itself in the midst of simmering conflicts and crises in its near and wider neighbourhood. Increasing numbers of international actors have become involved in the crises that mark today's security environment in Europe. An increasing number of international and regional organisations have been created including the UN, the NATO, the EU and the OSCE, who have all done their stint in securing Europe and its borders from external threats. Interestingly, states often prefer to create new organisations with overlapping functions and mandates in the same policy area instead of reforming the existing ones, thus adding to the growing proliferation of international and regional security organisations (Eilstrup-Sangiovanni 2020; Hofmann 2019). It would be naive to believe, however, that these organisations have the same share in contributing to peace, security and stability and that they maintain closer ties among each other. One salient example in which two overlapping organisations have forged exchanges and interactions in the Euro-Atlantic space is the relationship between the EU and NATO.

With the emergence and development of European capabilities and policies in the field of foreign, security and defence affairs through the introduction of the CFSP and CSDP in the Treaty of Maastricht in 1991, new questions of division of labour and institutional overlaps arose. What has been most striking is the question of why it has become necessary to create new structures and capacities alongside NATO's already existing military planning structures and capabilities and how the co-existence of similar security organisations in Europe will look like – will they cooperate or compete with each other. In fact, not only do the EU and NATO cover a similar geographical scope and share common norms and values, but above all, they share a high degree of membership overlap: 21 of NATO's 30 member states are also members of the EU. In addition, the two organisations have a similar origin: the idea to formalise cooperation among states in the Euro-Atlantic region to prevent future conflicts and deter new aggression in the aftermath of the Second World War.

In the study of international organisations and their interactions with each other in the same policy field, member states play a crucial role in designing, shaping and controlling the direction of external relationships.

DOI: 10.4324/9781003170068-1

Inevitably, questions that arise from this perspective concern the position of states in interorganisational relations and their contribution to shaping and directing the EU–NATO relationship. What roles do member states take in the relationship between the EU and NATO in the area of foreign, security and defence affairs? What is more, considering the developments of the EU–NATO relationship since the end of the Cold War; how do member states contribute to the functionality and dysfunctionality of this particular relationship?

Even though the literature on EU–NATO cooperation to date has mushroomed to examine their relationship from different perspectives, including the historical developments, practical cooperation in crisis management operations, the institutional structures as well as competition (see, for example, de Wijk 2004; Duke 2008; Flockhart 2011; Gebhard and Smith 2015; Græger 2016; Græger and Haugevik 2011; Hofmann 2009; Howorth and Keeler 2003; Major and Mölling 2009; Muratore 2010; Ojanen 2006; Reichard 2006; Smith 2011; Whitman 2004), this literature does not put a greater emphasis on the role of member states in shaping the EU–NATO relationship. This book contributes to the ongoing debate on cooperation among international organisations in the field of foreign, security and defence policy by focusing on the EU–NATO relationship and the particular role of member states. The first aim is thus to contribute to the understanding of the evolution, structures and interactions of EU–NATO cooperation. The time frame of interest for this study is from the end of the Cold War in 1991 to 2021, covering three decades of the development of this particular relationship. While looking at this special interorganisational cooperation, the role of member states will be at the centre of attention. This research thus examines the means that member states have at their disposal to circumvent institutional and legal barriers to shape EU–NATO cooperation.

The second purpose of this book is to contribute to the advancement of the theoretical approaches to the study of interorganisational cooperation. Conceptualising and theorising interorganisational relations in the International Relations Scholarship went a long way, although neither a common approach nor a clear conceptualisation exists. The present theoretical framework takes into account existing understandings and conceptualisations of international cooperation and foreign and security policy orientation, while also considering different theoretical approaches, such as interorganisationalism, network theory and international regime complexity. Developing a set of features of interorganisational interaction then helps to develop the typology of member states in interorganisational relations, which facilitates the analysis of the EU–NATO relationship from the member state perspective.

Since the EU and NATO share a high degree of overlap in their membership and in their functions, mandates and security policies, as well as some complementary and inter-bureaucratic institutional structures, the question remains why the two organisations still do not get on the way one would expect them based on these overlaps. As argued in this book, the very reason for the dysfunctionality of the EU–NATO relationship, at least to some extent, is found in states' behaviours, attitudes and approaches to using their membership in both organisations. While some states are outspoken supporters of the Atlantic Alliance – the so-called Atlanticists – others are labelled as Europeanists, that is, those favouring the EU's approach to crisis management (Cornish and Edwards 2001: 589). Yet, this categorisation does not ultimately explain what role states actually play in EU–NATO cooperation. The endeavour to examine the role of member states is thus guided by the following questions: *why and how do member states contribute to the (dys-)functionality of the EU–NATO interorganisational relationship? How do different national features shape member states' roles and positions in the relationship between the EU and NATO?* In this context, national features refer to member states' historical experiences, domestic particularities and restraints, geopolitical location and military capabilities. Given that states have varying perceptions, positions, ambitions and capabilities as well as differences in their bilateral and minilateral relations with other member states, this research further addresses the question: *how do states' use of minilateral and bilateral relationships affect EU–NATO cooperation?*

This book provides a new angle to the interorganisational relationship between the EU and NATO by exploring the different positions of member states. It argues that member states play a crucial role in steering and influencing the direction of the EU–NATO relationship based on their national attributes, foreign and security policy orientation and their partnerships with other member states in the Euro-Atlantic security community. States' bilateral and minilateral relationships as well as inter-state tensions strongly impact the developments and evolution of this interorganisational relationship. The state of the art of their relationship and the degree of enhanced cooperation between these two international security organisations has been an achievement by their secretariats, by individual key players and by their member states. The EU–NATO relationship has so far not yet yielded in any further formalisation as challenges and obstacles are still observable, which are primarily created and maintained by member states. The goal of this book is, therefore, to illustrate how member states are guided by their political strategies and foreign and security policy orientations on the one hand and by their capabilities, relationships and active engagement in security and defence affairs within the respective international security organisations on the other hand. By examining the role of member states in the EU–NATO relationship, this book seeks to enhance the scholarly work in these fields of study by adding the perspective of member states to the analysis. To investigate the particular roles and contributions of member states, a broader understanding of the EU–NATO relationship is required. In order to do so, this introductory chapter pictures the historical and institutional developments of their relationship and highlights why member states need to receive greater considerations.

The EU–NATO relationship in perspective

The relationship between the EU and NATO has experienced many rollercoaster moments since the beginning of their interactions. While it has seen constant progress, there have also been periods of stagnation. Both Howorth (2009) and Flockhart (2014) even claim that their relationship was not only unsatisfactory but also dysfunctional, and therefore, 'the political relationship between NATO and the EU requires careful thought and management' (Moens 2003: 32). Their relationship has consequently been summarised by Flockhart (2014: 75) in the following:

> In a nutshell, the EU-NATO relationship has been summarised as a relationship that has developed from parallel but separate existences during the Cold War, to intense interinstitutional rivalry during the 1990s, to a 'strategic partnership' defined by the EU-NATO Declaration on European Security and Defence Policy in 2002, but ending as a 'frozen conflict' following the admission of Cyprus to the EU in 2004.

The development of the EU–NATO relationship has its origins in informal meetings, which first took place in 1997 between then NATO Secretary General Javier Solana, European Commission Jacques Santer and Commissioner Hans van den Broek (Reichard 2006). With the appointment of Javier Solana as Secretary General of the Council of the EU and the Union's first High Representative in June 1999 and former British Defence Secretary George Robertson as NATO Secretary General in the same year, informal talks were continued during lunch meetings. This framework of interactions helped to further advance EU–NATO cooperation informally and to pave the way for a closer relationship. Both individuals took a very proactive approach in both EU–NATO cooperation and crisis management. Their personal relationship as well as their common interest in finding a joint approach to solve the Balkan conflicts, which were simmering at the Euro-Atlantic community's external border, have created a window of opportunity for 'some kind of EU–NATO institutional connection' (Reichard 2006: 123). Especially Javier Solana and George Robertson, as well as former US ambassador to NATO Alexander Vershbow, envisaged a permanent institutionalisation between the two organisations in the future (de Wijk 2004; Reichard 2006; Vershbow 1999). In fact, the best period of cooperation between the EU and NATO has been perceived during the 'Solana-Robertson connection', as it was the first time that organisations, instead of states, undertook joint efforts to solve a conflict. What is more, they were more interested in solving the issue than in the bureaucracy in Brussels (NATO Official 3).

In the late 1990s and early 2000s, informal meetings and exchanges took place between the EU and NATO on all levels[1]. The first informal meeting between the PSC and the NAC was held on 19 September 2000, which subsequently led to a routine of three meetings per year. Informal exchanges also occurred between the Head of the EU Interim Military Staff and NATO's DSACEUR since March 2000 (Messervy-Whiting 2005). These exchanges then triggered meetings at other levels, for example, at the ministerial level in May 2001, and between the organisation's military committees in the same year. Throughout their interactions, the meetings between the PSC and NAC 'became the key meeting format in all important areas of cooperation' (Reichard 2006: 126). Once both organisations became more familiar with their counterparts and had the chance to build up trust, learned about each other's procedures and modalities and internalised a routine of exchanges, relations started to become more formal (EU Official 1). As illustrated by the step-by-step rapprochement through several arrangements, agreements and declarations, EU–NATO cooperation moved 'from a parallel to a more integrated relationship' (Schleich 2014: 187).

One of the first steps towards formalising the EU–NATO relationship was the signing of the EU–NATO Declaration on ESDP on 16 December 2002, which supported the EU to achieve its capability goals as set out in its Headline Goals (HG) and helped to improve the EU–NATO relationship as a whole (NATO 2002). According to the 2002 Declaration, their cooperation shall be based on the principles of partnership, mutual consultation, equality, respect for each other's member states and the development of military capabilities benefitting both organisations. It further contains provisions concerning the involvement of non-EU European NATO members within the EU's security and defence policy. The 2002 Declaration labels the EU–NATO relationship as a 'strategic partnership', giving it an even greater importance as well as providing enough 'room for manoeuvre and flexibility' for both organisations (Touzovskaia 2006). However, some member states were not pleased with the wide scope of cooperation as they feared that NATO might be able to restrict the EU in the pursuit of its security and defence policy (NATO Official 2).

In the following year, both organisations focused on capability improvements for crisis management operations. In May 2003, the NATO–EU Capability Group was established to address shortfalls and ensure coherence in developing and acquiring capabilities. Resulting from exchanges of letters between Solana and Robertson, the EU and NATO eventually agreed on the so-called Berlin Plus arrangements in 2003, which are classified and thus not available to the public. The negotiations leading to these arrangements made reference to the already existing arrangements under the Berlin Accords between NATO and the WEU from 1996 as well as to the latter's (and the EU's) crisis management capacities and responsibilities as outlined in the Petersberg Tasks (NATO 1996; also see WEU 1992). More serious discussions began at the Washington summit of the Alliance in 1999, where NATO allies agreed on the provisions for making NATO military assets and capabilities available for EU-led operations (NATO 1999). As it had already outlined in the 1999 Helsinki Presidency Conclusions, the EU desired to conduct military crisis management operations 'where NATO as a whole does not get engaged' (EU 1999). However, it did not have adequate capabilities to do so, but with the Berlin Plus arrangements it would move closer to conducting autonomous military operations in its near proximity. According to the Berlin Plus arrangements, NATO assures the EU access to its military capabilities and assets for crisis management operations, including its planning capability. They further include consultation arrangements on the use of capabilities as well as on discussing further capability requirements. With the formalising of consultations and the use of capabilities, the Berlin Plus arrangements were thus perceived as a major breakthrough and 'landmark' for EU–NATO relations as they outline more concretely the principles for practical cooperation (CEU 2003; Ojanen 2006; Reichard 2004, 2006).

Despite the efforts on the institutional and staff-to-staff levels as well as on the operational level, as demonstrated in FYRoM/North Macedonia[2] and Bosnia and Herzegovina, the period of EU–NATO relations between 2004 and 2014 was labelled as a 'frozen conflict' and 'the end of the honeymoon' (Flockhart 2014: 75, 84; also see Acikmese and Triantaphyllou 2012: 564; Hofmann and Reynolds 2007: 2). Both organisations acknowledged the mutual benefits of their relationship but were not able to overcome a number of intervening political obstacles (Smith 2011). First, with the EU's big bang enlargement in 2004, Cyprus joined the club whilst facing a veto from Turkey concerning closer cooperation with NATO. The so-called *Cyprus issue* has been named as one of the most insurmountable obstacles to date, yet it is not the only issue posed by member states that create problems for EU–NATO cooperation (Reichard 2006; Smith and Gebhard 2017). Second, national interests have obstructed in pushing closer EU–NATO cooperation forward. While some states prefer enhanced cooperation, others perceive it as a threat to the EU's autonomy due to the dominance of NATO. In contrast, the push by some EU member states, notably France, for European strategic autonomy has been perceived as undermining NATO's role in European security and defence. The diverging strategic interests and threat perceptions by member states in both the EU and NATO create additional tensions within the organisations that disallow exchanges and cooperative endeavours (cf. Zięba 2018). Third, operational conduct depends on military actors and their capabilities. However, these are guided by the principles given by policymakers. If the latter are not able to agree on the legal and institutional frameworks for cooperation, the former cannot act. The same accounts for their capabilities and capacities; if adequate resources are not available, the actors cannot engage. Lastly, the 'participation problem' relating to the deadlock created by the Cyprus issue and the hostage-taking concerning Cyprus and Turkey's memberships cause a profound hurdle for EU–NATO cooperation. Consequently, most exchanges occur on the international staff-to-staff level through the office of the DSACEUR, where 'the "real business" of EU–NATO cooperation is being sustained, especially with regard to facilitating informal cooperation for non-Berlin Plus operations where both organisations are deployed' (Smith 2011: 244–245). Most information exchanges and practical cooperation still occur through informal channels on the lowest level of cooperation and on practical issues (Duke 2008; Græger 2016, 2017).

The year 2016 played a crucial part in many regards for the relationship between the EU and NATO. On 28 June 2016, the High Representative of the European Union for Foreign Affairs and Security Policy Federica Mogherini presented the EU Global Strategy at the EU Summit in Brussels (EU 2016). A few weeks later, on 9 July 2016, the President of the European Council, the President of the European Commission and the Secretary General of NATO adopted the Joint Declaration at the NATO Summit in Warsaw (NATO 2016a). While this does not embody an official cooperation and partnership agreement, it presents a major milestone for revitalising and raising the significance of this interorganisational relationship. It reaffirms the strengthening of the EU–NATO relationship and highlights the need to foster cooperation for enhancing European security. In the follow-up, the EU and NATO agreed on the implementation plan on 6 December 2016, which sets out the practical realisation of their cooperation efforts. Cooperation has thus shifted to seven key areas: (1) countering hybrid threats, (2) operational cooperation including maritime issues, (3) cyber security and defence, (4) defence capabilities, (5) defence industry and research, (6) exercises and (7) defence and security capacity building (CEU 2016). Within these areas of cooperation, 42 concrete actions have been agreed upon to be implemented, which are monitored through frequent progress reports every six months. To ensure further advances and to create new incentives for cooperation, the Council of the EU and the NAC agreed additional 34 actions in December 2017 (NATO 2018). EU–NATO cooperation now seems to be an implemented norm and a daily practice, as shown by the participation of each other's ministerial meetings and frequent consultations. Although progress in all areas of cooperation has been recorded, both organisations acknowledge that most proposals and actions have a long-term perspective that require continuous efforts and the need to intensify cooperation between the EU and NATO on both institutional and operational levels.

On the EU side, the introduction of the EUGS in 2016 and the establishment of new mechanisms also contributed to furthering cooperation with NATO. The EUGS equips the EU with strategic guidance in its foreign, security and defence policy, for which the partnership with NATO plays a vital part for Europe's security. At the same time, the EU seeks to act autonomously and therefore wishes to devise and strengthen its autonomy while concurrently acting in cooperation with NATO (EU 2016). As already outlined in the 2009 Lisbon Treaty, the EU envisioned new tools and mechanisms that were eventually introduced in 2017, such as the European Defence Fund (EDF), the Military Planning and Conduct Capacity (MPCC), the Coordinated Annual Review on Defence (CARD) and Permanent Structured Cooperation (PESCO). These mechanisms and instruments aim at improving European states' defence capacities and capabilities through joint procurement projects and working towards integrated forces, combining pooling, sharing and dividing tasks and responsibilities (Biscop 2017). Nevertheless, the establishment of PESCO has led to criticism concerning the future of EU–NATO cooperation due to the renewed idea of a European army and the risk of duplication. However, such concerns were annihilated by Mogherini who emphasised that these mechanisms are seen as complementary and will serve to enhance the EU's capability to make cooperation with NATO more effective and fruitful (EEAS 2018).

With the most recent events – especially the signing of the Joint Declaration by the President of the European Commission, the President of the European Council and the Secretary General of NATO in July 2016 and the subsequent implementation plans in 2016 and 2018 – and newly shared security threats and challenges coming from their Eastern and Southern borders, this relationship has experienced a revival. These events gave the relationship not only a new direction, but also a new momentum for future cooperation. While these achievements sound prosperous and promising, new challenges and obstacles have emerged for the EU–NATO relationship. Bilateral disputes among member states, such as the tensions between Austria and Turkey as well as between the latter and both Germany and the Netherlands, have disallowed a new stimulus and even posed new obstacles that need to be considered in implementing the proposals (NATO Official 1). Moreover, the changes on the domestic level in some member states, for example, the UK's decision to leave the EU in 2016 that was finalised in 2020 (the so-called Brexit), Donald Trump's presidency and the open critique of NATO and security partnerships, France's renewed drive for European strategic autonomy under Emmanuel Macron as well as new types of external security threats coming from both the East and the South put additional strains on the EU–NATO relationship, affecting the future of their cooperation.

Key challenges and obstacles

Some of the key challenges are of institutional nature; others have emerged from divergences in the organisations' approaches to security and defence, the increasing overlap of activities and responsibilities and tensions among their member states. One of the often-cited problems is the institutional nature of the EU–NATO relationship and the 'problem of institutional incompatibility' (Gebhard and Smith 2015: 113). Actors within NATO are not sure of their counterparts in the EU security and defence structure and whom to address in particular circumstances. Despite the similar structures, communication between the respective organisations has also not been labelled as successful. Consequently, EU–NATO relations are faced with the absence of arrangements regarding communication, cooperation and command (Gebhard and Smith 2015; Smith 2011). Nevertheless, over the years, informal working procedures have allowed bureaucrats on both sides to identify their counterparts and create a working routine with more frequent exchanges (Græger 2016). With the higher frequency of exchanges supported by the Joint Declaration, staff on both sides found a working routine of interacting with their counterparts that helped to advance towards a common agenda (EU Official 2; NATO Official 3).

Several additional obstacles and challenges have been identified, including the lack of a level playing field and differences in the military capabilities of both organisations as well as gaps in capabilities, sovereignty, leadership procurement and technology, which prevent a well-functioning EU–NATO relationship. These challenges particularly have an impact on interoperability and the division of labour between the two organisations (cf. Bialos 2005; Coonen 2006; Fiott 2017; Græger and Haugevik 2011; Muratore 2010; Reichard 2006; Schmidt 2006; Sperling 2004; Whitman 2004; Yost 2003). Similarly, Robert Kagan's (2003: 3) infamous distinction that 'Americans are from Mars and Europeans are from Venus' has translated into a debate on the power and capability gap between the United States[3] and Europe and between NATO and the EU. Flockhart (2011) used the wordplay of Tarzan and Jane to attribute the hard power approach to crisis management to the EU and the soft power approach to NATO. This has matched the initial division of labour between NATO and the EU – the Atlantic Alliance as the military alliance and the EU as the economic actor in Europe. Yet, the EU's objective to become a security actor capable of conducting autonomous military crisis management operations has experienced backlashes because of its inadequate capabilities. Former Belgian Foreign Minister Mark Eyskens therefore called the EU 'an economic giant, a political dwarf and a military worm' in a statement in 1991 (Whitney 1991).

The capabilities gap is an underlying problem within both organisations as well as in the EU–NATO relationship, as highlighted in the Balkan wars in the 1990s and in Afghanistan and Iraq in the early 2000s. In Kosovo, the EU's common foreign, security and defence tools and instruments were not operable as planned and NATO eventually stepped in to conduct its military intervention. Similarly in Afghanistan, the EU was mandated to establish sustainable civil police and law enforcement structures through its civilian mission EUPOL Afghanistan, but needed NATO's support to do so (Sperling 2004; Yost 2003). Three main reasons for the primacy of NATO military power and the EU's weak capabilities are money, institutional resistance and the lack of political will (Bialos 2005: 55). Member states' cultural and historical perspectives can be considered as additional explanatory factors. Throughout the EU–NATO relationship, the capabilities gap is not the only recognisable gap, but it 'should be defined as an aggregate of many gaps' (Yost 2003: 83).

In 2016, NATO's operational defence budget amounted to $913 billion (based on the 2015 prices and exchange rates), which increased to $1,028 billion in 2020 (NATO 2017, 2020).[4] Therein, the US is the major contributor to NATO's operational defence budget. In contrast, the EU possesses a multitude of financial instruments for foreign, security and defence affairs.

Its operational budget accounted for €205 billion in 2016 (EDA 2016), which reflected the decline of European defence budgets following the 2008 and 2011 financial and economic crises. With the introduction of new instruments including the EDF in 2016, the operationalisation of the EPF since 2021 and the adoption of the Multiannual Financial Framework (MAFF) for 2021–2027, the EU devoted a higher share to security and defence. In financial terms, this means that the EU's cumulative defence expenditure, based on its member states' defence expenditures, accounts for €186 billion in 2019 with €13.2 billion being devoted by the MAFF and €8 billion by the EDF. The EDF is solely split into two dimensions, defence research and capability development (CEU 2021; EDA 2020). In addition, with the launch of the EPF, an off-budget instrument of €5 billion to fund security and defence activities such as CSDP missions and operations to replace the Athena mechanism was created, and with the Connecting Europe Facility (CEF) for 2021–2017, another €1.5 billion was made available for military mobility (EP 2020). Prior to the introduction of the EPF, missions and operations were funded through the intergovernmental Athena mechanism based on the principle of 'costs lie where they fall', that is, the costs were covered partially through common costs and partially by member states based on their gross national income.

Despite the high degree of membership overlap – the overlapping 22 states (including the UK until 2020) pay financial contributions to both organisations – there is a financial imbalance between the EU and NATO and member states differ in their national contributions to both organisations (see figure 1 in EDA 2020 and graph 5 in NATO 2020). With the idea of burden sharing and common funding, old and long-lasting disputes among member states re-emerged and new problematic issues arose. Among the reasons are the diverging security interests and the different threat perceptions by member states as well as the commitments to other international cooperation and alliance efforts (Eilstrup-Sangiovanni 2014; Nováky 2016). Although all member states enjoy the security and defence provided through both organisations, those with higher contributions accuse other member states of free-riding. Central and Eastern European member states as well as Germany are frequent targets of such accusations since they do not meet NATO's objective and, in the case of Germany, it does not have a respective defence budget compared to its economic power. The US is especially concerned about decreasing defence budgets because 'Europe's undersupply of military security' can undermine NATO's accountability and capability to act not only in collective defence but also in military crisis management operations (Sperling 2004: 453; also see Mattelaer 2016).

However, in contrast to some NATO member states, the majority of European armies face dual obligations in light of advancing and funding their capabilities. They have to meet the demands of NATO's 1999 Defence Capabilities Initiative (DCI), the capability commitments set out at the 2002 Prague Summit and at the 2014 Wales Summit as well as targets set out in the EU's HG in 2003 and 2010 and the Capability Development Plan introduced by the EDA (Sperling 2004; Yost 2003). This therefore reflects 'a three-way stretch' between the EU, NATO and national obligations, which explains the shortfalls of European military assets and capabilities (Sperling 2004: 457). Most member states argue that they only have a single set of forces at their disposal that need to be distributed and committed to either EU or NATO crisis management operations in a calculated and cautious manner (British Official 1; Estonian Official 1; German Officials 2; Romanian Official 1). To counter the shortfalls in military capabilities and resources, the EU–NATO Capability Group was set up in 2003 to coordinate their capability development efforts. This was crucial to avoid 'unnecessary duplication' as requested by the US (Albright 1998). Directed to serve as the 'linchpin of coordination' between them, its abilities were constrained due to the political differences of the EU, NATO and their members (Marsh and Rees 2012: 55). Consequently, the EU–NATO Capability Group mainly conducts cross-briefings and consultations to keep each side updated about armament and capability improvements but did not meet between February and June 2017 due to political differences (French Official 1). Since resuming consultations and exchanges in the Capability Group, improvements have been recorded concerning interoperability, transparency and complementarity between NATO and the EU (NATO 2019).

Shortfalls in capabilities and imbalances in military expenditures have negative impacts in other areas relevant for EU–NATO cooperation. Lacking interoperability and the absence of a clear division of labour pose continuous challenges and yield questions over capability procurement plans and harmonisation of assets and resources. Cooperation and interoperability are essential for conducting operations in a holistic fashion due to both organisations' varying comparative advantages. Internally, NATO has submitted a guide for interoperability in joint operations in which it developed standardisation policies and practices (NATO 2006). The EU constantly improves its internal interoperability through several mechanisms that coordinate the activities of its instruments and tools, such as the civil–military coordination and the consultation and exchange procedures of the relevent EU institutions, that is, the EEAS, European Commission and the Council. It has thereby internalised a 'culture of coordination' within its own structures (Siedschlag and Eder 2006: 64). On the interorganisational level, the lack of an interoperability framework has become evident in the area of classified information. Due to their different classification systems as well as diverging views on handling classified, even information with regards to Berlin Plus are not easily shared among both organisations and their member states (NATO Official 3; Reichard 2006). A standardised classification system would therefore enhance the interoperability between the two organisations. Similarly, a more harmonised process of procurement as well as research and development would constitute an important contribution to both a higher level of interoperability and reducing the capability gap. An example in which interoperability and cooperation in general have been improved, however, are exercises, trainings and military mobility, that is, where cooperation between the EU and NATO facilitates the movement of troops and capabilities across Europe (cf. Drent, Kruijver and Zandee 2019; NATO 2021).

A clearly defined division of labour and responsibilities has been proposed to reduce the capabilities and interoperability gaps. In interorganisational relations, a balanced distribution of power and capabilities leads to the co-existence of governance structures and ultimately to a division of labour (Gehring and Faude 2014). During the Cold War, each organisation had their own specific tasks and responsibilities: NATO was in charge of collective defence and the EU was primarily responsible for economic, social and political integration. As a result of their transformation processes since 1990, both organisations sought new tasks and responsibilities. Initially, a division of labour was not desired by either the EU or NATO as they aimed at complementarity, and the issue has since troubled their relationship (cf. Hagman 2002; Heise and Schmidt 2005; Ojanen 2006; Reichard 2006; Schleich 2014; Schmidt 2006; Varwick 2006; Whitman 2004). For example, Varwick claims that the outline of a division of labour is one in which NATO 'would be responsible for the conduct of more robust combat missions where US participation is necessary, while the EU would mainly undertake peace-keeping operations' (Varwick 2006: 15). Furthermore, the lack of military capabilities in the EU, the lack of civilian capabilities in NATO and their differing approaches to crisis management call for both complementarity and a division of labour to make use of each other's comparative advantages. Without a clear task-related and functional division of labour, both organisations run the risk of duplicating important capabilities and entering into rivalry over these resources from their member states (Biermann 2008; Heise and Schmidt 2005). During the Balkans wars, such a division of tasks was clearer because of the limitations of the CSDP's tools and instruments. For instance, in North Macedonia, NATO's Operation Harvest served as the security provider and the EU's Operation Concordia concentrated primarily on economic assistance (Mace 2004). Yet, with the changing nature of warfare and the shift from traditional towards non-traditional and hybrid warfare, as illustrated in the Ukraine conflict since 2014, a division of tasks is less obvious and greater cooperation, interoperability and harmonisations are essential. This is also due to the various capabilities and resources, which both organisations have acquired and specialised in, as well as the mandates given by their member states (Hofmann 2019; Kristi and Järvenpää 2017; Mälksoo 2018).

Member states themselves have provided multiple sources of tensions between the EU and NATO in addition to the already existing gaps and challenges. Particularly, disputes between individual members as well as the issue of discrimination of non-members are of great significance. The most prominent examples of inter-state tension affecting EU–NATO cooperation are the still unresolved disputes between Cyprus, Turkey and Greece (see

Acikmese and Triantaphyllou 2012; Duke 2008; Græger and Haugevik 2011; Marsh and Rees 2012; Smith 2011) as well as the frequent tensions and disagreements between France and the US and between France and the UK. In addition, the single membership of certain states such as Denmark, Malta and Turkey as well as the use of states' membership for their national interests pose challenges for EU–NATO cooperation (cf. Martill and Sus 2018; Perruche 2014; Rodt 2017; Tiilikainen 2006; Tofte 2003). Because states maintain their sovereignty in security and defence and have the ability to shape the organisation's external relations, their own bilateral partnerships and use of memberships significantly impact the EU–NATO relationship.

While the Cyprus issue has often been used as an alibi and key reason for the stalemate, other member states have also put a strain on the EU–NATO relation. Most notably, the UK's decision to leave the EU in 2016, which was finalised in 2020, as well as the US foreign policy approach under Donald Trump present new challenges. With Britain's withdrawal, the largest military power left the EU, which creates new asymmetries, especially within the military capabilities dimension, between the EU and NATO. The Franco-British axis has traditionally been the foundation of European security and driver behind CSDP. With the renewed leadership by France and Germany, also supported by Italy and Poland, new capabilities and avenues for security and defence cooperation had to be forged to keep up with the EU's capability plans and to fill the gap left by the UK (Bond 2016). In contrast, Brexit has also been identified as a potential enabler for EU–NATO cooperation in the future. The UK's limited resources would result in the increase of its full commitment in and contributions to NATO (Martill and Sus 2018; von Voss and Schütz 2018). Given its geographical location and overlapping security interests, it is likely that Britain will still pursue to act as a transatlantic bridge through its extensive bilateral and minilateral security relations. Although the security and defence dimension has largely been left out of the EU–UK agreement, it has been crystallised that Britain will seek a close tie with its European partners and the EU in areas where both sides find cooperation necessary (Martill and Sus 2018; Whitman 2016, 2020). Similarly, the election of Donald Trump as the US President in 2016 and his 'distaste for these institutions' (Walt 2018) has put strains on the EU–NATO relationship. Because of his claim that 'NATO is obsolete', his accusations of European allies as free-riders in NATO and the unilateral foreign policy manoeuvres under the slogan of 'America First', the US has been perceived as a less reliable partner complicating Euro-Atlantic security cooperation (Howorth 2018; Kaufman 2017; Sperling and Webber 2019). In addition to increasing external risks as well as divergences over threat perceptions and security interests, especially between members from the South and East, the foreign policy behaviour by a number of member states, including France, Turkey and the US, therefore begs the question of member states' ability to shape the EU–NATO relationship.

Analysing member states in EU–NATO cooperation

Besides the acclaimed problem of institutional incompatibility and the lack of consensus about the roles of each organisation, the 'overlapping but differentiated membership' poses another obstacle for closer cooperation (Marsh and Rees 2012: 55). It has been highlighted that a 'constant feature of the EU–NATO relationship that complicates its analysis is that the membership of the two organisations largely overlaps' (Reichard 2006: 6). Member states' behaviour varies in each organisation, they pursue their own interests and make use of their memberships in different ways. Traditionally, some member states see NATO as the main forum for collective defence and crisis management, whereas they regard the EU as an economic actor instead of a security and military one. Over time, however, member states' views have shifted as indicated by the development of CSDP and the enthusiasm for launching new policy instruments, which ultimately affect the evolution of the EU–NATO relationship. This was also reflected in the institutionalisation of security and defence policies as well as in the evolution of the strategic cultures of both organisations (Cornish and Edwards 2001; Juncos 2017).

Membership is a key element to understand the development of the EU–NATO relationship. Generally, member states are vital components of both international organisations and interorganisational relationships since they provide the foundation of interactions, have the decision-making powers, delegate mandates and sovereignty to the organisations and provide resources to their functioning (Abbott and Snidal 1998; Koch 2008; Koops 2017). However, membership can take different forms in international organisations. It can be distinguished between political and administrative memberships, where the latter refers to the institutions and bureaucratic bodies that run the everyday activities of organisations. Political membership, in contrast, consists of member states and their governments that actively join organisations, or withdraw from them, and steer the direction based on their national interests (Koch 2008). Membership can be furthermore categorised into single and multiple memberships. Whereas single members possess the membership in only one relevant organisation in an interorganisational relationship, multiple members enjoy the membership of both or all participating organisations. Similarly, member states can be distinguished between old or original and new or subsequent members based on their accession to an organisation (Gehring and Faude 2014; Gehring and Oberthür 2009; Magliveras 2011).

As of 2021, the EU consists of 27 member states and NATO consists of 30 member states with an overlap of 21 states (see Figure 1.1; Table 1.1). The overlapping states possess membership in both organisations and enjoy full decision-making powers. Among the EU and NATO, single and multiple as well as original and subsequent members are easily identifiable. They can also be categorised either in the camp of Atlanticists, for example, the Netherlands, Spain and the UK, or in the camp of Europeanists, for example, Belgium and France (Flockhart 2014; Gebhard and Smith 2015; Larrabee 2004). Both

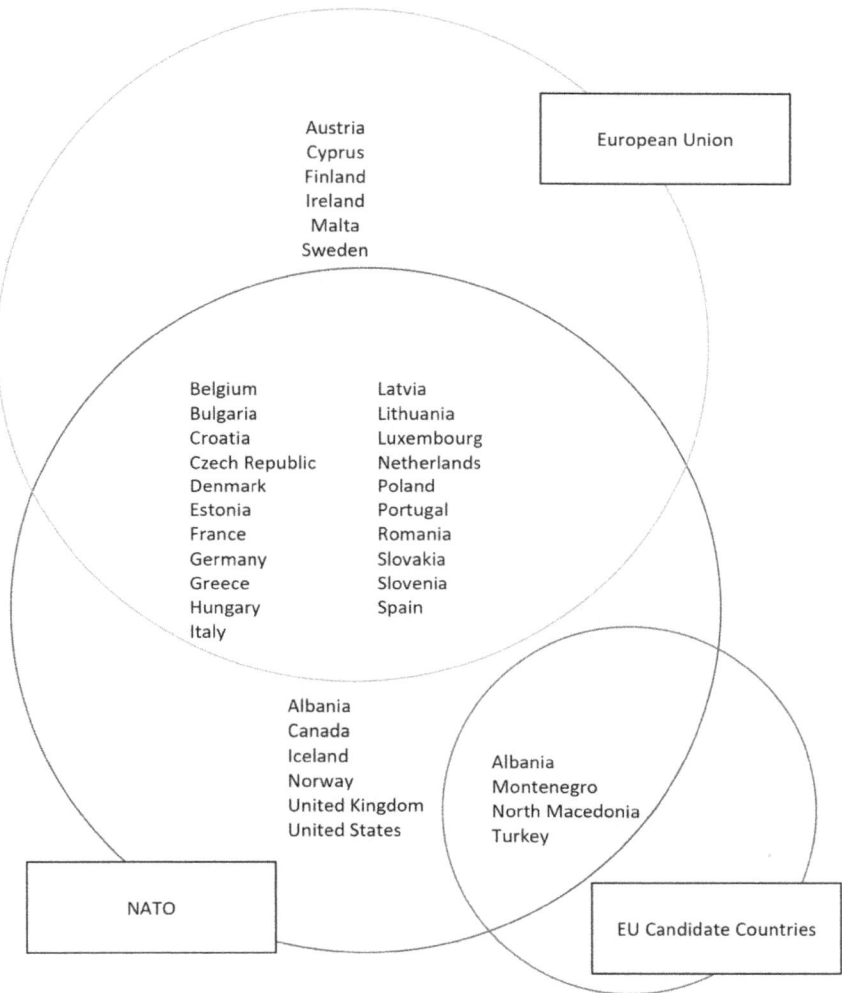

Figure 1.1 The EU and NATO membership overlap in 2021.

organisations developed a catalogue of accession criteria that states have to meet in order to join. They furthermore introduced mechanisms for candidate countries or those states aligned who do not wish to join or do not meet the criteria. For security relations with non-EU NATO member states, the EU establishes Framework Participation Agreements (FPAs) that enable third states to participate in operations and missions conducted through CSDP (Tardy 2014). Similarly, NATO maintains agreements with non-NATO EU partner countries through the Partnership for Peace (PfP) programme, which

Table 1.1 Membership overlap in the EU–NATO relationship

EU	NATO	Partner countries FPA	Partner countries PfP
	Albania	Albania	
Austria			Austria
Belgium	Belgium		
Bulgaria	Bulgaria		
	Canada	Canada	
Croatia	Croatia		
Cyprus			
Czech Republic	Czech Republic		
Denmark	Denmark		
Estonia	Estonia		
Finland			Finland
France	France		
Germany	Germany		
Greece	Greece		
Hungary	Hungary		
	Iceland	Iceland	
Ireland			Ireland
Italy	Italy		
Latvia	Latvia		
Lithuania	Lithuania		
Luxembourg	Luxembourg		
Malta			Malta
	Montenegro	Montenegro	
The Netherlands	The Netherlands		
	North Macedonia	North Macedonia	
	Norway	Norway	
Poland	Poland		
Portugal	Portugal		
Romania	Romania		
Slovakia	Slovakia		
Slovenia	Slovenia		
Spain	Spain		
Sweden			Sweden
	Turkey	Turkey	
UK	UK		
	US	US	

is designed to maintain bilateral security cooperation between NATO and its partner countries. It enables these states to participate in NATO-led operations and prepares candidate countries for future accession (NATO 2016b). With regard to the membership landscape in the EU–NATO relationship, a few countries represent special cases. Cyprus is the only state which is considered to be a truly single member state, as it neither participates in NATO's PfP programme nor does it maintain any other formalised partnership with NATO. With its CSDP opt-out, Denmark is technically considered a single member, but is a *de facto* multiple member state. Lastly, because the UK officially withdrew from the EU in 2020 and because the EU–UK Trade and Cooperation Agreement of 2021 does not include any provisions for security and defence cooperation, it is still primarily treated as a multiple member state for the present analysis.

As members of international organisations, states can make use of a number of political strategies that impact interorganisational relations. For example, they can choose to contribute actively and promote closer cooperation through bargaining and trade-offs. In contrast, they are also able to obstruct and block interorganisational interactions. Forum-shopping is a common approach in which member states choose one particular international organisation over another to realise their interests and goals (Gehring and Oberthür 2009). Other political strategies applied by member states include hostage-taking, turf battles, muddling through and brokering (Alter and Meunier 2009; Goddard 2009; Hofmann 2009, 2019). Member states have utilised one of these strategies on several occasions. One example is Turkey's extensive use of hostage-taking when it comes to fostering closer cooperation by blocking the accession of Cyprus to NATO (Acikmese and Triantaphyllou 2012). France's behaviour in the EU and NATO and primarily its support for European strategic autonomy has been perceived as a way of hostage-taking in NATO, and thus as a form of obstructing reforms to allow the EU to take on certain responsibilities and tasks (NATO Official 2).

In addition to the membership overlap and the divergences of member states' preferences and interests as well as their strategies in pursing these, three issues have crystallised that highlight how member states shape the EU–NATO relationship: the role of groups of interest, tensions among member states in both organisations and states' 'schizophrenic' behaviour. Apart from cooperating through international organisations, member states also maintain bilateral and minilateral partnerships outside these formal frameworks. Such bilateral and minilateral relationships lead to networks of like-minded states and allow to form coalitions to promote, delay or oppose initiatives and policies. Through these coalitions, member states can informally influence decisions that have underlying implications for the direction of EU–NATO interactions. Some member states also stand out with their ambiguous and inconsistent behaviour in international negotiations that transmits wrong signals to other member states and thus create incoherence and confusion (EU Official 1). Lastly, tensions and disputes among members have been an increasingly dominant factor and specifically an obstacle to furthering EU–NATO cooperation in both legal and practical terms (Acikmese and Triantaphyllou 2012; Bilgin 2003; Duke 2008; Smith 2011). Since cooperation between the EU and NATO heavily relies on the cooperation and interactions among their member states, the latter have a greater leverage in designing and shaping this interorganisational relationship. This research therefore takes a closer look by adding the member states' perspective and focusing on the impact of member states' roles, interactions and behaviour on shaping EU–NATO cooperation.

Minilateral relationships and groups of interest

Throughout the evolution of the EU and NATO on the one hand and their interorganisational relationship on the other hand, specific groups of interest or coalition groups have emerged. These groups consist of like-minded and closely aligned member states in terms of their security and defence policies, threat perceptions and strategic interests. Especially within Europe, a trend towards minilateralism in defence cooperation has been recorded. In comparison to multilateral frameworks such as the EU and NATO, which member states often see as lacking the appropriate efficiency and effectiveness in developing new initiatives and taking decisions on new proposals, minilateral cooperation has become a helpful tool to realise new ideas. Minilateral cooperation is comprised of two or more states that share a common goal and that can be operated, formally or informally, within multilateral frameworks (Pannier 2015). Within both the EU and NATO, minilateral cooperation has taken the form of groups of interests or coalition groups. They facilitate member states to identify other states as coalition partners that share similar ideas, threat perceptions and viewpoints. In some cases, these states are located in the same geographical region, for example, the Nordics, Central and Eastern Europe or Southern Europe. The regional divide particularly between the South and the East often illustrates a problem of convergence in both organisations since some Eastern European member states put a greater emphasis on deterrence and defence, whereas Southern European states focus on counterterrorism, illegal migration and maritime security in the Mediterranean Sea (British Official 1).

In the EU–NATO relationship, there are a number of such coalition groups that are most prominent. The 'Friends of Europe' in NATO is a group comprised of Belgium, France, Germany, the Netherlands, Slovakia, Spain, the UK and the US (Cypriot Official 2; NATO Official 3). Except for the US, these states are all multiple members and among those with the biggest share of the defence budget in the EU. In addition, they put an emphasis on EU–NATO cooperation, though from different perspectives and with different objectives in mind. Another group is 'the Quint' formed by France, Germany, Italy, the UK and the US, which meets regularly prior to meetings of the NAC or of the EU Military Committee (EUMC) (German Official 2). During these meetings, the military representatives and other national representatives discuss their positions on a crisis or conflict, or any other crucial topic, in an informal way. This forum serves to exchange views and helps to formulate a common position in order to form a coalition in the decision-making process. The 'Big Three' or 'E3', which consists of France, Germany and the UK, is another prominent group. Despite the divergences of historical experiences and their different views on the use of force, a policy convergence on some security and defence matters has been recorded. This trilateral framework is regarded as vital for advancing defence in Europe, particularly with the UK's withdrawal from the EU (Billon-Galland, Raines and Whitman 2020; Pannier and Schmitt 2014). These three countries are not only the major economic powers in Europe, but they also possessed the highest military expenditures and largest share in the EU's operational defence budget in 2016 (EDA 2016). The Visegrád Group is another prominent group of member states, which often meets informally as well as formally to discuss issues of security, defence and foreign policy. It is a political alliance of Czech Republic, Hungary, Poland and Slovakia. Compared to other coalition groups, the Visegrád group collaborates on a more formalised basis. All four states sought simultaneous accession to both EU and NATO and see membership as well as EU–NATO cooperation crucial for their own security and defence and for the realisation of their national interests (Törő 2011). All of these groups of interest help to foster coalitions as they provide greater leverage in multilateral negotiations and allow for informal discussions before decisions are taken in the EU and NATO, whereby they seek to avoid vetoes and the creation of new obstacles.

Inter-member-state tensions

Disagreements among member states over the appropriate approach to crisis management, the design of the EU–NATO relationship as well as the level of intensity and scope of their cooperation have hampered the progress of convergence (Manners and Whitman 2001; Marsh and Rees 2012; Schleich 2014; Varwick and Koops 2009; Winn 2003). In EU–NATO cooperation, especially the Cyprus issue plays a crucial role as it represents a well-known obstacle for enhanced cooperation. Historically, the conflict between Greece and Turkey dates back to before either organisation was founded. Both states became NATO members in 1952, Greece later joined the EU in 1981 and Turkey became a candidate country in 2005. With the invasion of the Turkish army on the Cypriot island in 1974 and the Turkish non-recognition of the Republic of Cyprus as a sovereign state, the dispute between the three countries culminated. The developments have since affected the cooperation between the EU and NATO. Interestingly, even though the three guarantors of Cyprus – Greece, Turkey and the UK – are all alliance members, the country rejected NATO membership and opted for the Non-Alignment Movement (Ker-Lindsay 2010). The EU–NATO relationship was regarded as moderate until Cyprus became a member state of the EU in the 2004 enlargement round, which changed the cooperation dynamics (Biermann 2015). In short, the unresolved Cyprus–Greece–Turkey dispute and Cyprus's EU membership caused obstacles for the EU–NATO relationship in multiple dimensions. First, the 2002 Security of Information Agreement (EU 2003c) only includes the exchange of classified information between the two organisations and all the member states as long as a bilateral agreement on information sharing exists for non-members. When this agreement was drafted, Turkish representatives took careful accounts of the correct wording in case of a potential EU membership of Cyprus to ensure that it would not be included in an exchange of classified information (NATO Official 2).

NATO's PfP programme and the EU's FPA account for such bilateral security of information agreements, but such an agreement does not exist between NATO and Cyprus due to Turkey's veto (Acikmese and Triantaphyllou 2012). As a result, formal exchanges on the PSC and NAC level, therefore, only occur on the issues of Operation Concordia in North Macedonia and Operation Althea in Bosnia and Herzegovina through the provisions of the Berlin Plus arrangements. Formal negotiations on issues not related to Berlin Plus thus exclude Cyprus. To improve the situation and to make progress, the PSC and NAC increasingly meet in informal settings (Cypriot Official 2; EU Official 1). Although the reunification of the Republic of Cyprus and Northern Cyprus with the subsequent accession to NATO's PfP programme and Turkey's concurrent accession to the EU have been proposed as possible solutions to overcome the problem of information security, a viable solution is not yet in sight (Cypriot Official 1; Cypriot Official 2). Consequently, the likelihood of closer EU–NATO cooperation is still entrapped in the double veto of these two countries.

The traditional divergences and tensions of France with both the UK and the US have been perceived as additional obstacles. Both France and Britain are among the militarily powerful states in Europe, in possession of nuclear weapons, but their views often diverge over the purpose of NATO and CSDP. Yet, with the Saint-Malo Declaration in 1998 and the bilateral defence cooperation through the Lancaster House Treaties in 2010, their tensions have become a minor issue for fostering the EU–NATO relationship (EUISS 2000; Ostermann 2015). First, France agreed to the British demand that the EU will be able to further develop its security and defence policy and its military capabilities under the condition of closer EU–NATO cooperation. Second, with enhanced bilateral defence cooperation, France and the UK have built the core of European security for both the EU and NATO. In addition, the Franco-American divergences were primarily reasoned in France's withdrawal from NATO's military command structures. However, with its return and the improved bilateral relations under Barak Obama and Nicolas Sarkozy, their divergences play a less significant role for EU–NATO cooperation (cf. Perruche 2014). But France's renewed ambition for European strategic autonomy is also a distinctive thorn for many Atlanticists, including the UK and the US.

States' 'schizophrenic' behaviour

Member states pursue specific interest with their memberships in international organisations. Due to the high degree of functional overlap and domain similarity of the EU and NATO in security and defence, that is, the overlap or similarity of policy domains in which they have competences and mandates (Biermann and Koops 2017; Gehring and Oberthür 2009), member states have to take important decisions about which organisation should be tasked with a specific issue or policy area. In some cases, it has been observed that certain member states act in 'schizophrenia' (EU Official 1). This means that a member state expresses its view on an issue positively in one organisation, but negatively on the same issue in the other. A prime example of this is the behaviour of the French foreign minister during the negotiations on the EU's takeover of NATO's operations in the Western Balkans, notably in Bosnia and Herzegovina and in Kosovo. The French representative emphasised the French support for a takeover in EU negotiations in the PSC, but the French representative in the NAC expressed concerns about the EU's readiness, hence showing scepticism and disagreement over a potential takeover (NATO Official 2).

Another illustrative example is the case of Turkey when discussing closer EU–NATO cooperation. In NATO negotiations it has voiced its consent to deepening relations with the EU, but concurrently vetoed Cyprus's accession to NATO's PfP programme, which would be fundamental to overcome many stalemates in this relationship (EU Official 3; NATO Official 2). This schizophrenia of member states is not uncommon and has been observed at numerous occasions. It serves to play off NATO and the EU against each other to obstruct further progress in their cooperation. This behaviour, however, is to a certain extent dependent on what member states' representatives partake in the negotiations and decision-makings. Whereas some military representatives and ambassadors to the NAC and the PSC receive joint instructions from their Ministry of Defence and Ministry of Foreign Affairs, other member states either receive separate instructions and guidance or make diverging decisions within their national delegations to the respective organisations.

A note on sources, methodology and typologies

The research in this book is based on the examination of the strategies, interests and preferences of member states concerning their attitudes towards interorganisational cooperation between the EU and NATO. It examines how they seek to exert influence on the design, structures and formalisation of this relationship. To do so, this book relies on a qualitative research design with an application of an inductive and deductive approach to social inquiry using document analysis of primary and secondary sources and the conduct of semi-structured interviews (cf. Lamont 2015). It makes observations of the EU–NATO relationship based on the examination of secondary literature and strategic documents published by both organisations and their member states. Since this empirical examination consists of a contemporary phenomenon, conducting semi-structured interviews with representatives from the organisations and their member states supports this research. With the help of these observations, theoretical propositions are generated, which help to identify and formulate the typology for the study of member states in interorganisational interaction. These observations and the newly generated knowledge from the national strategy documents allow to formulate assumptions about member states' choices and behaviour for which an understanding of their preferences and viewpoints is paramount.

Primary and secondary sources have been examined, including official documents, statements and transcript of speeches by both the EU and NATO as well as member states' ministries and governments. For analysing EU–NATO cooperation, three documents are most salient: the 2002 EU–NATO Declaration on the ESDP (EU 2002; NATO 2002), the 2003 EU–NATO framework for permanent relations and Berlin Plus (EU 2003a) and the 2016 Joint Declaration by the President of the European Council, the President of the European Commission and the Secretary General of NATO as well as the follow-up implementation plans and progress reports (NATO 2016a; 2019). Strategic concepts, security strategies and press releases from both organisations, including NATO's Strategic Concepts (NATO 1991, 2010) and the EU's Security Strategy and Global Strategy (EU 2003b, 2016), and other relevant documents such as the 1998 Franco-British Saint-Malo Declaration (EUISS 2000) have been considered. Member states' security and defence strategy documents produced by their Ministry of Defence, Ministry of Foreign Affairs, Prime Minister's Offices or Parliaments helped to align their positions on the EU–NATO relationship and to cross-check the findings with the statements from the interviews. These national documents are particularly crucial to categorise each member state and to identify their orientations in foreign, security and defence affairs, as they contain vital information on the member states' strategic cultures and security interests. Derived from the knowledge that has been gained from the secondary literature, these national strategy papers have been examined based on a set of keywords, including 'EU', 'NATO', 'EU–NATO', 'CSDP', 'CFSP', 'cooperation', 'collaboration', 'strategic partnership(s)', 'partner', 'interorganisational' (or, alternatively, 'inter-organisational'), 'PfP' or 'Partnership for Peace', 'FPA' (or 'Framework Participation Agreement'), 'crisis management', '(military) operations', 'security' and 'defence'. These keywords have been chosen according to their relevance for the overall research aim and to ascertain member states' foreign and security policy strategies towards the EU and NATO.

A total of 28 face-to-face semi-structured interviews with national representatives, individually or in small groups, and with officials and representatives from different member states, the EU and NATO were carried out in Berlin and Brussels between February 2017 and February 2018 (see Appendix A). The conduct of interviews was grounded in random and non-random sampling as well as the so-called snowball sampling of interview partners (Lamont 2015: 147), which helped to gain access to participants from both organisations and their member states who would have otherwise not been accessible. Interviewing representatives from the EU, NATO and their member states played an essential part in the generation of knowledge on member states' behaviours, perceptions and approaches to EU–NATO cooperation since they provided first-hand access to information and national policies that supplemented the findings from the national security and defence documents. They furthermore allowed to dig deeper into member states' perspectives, attitudes and perceptions that enabled to identify their positions and roles within the EU–NATO relationship.

Since this research is interested in investigating the positions that member states take and how they make use of these roles to shape the development of the EU–NATO relationship, this yields the question how member states are categorised. Typologies are analytical tools that help to explain and predict certain phenomena such as the motives, behaviour and roles of member states in the EU–NATO relationship. Typologies can be defined as 'organised systems of types' (Collier, LaPorte and Seawright 2012: 217) and relate to classification, which is 'both a process and an end result' in which 'the ordering of entities into groups or classes on the basis of their similarity' provide the foundation (Bailey 1994: 1–2). Distinctive types of typologies have been identified including conceptual typologies, descriptive and explanatory typologies and multidimensional and unidimensional typologies (Bailey 1994; Collier, LaPorte and Seawright 2012). This research pursues the development and testing of a descriptive typology that allows to categorise member states based on their similar views on and positions in the EU–NATO relationship. While an ideal type is proposed, it is acknowledged that none of the member states represent this ideal type, though member states in each type nevertheless share a set of characteristics reflecting the ideal type.

The goal of typologies and classifications is to explain, predict and identify specific patterns of behaviour and attitudes by states. They also allow to synthesise complex ideas and multiple strands of analysis into a simplified understanding of phenomena, which reduces the overall complexity (Bailey 1994; Collier, LaPorte and Seawright 2012). The categorisation into types based on similar criteria and characteristics increases the predictability of its entities due to the presumption of their characteristics, such as attitudes, opinions and patterns of behaviour. This enables to formulate responses and to make amendments and changes. Yet, it is impossible to objectively classify and categorise entities into types due to different understandings and viewpoints of the data as well as the subjective interpretation of the categorisation criteria. Typologies have been accused of being rather static than dynamic and have also been criticised for being incomplete, imperfect or non-permanent with often undetermined characteristics (Bailey 1994; Smith 2002). This leads to the problem of boundary cases and fluid cases, or what Rodt identifies as 'swing states' (Rodt 2017: 139), concerning the categorisation of member states. Boundary cases therefore refer to those states that adopt and fulfil characteristics of more than one type. Throughout this book, a number of such boundary cases and swing states are identified. Domestic politics in the form of the change of governments and party coalitions as well as external shocks, such as the 9/11 terrorist attacks and the 2015 refugee and migration crisis, significantly shape states' foreign and security policy orientations (cf. Hofmann 2017). These changes and the existence of boundary cases add to the complexity of typologies and complicate predictions of state behaviour, thus disallowing policymakers to make clear calculations and interpretations for their decisions on security and defence matters.

The development of the typology of member states in interorganisational relations relies on a set of selection criteria including attitudes towards interorganisational cooperation in security and defence (positive, negative, balanced, indifferent), level of active promotion of closer interorganisational cooperation (absent, low, medium, high), view on division of labour between the respective international organisations (positive, negative, balanced, indifferent), level of engagement in negotiations (absent, low, medium, high) and material contributions to the international organisations and their operations (absent, low, medium, high). The sources and data have been examined according to these criteria to categorise each EU and NATO member state. While every single member state is considered for the investigation, some states receive greater attention because of the availability and access to information and data. More data is available for certain actors, such as bigger states with more military capabilities and resources including France, Germany and the UK, or specific groups of states, such as the Baltics, Nordics and the Cyprus–Greece–Turkey triad. The analysis therefore shifts to these states to illustrate the extent to which they represent each type of member states in interorganisational relations.

Structure of the book

Building upon this introductory chapter on the background of the EU–NATO interorganisational relationship, chapter 2 sets out the theoretical and analytical framework of this book. It adopts a conceptualisation of interorganisational cooperation that builds on the existing scholarly literature and theoretical debates on cooperation in international relations and particularly in foreign, security and defence affairs. The aim is to embed the phenomenon of interorganisational interaction into existing scholarly works and to establish a robust theoretical framework for the empirical analysis. The chapter then establishes a set of features of interorganisational cooperation that help to develop the typology of member states in interorganisational relations, which presents the key element of this research and poses the theoretical bedrock for the subsequent empirical chapters.

Chapters 3, 4, 5 and 6 present the empirical analyses of the four types of member states in the EU–NATO interorganisational relationship. These chapters examine the extent to which member states exert influence, behave and participate in the interactions between the EU and NATO. The focal point of these chapters is to illustrate each type of member state and to provide evidence of their actions, behaviour and approaches to interorganisational cooperation in security and defence. Furthermore, the aim is to examine the extent to which they contribute to the evolution of the EU–NATO relationship. Chapter 3 introduces the group of advocates, which contribute significantly to the advancement of this interorganisational relationship. The chapter gives insights into their behaviour and activities that enhance cooperation, which reveals their continuous efforts to promote this relationship. Chapter 4 examines how blockers hamper EU–NATO cooperation and illustrates exemplary actions through which they try to decelerate interorganisational relations. Blockers play a crucial part and provide a reminder about the challenges posed by member states. Chapter 5 introduces the group of balancers. It shows how these states seek to make a contribution to EU–NATO cooperation by mediating and balancing among other member states. A central feature is their attempt to act as brokers in interorganisational interaction while having to meet numerous internal and external pressures. In the last empirical chapter, chapter 6, the group of neutrals receives greater attention. This chapter outlines their positions and demonstrates how these states, which usually have little influence, play their significant share in the interactions between the EU and NATO.

The concluding chapter then summarises the key theoretical and empirical findings. Based on the analysis, it assesses how this research and its findings will impact the future development of the EU–NATO interorganisational relationship. The chapter highlights the significance of member states in interorganisational relations and suggests an outlook for future exploration of the EU–NATO relationship and member states' behaviour and contributions in international security organisations.

Notes

1 For an overview of formal and informal meetings between 2001 and 2009 see table 1 in Smith 2011.
2 Formerly known as the Former Yugoslav Republic of Macedonia (FYRoM) until the name changed in 2019.
3 When analysing the capabilities gap, NATO and the US are often used interchangeably because of the large US contribution to NATO's military capabilities.
4 Numbers and figures for 2020 are estimates and already include Montenegro and North Macedonia.

References

Abbott, Kenneth W. and Duncan Snidal (1998) 'Why states act through formal international organisations', *The Journal of Conflict Resolution*, 42(1): 3–32.
Acikmese, Sinem Akgul and Dimitrios Triantaphyllou (2012) 'The NATO-EU-Turkey trilogy: The impact of the Cyprus conundrum', *Southeast European and Black Sea Studies*, 12(4): 555–573.
Albright, Madeleine K. (1998) *Speech and Press Conference Held at North Atlantic Council, NATO HQ in Brussels on 8 December 1998*, www.nato.int/docu/speech/1998/s981208x.htm (accessed on 21/12/2017).
Bailey, Kenneth D. (1994) *Typologies and Taxonomies: An Introduction to Classification Techniques*, Thousand Oaks; London: SAGE Publications.
Bialos, Jeffrey P. (2005) 'The United States, Europe and the interoperability gap', *The International Spectator*, 40(2): 53–62.

Biermann, Rafael (2008) 'Rivalry among international organisations'. *Paper presented at Konferenz Internationale Beziehungen und Organisationsforschung: Stand und Perspektiven*, Munich, 18–19 September 2008.

Biermann, Rafael (2015) 'Designing cooperation among international organisations: The quest for autonomy, the dual-consensus rule, and cooperation failure', *Journal of International Organisation Studies*, 6(2): 45–66.

Biermann, Rafael and Joachim A. Koops (2017) *Palgrave Handbook of Interorganisational Relations in World Politics*, New York, Basingstoke: Palgrave Macmillan.

Bilgin, Pinar (2003) 'The 'peculiarity' of Turkey's position on EU-NATO military/ security cooperation: A rejoinder to Missiroli', *Security Dialogue*, 34(4): 345–349.

Billon-Galland, Alice, Thomas Raines and Richard G. Whitman (2020) 'The future of the E3: Post-Brexit cooperation between the UK, France and Germany', *Chatham House Research Papers*, London: Chatham House.

Biscop, Sven (2017) 'European defence: What's in the CARDs for PESCO?' *Egmont Security Policy Brief*, 91: 1–6.

Bond, Ian (2016) 'NATO, the EU and Brexit: Joining forces?' *Centre for European Reform Insight*, 1–4.

Collier, David, Jody LaPorte and Jason Seawright (2012) 'Putting typologies to work: Concept formation, measurement and analytical rigour', *Political Research Quarterly*, 65(1): 217–232.

Coonen, Stephen J. (2006) 'The widening military capabilities gap between the United States and Europe: Does it matter?' *Parameters*, 36(3): 67–84.

Cornish, Paul and Geoffrey Edwards (2001) 'Beyond the EU/NATO dichotomy: The beginnings of a European strategic culture', *International Affairs*, 77(3): 587–603.

Council of the European Union (2003) *EU-NATO: The Framework for Permanent Relations Under Berlin Plus*, www.consilium.europa.eu/uedocs/cmsUpload/03-11-11%20Berlin%20Plus%20press%20note%20BL.pdf (accessed on 17/07/2016).

Council of the European Union (2016) *Council Conclusions on the Implementation of the Joint Declaration by the President of the European Council, the President of the European Commission and the Secretary General of the North Atlantic Treaty Organisation, 14802/17*.

Council of the European Union (2021) *Multiannual Financial Framework 2021–2027 and Next Generation EU*, www.consilium.europa.eu/media/47567/mff-2021-2027_rev.pdf (accessed on 16/03/2021).

de Wijk, Rob (2004) 'The reform of ESDP and EU-NATO cooperation', *The International Spectator*, 1: 71–82.

Drent, Margriet, Kimberley Kruijver and Dick Zandee (2019) *Military Mobility and the EU-NATO Conundrum*. The Hague: The Clingendael Institute.

Duke, Simon (2008) 'The future of EU–NATO relations: A case of mutual irrelevance through competition?' *Journal of European Integration*, 30(1): 27–43.

EEAS (2018) *Remarks by High Representative/Vice-President Federica Mogherini at the Press Conference Following the Foreign Affairs Council (Defence)*. Speech held on 6 March 2018, https://eeas.europa.eu/headquarters/headquarters-homepage/40897/remarks-hrvp-mogherini-press-conference-following-foreign-affairs-council-defence_en (accessed on 03/11/2018).

Eilstrup-Sangiovanni, Mette (2014) 'Europe's defence dilemma', *The International Spectator*, 49(2): 83–116.

Eilstrup-Sangiovanni, Mette (2020) 'Death of international organisations: The organisational ecology of intergovernmental organisations, 1815–2015', *The Review of International Organisations*, 15(2): 339–370.

European Defence Agency (2016) *National Defence Data 2013–2014 and 2015 (est.) of the 27 EDA Member States*, http://eda.europa.eu/docs/default-source/documents/eda-national-defence-data-2013-2014-(2015-est)5397973fa4d264cfa776ff000087ef0f.pdf (accessed on 24/07/2017).

European Defence Agency (2020) *Defence Data 2018–2019: Key Findings and Analysis*, https://eda.europa.eu/publications-and-data/brochures/defence-data-2018-2019 (accessed on 16/03/2021).

European Parliament (2020) *Connecting Europe Facility 2021–2027: Financing key EU Infrastructure Networks*, www.europarl.europa.eu/RegData/etudes/BRIE/2018/628247/EPRS_BRI(2018)628247_EN.pdf (accessed on 16/03/2021).

European Union (1999) *Presidency Conclusions of European Council, Helsinki, 10–11 December 1999*, www.consilium.europa.eu/media/21046/helsinki-european-council-presidency-conclusions.pdf (accessed on 26/05/2016).

European Union (2002) *European Union-NATO Declaration on the European Security and Defence Policy*, http://eur-lex.europa.eu/legal-content/EN/TXT/?uri=URISERV%3Al33243 (accessed on 25/02/2017).

European Union (2003a) *EU-NATO Framework for Permanent Relations and Berlin Plus*, www.consilium.europa.eu/uedocs/cmsUpload/031111%20Berlin%20Plus%20press%20note%20BL.pdf (accessed on 25/02/2017).

European Union (2003b) *European Security Strategy: A Secure Europe in a Better World*, Brussels: European Union.

European Union (2003c) 'Agreement between the European Union and the North Atlantic Treaty Organisation on the security of information', *Official Journal of the EU*, L80/36.

European Union (2016) *Shared Vision, Common Action: A Stronger Europe – A Global Strategy for the European Union's Foreign and Security Policy*, Brussels: European Union.

European Union Institute for Security Studies (2000) *Joint Declaration Issued at the British-French Summit*, Saint-Malo, France, 3–4 December 1998, www.consilium.europa.eu/uedocs/cmsUpload/FrenchBritish%20Summit%20Declaration,%20Saint-Malo,%201998%20-%20EN.pdf (accessed on 23/02/2017).

Fiott, Daniel (2017) 'A revolution too far? US defence innovation, Europe and NATO's military-technological gap', *Journal of Strategic Studies*, 40(3): 417–437.

Flockhart, Trine (2011) ' "Me Tarzan - You Jane": The EU and NATO and the reversal of roles', *Perspectives on European Politics and Society*, 12(3): 263–282.

Flockhart, Trine (2014) 'NATO and EU: A "strategic partnership" or a practice of "muddling through"?' *In*: Liselotte, Odgaard (ed.) *Strategy in NATO: Preparing for an Imperfect World*, Basingstoke, New York: Palgrave Macmillan, 75–89.

Gebhard, Carmen and Simon J. Smith (2015) 'The two faces of EU-NATO cooperation: Counter-piracy operations off the Somali coast', *Cooperation and Conflict*, 50(1): 107–127.

Gehring, Thomas and Benjamin Faude (2014) 'A theory of emerging order within international complexes: How competition among regulatory international institutions leads to institutional adaptation and division of labour', *Review of International Organisations*, 9(4): 471–498.

Gehring, Thomas and Sebastian Oberthür (2009) 'The causal mechanisms of interaction between international institutions', *European Journal of International Relations*, 15(1): 125–156.

Goddard, Stacie E. (2009) 'Brokering change: Networks and entrepreneurs in international politics', *International Theory*, 1(2): 249–281.

Græger, Nina (2016) 'European security as practice: EU-NATO communities of practice in the making?' *European Security*, 25(4): 478–501.

Græger, Nina (2017) 'Grasping the everyday and extraordinary in EU-NATO relations: The added value of practice approaches', *European Security*, 26(3): 340–358.

Græger, Nina and Kristin M. Haugevik (2011) 'The EU's performance with and within NATO: Assessing objectives, outcomes and organisational practices', *European Integration*, 33(6): 743–757.

Hagman, Hans-Christian (2002) *European Crisis Management and Defence: The Search for Capabilities*, Oxford: Oxford University Press for The International Institute for Strategic Studies.

Heise, Volker and Peter Schmidt (2005) 'NATO und EU: Auf dem Weg zu einer strategischen Partnerschaft?' *In*: Jäger Thomas, Alexander Höse and Kai Oppermann (eds) *Transatlantische Beziehungen: Sicherheit – Wirtschaft – Öffentlichkeit*, Wiesbaden: VS Verlag für Sozialwissenschaften, 65–86.

Hofmann, Stephanie C. (2009) 'Overlapping institutions in the realm of international security: The case of NATO and ESDP', *Perspectives on Politics*, 7(1): 45–51.

Hofmann, Stephanie C. (2017) 'Party preferences and institutional transformation: revisiting France's relationship with NATO (and the common wisdom on Gaullism)', *Journal of Strategic Studies*, 40(4): 505–531.

Hofmann, Stephanie C. (2019) 'The politics of overlapping organisations: hostage-taking, forum-shopping and brokering', *Journal of European Public Policy*, 26(6): 883–905.

Hofmann, Stephanie C. and Christopher Reynolds (2007) 'EU-NATO relations: Time to thaw the "frozen conflict"', *SWP Comments*, 12: 1–9.

Howorth, Jolyon (2009) 'NATO and ESDP: Institutional complexities and political realities', *Politique Etrangère*, 5: 95–106.

Howorth, Jolyon (2018) 'EU-NATO cooperation and strategic autonomy: Logical contradiction or Ariadne's thread?' *KFG Working Paper*, 90: 1–21.

Howorth, Jolyon and John T.S. Keeler (2003) *Defending Europe: The EU, NATO and the Quest for European Autonomy*, New York, Basingstoke: Palgrave Macmillan.

Juncos, Ana E. (2017) 'Security and defence'. *In*: Hadfield, Amelia et al. (eds) *Foreign Policies of EU Member States: Continuity and Europeanisation*, Abingdon: Routledge, 115–130.

Kagan, Robert (2003) *Of Power and Paradise: America and Europe in the New World Order*, New York: Alfred A. Knopf/Random House Publisher.

Kaufman, Joyce P. (2017) 'The US perspective on NATO under Trump: Lessons of the past and prospects for the future', *International Affairs*, 93(2): 251–266.

Ker-Lindsay, James (2010) 'Shifting alignments: The external orientation of Cyprus since independence', *The Cyprus Review*, 22(2): 67–74.

Koch, Martin (2008) *Verselbstständigungsprozesse Internationaler Organisationen*, Wiesbaden: VS Verlag für Sozialwissenschaften.

Koops, Joachim A. (2017) 'Inter-organisationalism in international relations: A multilevel framework of analysis'. *In*: Biermann, Rafael and Joachim A. Koops (eds) *Palgrave Handbook of Inter-Organisational Relations in World Politics*, New York, Basingstoke: Palgrave Macmillan, 189–216.

Kristi, Raik and Pauli Järvenpää (2017) *A New Era of EU-NATO Cooperation: How to Make the Best of a Marriage of Necessity*, Tallinn: International Centre for Defence and Security.

Lamont, Christopher (2015) *Research Methods in International Relations*, London: SAGE Publications Ltd.

Larrabee, F. Stephen (2004) 'ESDP and NATO: Assuring complementarity', *The International Spectator*, 39(1): 51–70.

Mace, Catriona (2004) 'Operation Concordia: Developing a 'European' approach to crisis management?' *International Peacekeeping*, 11(3): 474–490.

Magliveras, Konstantinos D. (2011) 'Membership in international organisations'. *In*: Klabbers, Jan and Asa Wallendahl (eds) *Research Handbook on the Law of International Organisations*, Cheltenham and Northampton: Edward Elgar Publishing, 84–107.

Major, Claudia and Christian Mölling (2009) 'More than wishful thinking? The EU, UN, NATO and the comprehensive approach to military crisis management', *Studia Diplomatica*, 62(3): 21–28.

Mälksoo, Maria (2018) 'Countering hybrid warfare as ontological security management: The emerging practices of the EU and NATO', *European Security*, 27(3): 374–392.

Manners, Ian and Richard G. Whitman (2001) *The Foreign Policies of European Union Member States*, Manchester: Manchester University Press.

Marsh, Steve and Wyn Rees (2012) *The European Union in the Security of Europe: From Cold War to Terror War*, Abingdon: Routledge.

Martill, Benjamin and Monika Sus (2018) 'Post-Brexit EU/UK security cooperation: NATO, CSDP+, or "French connection"?' *The British Journal of Politics and International Relations*, 20(4): 846–863.

Mattelaer, Alexander (2016) 'US leadership and NATO: Revisiting the principles of NATO burden-sharing', *Parameters*, 46(1): 25–33.

Moens, Alexander (2003) 'ESDP, the United States and the Atlantic Alliance'. *In*: Howorth, Jolyon and John T.S. Keeler (eds) *Defending Europe: The EU, NATO and the Quest for European Autonomy*, Basingstoke: Palgrave Macmillan, 25–37.

Muratore, Andrew (2010) 'EU-NATO co-operation and the pirates of the Gulf of Aden', *Australian Journal of Maritime and Ocean Affairs*, 2(3): 90–101.

NATO (1991) *The Alliance's New Strategic Concept*. Brussels: NATO.

NATO (1996) Final Communiqué of the Ministerial Meeting of the North Atlantic Council in Berlin on 3 June 1996. Press Communiqué M-NAC-1(96)63.

NATO (1999) *The Washington Declaration Signed and Issued by the Heads of State and Government Participating in the Meeting of the North Atlantic Council in Washington D.C. on 23rd and 24th April 1999. Press Release NAC-S(99)63.*

NATO (2002) *EU-NATO Declaration on the European Security and Defence Policy*, www.nato.int/cps/en/natolive/official_texts_19544.htm (accessed on 25/02/2017).

NATO (2006) *Backgrounder: Interoperability for Joint Operations*, www.nato.int/cps/en/natolive/topics_82679.htm (accessed on 24/07/2017).

NATO (2010) *Active Engagement, Modern Defence: Strategic Concept for the Defence and Security of Members of the North Atlantic Treaty Organisation*, Brussels: NATO.

NATO (2016a) *Joint Declaration by the President of the European Council, the President of the European Commission, and the Secretary General of the North Atlantic Treaty*

Organisation, www.nato.int/nato_static_fl2014/assets/pdf/pdf_2016_07/20160708_160708-joint-NATO-EU-declaration.pdf (accessed on 10/07/2016).

NATO (2016b) *Partnership for Peace Programme. Last updated on 7 April 2016*, www.nato.int/cps/en/natolive/topics_50349.htm (accessed on 16/02/2017).

NATO (2017) *Defence Expenditure of NATO Countries (2009–2016), NATO Press Release, Communiqué No. PR/CP(2017)045 (March 2017).*

NATO (2018) *Third Progress Report on the Implementation of the Common Set of Proposals by EU and NATO Councils on 6 December 2016 and 5 December 2017.* Published on 8 June 2018, www.nato.int/nato_static_fl2014/assets/pdf/pdf_2018_06/20180608_180608-3rd-Joint-progress-report-EU-NATO-eng.pdf (accessed on 03/11/2018).

NATO (2019) *Fourth Progress Report on the Implementation of the Common Set of Proposals Endorsed by NATO and EU Councils on 6 December 2016 and 5 December 2017. Published on 17 June 2019*, www.nato.int/nato_static_fl2014/assets/pdf/pdf_2019_06/190617-4th-Joint-progress-report-EU-NATO-eng.pdf (accessed on 24/07/2020).

NATO (2020) *Defence Expenditure of NATO Countries (2013–2020)*, www.nato.int/cps/en/natohq/news_178975.htm (accessed on 15/02/2021).

NATO (2021) *Directors General of the NATO and EU International Military Staff Meet to Assess Ongoing Cooperation.* Published on 16 March 2021, updated on 18 March 2021, www.nato.int/cps/en/natohq/news_182298.htm (accessed on 21/03/2021).

Nováky, Niklas I.M. (2016) 'Who wants to pay more? The European Union's military operations and the dispute over financial burden sharing', *European Security*, 25(2): 216–236.

Ojanen, Hanna (2006) 'The EU and NATO: Two competing models for a common defence policy', *Journal of Common Market Studies*, 44(1): 57–76.

Ostermann, Falk (2015) 'The end of ambivalence and the triumph of pragmatism? Franco-British defence cooperation and European and Atlantic defence policy traditions', *International Relations*, 29(3): 334–347.

Pannier, Alice (2015) 'Le «minilatéralisme»: une nouvelle forme de coopération de défense', *Politique Etrangère*, 1: 37–48.

Pannier, Alice and Olivier Schmitt (2014) 'Institutionalised cooperation and policy convergence in European defence: Lessons from the relations between France, Germany and the UK', *European Security*, 23(3): 270–289.

Perruche, Jean-Paul (2014) 'From exception to facilitator: What place for France in the EU/NATO partnership in the post-Cold War global world?' *Journal of Transatlantic Studies*, 12(4): 432–442.

Reichard, Martin (2004) 'Some legal issues concerning the EU-NATO Berlin Plus agreement', *Nordic Journal of International Law*, 73(1): 37–67.

Reichard, Martin (2006) *The EU-NATO Relationship: A Legal and Political Perspective*, Abingdon: Routledge.

Rodt, Annemarie Peen (2017) 'Member states policy towards EU military operations'. *In*: Hadfield, Amelia et al. (eds) *Foreign Policies of EU Member States: Continuity and Europeanisation*, Abingdon: Routledge, 131–147.

Schleich, Caja (2014) 'NATO and EU in conflict regulation: Interlocking institutions and division of labour', *Journal of Transatlantic Studies*, 12(2): 182–205.

Schmidt, Peter (2006) 'Die transatlantische Partnerschaft und ihre Bedeutung für das EU Krisenmanagement – Eine Skizze in vier Thesen'. *In*: Feichtinger, Walter and Carmen Gebhard (eds) *EU als Krisenmanager: Herausforderungen – Akteure – Instrumente*, Wien: Schriftenreihe der Landesverteidigungsakademie, 119–128.

Siedschlag, Alexander and Franz Eder (2006) 'Akteure und Zusammenspiel im EU- Krisenmanagement'. *In*: Feichtinger, Walter and Carmen Gebhard (eds) *EU als Krisenmanager: Herausforderungen – Akteure – Instrumente*, Wien: Landesverteidigungsakademie (LVAk)/Institut für Friedenssicherung und Konfliktmanagement (IFK), 61–90.

Smith, Kevin B. (2002) 'Typologies, taxonomies, and the benefits of policy classification', *Policy Studies Journal*, 30(3): 379–395.

Smith, Simon J. (2011) 'EU-NATO cooperation: A case of institutional fatigue?' *European Security*, 20(2): 243–264.

Smith, Simon J. and Carmen Gebhard (2017) 'EU-NATO relations: running on the fumes of informed deconfliction', *European Security*, 26(3): 303–314.

Sperling, James (2004) 'Capabilities traps and gaps: Symptom or cause of a troubled transatlantic relationship', *Contemporary Security Policy*, 25(3): 452–478.

Sperling, James and Mark Webber (2019) 'Trump's foreign policy and NATO: Exit and voice', *Review of International Studies*, 45(3): 511–526.

Tardy, Thierry (2014) 'CSDP: Getting third states on board', *EUISS Brief*, 6: 1–4.

Tiilikainen, Teija (2006) 'The Nordic countries and the EU-NATO relationship'. *In*: Bailes, Alyson J.K., Gunilla Herolf and Bengt Sundelius (eds) *Nordic Countries and the European Security and Defence Policy*, Stockholm: SIPRI, 50–66.

Tofte, Sunniva (2003) 'Non-EU NATO members and the issue of discrimination'. *In*: Howorth, Jolyon and John T.S. Keeler (eds) *Defending Europe: The EU, NATO and the Quest for European Autonomy*, Basingstoke: Palgrave Macmillan, 135–156.

Törö, Csaba (2011) *Visegrad Cooperation Within NATO and CSDP, V4 Papers, No. 2.*

Touzovskaia, Natalia (2006) 'EU-NATO relations: How close to "strategic partnership?"' *European Security*, 15(3): 235–258.

Varwick, Johannes (2006) 'European Union and NATO: Partnership, competition or rivalry?' *Kieler Analysen zur Sicherheitspolitik*, 18: 1–22.

Varwick, Johannes and Joachim A. Koops (2009) 'The European Union and NATO: 'Shrewd interorganisationalism' in the making?' *In*: Jørgensen, Knud Erik (ed.) *The European Union and International Organisations*, Abingdon: Routledge, 101–130.

Vershbow, Alexander (1999) *Next Steps on European Security and Defence: A US View*, Speech Held in Berlin, 17 December 1999.

von Voss, Alicia and Tobias Schütz (2018) 'The UK's potential role in enabling EU-NATO cooperation after Brexit', *In*: IISS and DGAP (eds) *Brexit and Defence: An Agenda for Constructive Dialogue in Support of European Security*, London: International Institute for Security Studies.

Walt, Stephen M. (2018) The EU and NATO and Trump – Oh My! *Foreign Policy: Voice*, Published on 2 July 2018, https://foreignpolicy.com/2018/07/02/the-eu-and-nato-and-trump-oh-my/ (accessed on 03/11/2018).

Western European Union (1992) *Petersberg Declaration. Western European Union Council of Ministers Meeting in Bonn on 19 June 1992*, www.weu.int/documents/920619peten.pdf (accessed on 26/05/2016).

Whitman, Richard G. (2004) 'NATO, the EU and ESDP: An emerging division of labour', *Contemporary Security Policy*, 25(3): 430–451.

Whitman, Richard G. (2016) 'The UK and EU foreign, security and defence policy after Brexit: Integrated, associated or detached?' *National Institute Economic Review*, 238(1): 43–50.

Whitman, Richard G. (2020) 'Missing in action: The EU-UK foreign, security and defence policy relationship after Brexit', *European View*, 19(2): 222–229.

Whitney, Craig R. (1991) War in the Gulf: Europe; Gulf Fighting Shatters Europeans' Fragile Unity, *New York Times,* Published on 25 January 1991, www.nytimes.com/1991/01/25/world/war-in-the-gulf-europe-gulf-fighting-shatters-europeans-fragile-unity.html?pagewanted=1 (accessed on 02/10/2017).

Winn, Neil (2003) 'Towards a common European security and defence policy? The debate on NATO, the European army and transatlantic security', *Geopolitics*, 8(2): 47–68.

Yost, David S. (2003) 'The US-European capabilities gap and the prospect for ESDP'. *In*: Howorth, Jolyon and John T.S. Keeler (eds) *Defending Europe: The EU, NATO and the Quest for European Autonomy*, Basingstoke: Palgrave Macmillan, 81–106.

Zięba, Ryszard (2018) *The Euro-Atlantic Security System in the 21st Century: From Cooperation to Crisis*, Berlin, Heidelberg, New York: Springer.

2   Theorising member states in interorganisational relations

To understand the relationship between the EU and NATO, including its functions and dysfunctions, it is vital to understand how member states shape interorganisational relations. This chapter is guided by the question of how relations between international organisations are understood and explained from a theoretical point of view and how the role of member states in interorganisational relations can be theorised. What drives the development of the theoretical framework are questions on the design of interactions and relationships between organisations with overlapping mandates in the same policy area and with a significant membership overlap. The research programme of interorganisational relations has become the main tool to analyse the EU–NATO relationship (Biermann and Koops 2017), yet the scholarly theoretical literature has so far not focused systematically on explaining the role of member states in shaping interorganisational relations.

Stephen D. Krasner's definition of international regimes has been widely acknowledged in the International Relations scholarship. He defines them as 'sets of implicit or explicit principles, norms, rules and decision-making procedures around which actors' expectations converge in a given area of international relations' (Krasner 1982: 186). International regimes are characterised as 'man-made' and 'social institutions' (Haas 1982: 210), which deal with immaterial and indirect processes. In contrast, international organisations consist not only of ideational and normative processes, but of 'brick and mortar' (Archer 2001: 2), in the form of material processes and physical presence. They include an independent bureaucratic structure as well as some autonomous decision-making power, which is distinct from their member states' decision-making powers (Barnett and Finnemore 1999, 2004; Bauer and Ege 2016; Reinalda and Verbeek 1998). In addition, international organisations have also been understood as arenas and forums, as actors in their own right and as social environments (Barnett and Finnemore 2004; Johnston 2001; Reinalda and Verbeek 1998). Organisations can act independently and autonomously from their member states by pursuing their own goals and policy objectives, whereby they can also influence and even trigger change in states' strategies and behaviour towards cooperative action through the process of socialisation and learning (Johnston 2001).

DOI: 10.4324/9781003170068-2

There are two major components that constitute and shape the activities, design and functioning of international organisations: member states and bureaucracies. International organisations have limited autonomy to develop further and to take actions and decisions on behalf of their members. They therefore include bureaucratic structures, such as sub-institutions and agencies, which deal with specific, commonly agreed issues and policy areas within a defined functional and geographical scope. Consequently, international organisations comprise specific characteristics and features, which impact their external relations and interactions with other actors (Biermann 2017). As Barnett and Finnemore (2004: 16) argue, international organisations 'are constituted as bureaucracies, and that bureaucratic character profoundly shapes the way they behave'. Bureaucracies are regarded as 'the collection of rules that define complex social tasks and establish a division of labour to accomplish them' (Barnett and Finnemore 2004: 18).

The secretariats of international bureaucracies are comprised of staff members that contribute information, knowledge, expertise and skills to the bureaucratic structures that organise and regulate international politics, and which can also shape the behaviour of states. Secretariats contribute to developing a distinctive bureaucratic culture of international organisations that rest on shared discourses, symbols and values for staff. These help to generate a certain group identity guiding their action and to adopt a certain type of collective identity, which relates to the extent to which international organisations have acquired their own identity, loyalty and spectrum of legal capacity (Wendt 1987, 1994). International organisations possess some autonomy over the direction of their policies and actions, which leads to the premise that they are 'partially independent actors' (Faude 2015: 296). Because of the bureaucratic power and extent of authority and autonomy that secretariats can exercise, for example, in regulating inter-state relations, international bureaucracies themselves alongside member states can trigger interorganisational relations (Barnett and Finnemore 1999, 2004; Bauer and Ege 2016). While international organisations include internal structures and procedures to allow their member states to cooperate, they themselves are able to cooperate with external actors via secretariats and liaison mechanisms.

Cooperation among international organisations in European security and defence has become an interesting as well as a relevant research topic, which has recently enjoyed increasing levels of scholarly attention, especially since the involvement of a growing number of international and national actors in the field (Biermann and Koops 2017; de Wijk 2004; Græger 2017; Græger and Haugevik 2011; Howorth and Keeler 2003; Koops 2017; Missiroli 2002). Different approaches to the study of cooperation in international relations have been applied to examine the interactions between organisations on the international level. These approaches range from traditional theories of international relations and European integration (Ojanen 2006) to institutionalism and organisation theories (Johnston 2001; Jönsson 1986, 2017), principal-agent models (Schleich 2014), socialisation theory, practice theory and ontological security (Adler and Greve 2009; Græger 2016, 2017) as well as concepts of security community (Adler 2008; Adler and Barnett 1998; Greve 2018).

What is more, the growing density of international organisations sparked debates on the interactions between overlapping organisations leading to the notion of regime complexes. Regime complexity describes 'the congeries of agreements and rules that intersect with regard to a particular issue or set of issues and conceptualises how the complexity of rules and institutions can, in and of itself, shape the politics of cooperation' (Alter and Raustiala 2018: 330). However, while regime complexity allows to examine relations between overlapping organisations, it neither considers the role nor accounts for the contributions by member states to the (dys-) functionality of interorganisational cooperation. In contrast, the emergence of interorganisationalism as a separate theoretical approach possesses tools and the ability to analyse the dynamics between organisations by examining the interactions on different levels, including the member state and inter-secretariat levels (Biermann 2009; Koops 2017).

The theoretical framework developed and applied in this book thus enhances the scholarship by providing an overview of the key features according to which interorganisational relationships can be examined. More importantly, it also adds the focus on member states as a new perspective to the analysis of interorganisational relations, which has so far received little attention. This chapter first provides a discussion of existing approaches in order to develop the theoretical framework of interorganisational relations. A set of features of interorganisational cooperation will be established to identify the occurrence of such phenomena. Subsequently, this chapter develops the typology of member states in interorganisational relations, which guides the empirical analysis.

Theorising interorganisational relations

Cooperation is a key component of international organisations. In line with Krasner's definition of international regimes, member states formalise their interactions and cooperation through agreeing on a set of rules, norms, values, practices and procedures, which they foster with the help of regimes and organisations. Alternative theoretical approaches to regime theory also seek to explain cooperation and the existence of international organisations. Neorealist scholars such as Mearsheimer (1994: 13) understand international institutions as means to help realise powerful states' interests and preferences in the international system. More precisely, he argues that states create and act through international institutions to 'maintain their share of world power'. In contrast, constructivists such as Jeffrey Checkel (2005) and Alastair Iain Johnston (2001) see the potential of international organisations to act as enablers for socialisation among member states, that is, the process of learning and internalising rules, norms and procedures that can create a common or collective identity.

A rather simple definition of cooperation is the working together of two or more actors who share the same end goal. In his understanding of cooperation theory, Axelrod (2006: 6) claims that individuals collaborate in order to 'pursue their self-interests without the aid of a central authority to force them to cooperate with each other'. Müller (2012: 607) refers to security cooperation as a distinctive form of cooperation, which he defines as 'relying on other states for national survival'. Hence, security cooperation among individual states 'occurs when states adjust their foreign policy and defence behaviour to the actual or anticipated preferences of others' (Jones 2007: 8). Cooperation can then be formalised through agreements and treaties of the participating actors. The processes of institutionalisation and the increased social interaction of actors promote the persistence of cooperation (Duffield 2013). In this context, Bailes and Cottey (2006) identify four different models of security cooperation: alliances, collective security, security regimes and security communities. The cooperation of states in the field of security and defence has triggered, for example, the creation of the Atlantic Alliance in 1949 and the EU with its CSDP in 1992.

Defining and mapping interorganisational relations

Taking the research programme of international regimes and regime complexity as the point of departure helps to develop a theoretical framework for the analysis of interorganisational cooperation. With the emergence of overlapping regimes, for example, in the issue areas of environmental politics and international trade, the idea of regime complexes emerged. Regime complexity is defined as an 'array of partially overlapping and non-hierarchical institutions governing a particular issue area' (Raustiala and Victor 2004: 279). It is seen as 'the presence of nested, partially overlapping and parallel international regimes that are not hierarchically ordered' (Alter and Meunier 2009: 13). The cumulating number of international organisations within the same policy area, such as in security policy, environmental policy or trade policy, can be seen in such networks, which Jönsson (1986) and Biermann (2008a) therefore label as 'interorganisational systems' and 'interorganisational networks' respectively. Rooted in the study of regime complexity, the literatures on institutional linkage and organisation theory explore regime interactions (see Gehring and Oberthür 2004; Jönsson 2017; Lipson 2017). They look at how the rules and norms of overlapping international regimes, including their agreements, conventions and treaties, affect one another (Gehring and Oberthür 2009). The aim is to analyse how these overlaps translate into either cooperation or competition between international regimes. Consequently, regimes affect each other if they have a functional relation or show some similarity (Lipson 2017). Related to the research programme of regime complexity is the study of organisational fields, which are defined as 'a community of organisations that partakes of a common meaning system and whose participants interact more frequently and fatefully with one another than with actors outside of the field' (Scott 1994: 207–208). The existence of such organisational fields requires a certain degree of homogeneity among members as well as overlaps and similarities of structures and bureaucracies to facilitate exchanges, interaction and cooperation. In addition, organisational fields are influenced by their members and, vice versa, members are influenced by those organisational fields in which they partake (DiMaggio and Powell 1983; Wooten and Sacco 2017). Furthermore, members of an organisational field share a common and collective goal.

While these theoretical approaches acknowledge the existence of overlapping and interacting international organisations, the focus is either on the power relations between member states and secretariats or on the contributions by the various actors at different levels of the international system (Koops 2017; Smith 2011). In the study of the EU–NATO relationship, most contributions circulate around the dominant themes of rivalry and competition between two organisations (Duke 2008; Ojanen 2006; Varwick 2006), the approaches to crisis management by the EU and NATO (Major and Mölling 2009; Schleich 2014) or the actors involved in EU–NATO cooperation, that is, individuals, states, international staff and military actors (Koops 2017; Smith 2011). Other studies also focus on the actual relationship between Europe and North America and between the EU and NATO (Kagan 2003; Reichard 2006; Sloan 2003) or on the issue of practical cooperation in crisis management operations (Gebhard and Smith 2015; Missiroli 2002; Schleich 2014). When both international organisations and member states are concerned, the applicability of these theoretical and conceptual approaches is limited and often does not account for the interactions between states and bureaucracies as well as between different international organisations in the same policy field. Moreover, the systemic analysis of member states, their behaviour and interactions have not been the focal points in the study of interorganisational relations. The concepts of regime interaction and regime complexity provide starting points for theorising interorganisational cooperation and analysing the relationship between the EU and NATO. The understanding of international organisations as actors in their own right and the acknowledgement that both states and international organisations with their secretariats shape international politics, provide relevant insights for theorising both interorganisational interaction and how member states shape these interactions. Yet, these existing approaches and analyses do not allow to fully study the mechanisms of cooperation and interactions between the EU and NATO. They also do not include the numerous actors involved in the study of relations between international organisations because approaches such as regime theory assume that international organisations affect behaviour, while not making assumptions about how states are able to shape interactions between organisations.

Deriving from the study of international organisations more broadly as well as from regime complexity and network analysis, Christer Jönsson

(1986) gives the observed phenomenon the name 'interorganisational theory'. He discusses the issue of the interrelations of international organisations and thereby takes a closer look at the networks in which they interact. He calls this observation 'interorganisational relations' (Jönsson 1986). In their approach to developing a theoretical and conceptual framework, Thomas Gehring and Sebastian Oberthür examine 'interinstitutional interaction' (2004, 2009; also see Gehring and Faude 2014). When seeking to explain the relations between international institutions and international organisations, both Howard Loewen (2006) and Stefan Jungcurt (2006) use the term 'interplay between international institutions'. The term interplay, however, refers solely to 'situations when the development, operation, effectiveness or broad consequences of one institution are significantly affected by the rules and programs of another' (Loewen 2006: 11), which does not include the possibility of collaboration and cooperation of the respective institutions.

In terms of actual exchanges, cooperation and interplay of international organisations, Joachim Koops (2007, 2012) and Rafael Biermann (2008a, 2009) label the observation 'interorganisationalism'. Biermann (2008a) goes even a step further by referring specifically the EU–NATO relationship as 'interorganisational networking' because of their shared efforts to create a wider group or system in which the organisations are increasingly interconnected. The notion of *interorganisational relations* – or alternatively, *interorganisational interaction* and *interorganisational cooperation* – points to the relations between international security organisations, particularly the relationship between the EU and NATO. It comprises the overall phenomenon of the connection of two or more international organisations and the way these actors regard and relate to as well as behave and exert influence towards each other. The term also encompasses the overall organisational setting as well as the whole architecture of the web of international security organisations. It includes the influences that can be exerted by actors within one of the organisations – for example, the secretariats, agencies or institutions such as the EU institutions and NATO departments – as well as by member states and key individual figures, thereby comprising the multiple actors involved.

Broadly speaking, interorganisational interaction occurs 'if one institution (the source institution) affects the development or performance of another institution (the target institution)' (Gehring and Oberthür 2009: 127). In addition, Koops (2012: 72) defines interorganisational relations as 'links, relationships and modes of interaction between two or more international organisations'. Consequently, the interactions between two organisations can take different forms, including exchanges of information and material resources, coordination of activities and the establishment of structured relationships.

Based on these definitions, international organisations can influence and shape each other's policies, procedures and institutions when interacting more regularly, whereby one organisation finds itself in a learning process in which it gets socialised. While learning is defined as a 'change in the cognitive structures of actors' and the change of their beliefs, procedures and structures, socialisation is a specific type of learning. It refers to a 'process by which social interaction leads novices to endorse "expected ways of thinking, feeling and acting"' (Johnston 2001: 494) as well as to a process of 'adaptation of certain rules of behaviour, "ways of doing things", stemming from interaction with members of the same group' (Juncos and Pomorska 2006: 3). Socialisation and learning among member states as well as among international organisations are likely to occur with increased interactions and overlaps. However, learning can be prevented by communication problems, lack of implementation due to shortage of resources and the frequent rotation of staff, whereby the learned processes get lost. Drawn from these definitions and conceptualisations, a set of features will be developed that further allow to define and characterise interorganisational relations.

Features of interorganisational relations

The theoretical framework draws on findings from different conceptualisations and theoretical approaches that investigate the connections and interplays of actors within a network in the same policy domain. Interorganisational relationships take different designs and are equipped with specific characteristics that define the degree and form of interactions. These features of interorganisational relations refer to the intensity, formality and set-up of interactions while also considering additional factors, such as the network of organisations and the institutional set-ups of the organisations.

As a precondition for organisations to enter an interorganisational relationship, they need to demonstrate a high degree of functional overlap and a higher degree of homogeneity in terms of interests, norms and rules. Gehring and Oberthür (2009) and Biermann (2008b) argue that particularly functional overlap triggers interorganisational relations due to already existing links and connections among international organisations. According to Faude (2015: 297), 'functional overlap occurs when an overlap between two or more international organisations exists in terms of membership and contextual governance areas'.[1] Functional overlap refers to the overlap of regulatory jurisdiction, tasks, geographical scope and membership, but can furthermore include, for example, geography, membership, responsibilities and organisational structures (Gehring and Oberthür 2009). Both member states and international secretariats can initiate functional overlap, which can take place either intended or unintended. Deriving from a sociological viewpoint on interorganisational interactions, 'the more organisations learn from each other and the more similar they tend to become, the easier their cooperation will become' (Koops 2007: 22). Organisations favouring exchanges and cooperation with other international organisations are thus more inclined to functional overlap.

Functional overlap is most commonly present when two or more organisations exist in the same policy area, which create a network of interconnected actors that depict the relationships and interactions between international organisations and their member states. Networks are defined as 'sets of relations that form structures, which in turn may constrain and enable agents' and as 'sets of ties between any set or sets of nodes' (Hafner-Burton, Kahler and Montgomery 2009: 560, 562). They consist of nodes which imply any actors, such as states, bureaucracies or international organisations, within these networks, as well as of ties which illustrate connections or relationships between nodes. The connections can be composed of dyads, triads and of a greater number of participating international actors. General characteristics and basic elements of networks include the interdependence among the nodes and units in a given network and constant interactions between the units and nodes to maintain fluid exchanges (Maoz 2012). Links between actors and thus the networks also follow specific purposes. First, they link international actors that have common values, rules and responsibilities. Second, networks enhance and facilitate interactions and dialogue between their nodes due to the increasing links among actors and because they enable access to important resources. The more links exist, the less likely it is that conflicts occur between the nodes (Dorussen and Ward 2008, Keck and Sikkink 1998). Therefore, a network serves as a 'mode of organisation that facilitates collective action and cooperation, exercises influence, or serves as a means of international governance' (Hafner-Burton, Kahler and Montgomery 2009: 560). Actors set up networks – or regime complexes – based on shared understandings of norms, rules and purposes as well as overlaps of policy domains. In this sense, networks 'reflect and promote similarity of interest and mutual understanding' (Dorussen and Ward 2008: 192) and the members of a network are 'bound together by shared values, a common discourse, and dense exchanges of information and service' (Keck and Sikkink 1998: 2).

Positioning and membership both in international organisations and in networks are central features of network analysis applicable to the study of interorganisational relations. It is important for nodes to position themselves in networks to receive access to crucial resources, such as information, and to have direct interactions and exchanges with other important nodes. Positioning is also a way of expressing power, in the sense of possessing capabilities and resources. For this reason, 'organisations constantly seek to enhance their own positions within a network, resulting in rivalry for interorganisational power and centrality within a network' (Koops 2012: 79). Joint membership of states in various international organisations within the same network is another form of power because joint memberships have the advantage of fostering linkages and exchanges. Moreover, both positioning and membership can influence the transformation of networks, for example, from informal to more formal networks (Dorussen and Ward 2008; Hafner-Burton, Kahler and Montgomery 2009). Both elements are important to explain organisational adaptation and change because group socialisation, which occurs through interactions with other nodes, can affect change within other nodes. The idea of networks and organisational fields can be transferred to interorganisational relations since numerous international organisations with a degree of overlap and similarity co-exist in a network in which they and their member states need to position themselves. The consideration of networks of international actors helps to position member states and allows to examine the linkages among international organisations.

Organisations can take specific positions and roles in networks, which can further promote stronger cooperation and intensify functional overlaps. Christer Jönsson (1986) and Patrick Doreian and Kayo Fujimoto (2004) focus on linking-pin organisations in interorganisational networks. These are defined as those organisations 'that have extensive and overlapping ties to different parts of the network' (Aldrich and Whetten 1981: 390) and therefore, they take an 'integrative role in interorganisational networks' (Doreian and Fujimoto 2004: 46). Linking-pin organisations or linking-pin actors serve as communication points between organisations and actors within interorganisational networks. This notion is transferable to the idea of boundary-role occupants, which connect two or more organisations in a given policy area.

In addition, interorganisational interaction occurs on several levels: international system, member states, individual, bureaucratic and inter-secretariat (inter-institutional) levels (Koops 2017; also see Waltz 1959). The *international system level* takes into account the neorealist assumptions that addresses the anarchic nature of the international system, which allows war to occur. The structure of the international system and the changes and developments thereof lead to opportunities, which can either enable or constrain state actions (Waltz 1959). This structure of the international system allows interorganisational interaction to take place, that is, the prevailing international order can either facilitate or impede cooperation between international actors.

The *member state level* considers the behaviour of states within the international system. As the foundation and building blocks of organisations, states play the central role. They thus possess the ability to initiate, trigger, hamper or even prevent cooperation with other states as well as between organisations. It is important to consider the extent to which member states can influence the emergence and design of interorganisational interaction. Member states lead negotiations between international organisations, maintain the necessary resources and means to approve or obstruct interorganisational relationships and possess the power to move these relationships forward to deepen cooperation. Nevertheless, states face certain limitations such as a lack of coherence among national institutions and ministries. They also encounter the problem of imperfect knowledge and information which leads to uncoordinated policies and different approaches within a state. Rivalries among member states in different international organisations can furthermore prevent interorganisational relations (Biermann 2008b; Koops 2017).

On the *individual level*, the focus is shifted towards the role of individual decision-makers and the relations between key figures, such as executive heads and liaison officers, who can initiate and foster but also hamper cooperation and create rivalries. According to Koops (2007: 27), the 'facilitation of greater interaction and socialisation between key leaders and boundary-role occupants of international organisations is as important as greater interorganisational interaction on the ground in the form of joint training exercises and desk-to-desk dialogues'. Boundary-role occupants are those actors that connect international organisations and thereby play the role of bridges or linkages within multilateral settings (Jönsson 1986). Even though executive heads, such as the NATO Secretary General and the EU High Representative, can be drivers as well as obstacles in deepening interorganisational interaction, interpersonal relations matter on all levels of the organisational hierarchy. In cases of well-working interpersonal relations, the emergence of interpersonal trust can transform into interorganisational trust. For example, the good relations between HR Federica Mogherini and NATO Secretary Jens Stoltenberg have been recorded as an exmaple of personal ties contributing to EU-NATO cooperation. Koops (2017: 23) suggests that the frequent rotation of personnel and key figures in liaison offices leads to an 'alumni effect', which can enhance mutual understandings and increase both interorganisational trust and the enthusiasm for cooperation.

Because of the special nature of interorganisational relations, exchanges and cooperation take place on two additional levels: the bureaucratic and the inter-secretariat levels. The *bureaucratic level* refers to administrative structures within international organisations, where the majority of procedural decisions are taken and the day-to-day management occurs (Barnett and Finnemore 2004; Koops 2007, 2017). On this level, liaison units, permanent committees and formal cooperation channels can be established. In addition, 'identities, loyalties and an organisational culture of bureaucracies can also influence a secretariat or subunit's behaviour and approach towards interorganisational cooperation' (Koops 2017: 205). To facilitate exchanges, some international organisations have even developed compatible or similar administrative structures. The *inter-secretariat level* includes jointly created cooperation channels, such as working groups and steering committees that support formal cooperation between organisations. Secretariats and institutional bodies have to update each other frequently through the joint cooperation channels to maintain and nurture efficient interorganisational interaction. Besides formal channels, informal cooperation plays a crucial role, especially in cases of institutional incompatibility or other institutional and legal barriers (Smith 2011), such as the issue of limited sharing of classified information and intelligence. On the inter-secretariat level, certain institutional aspects need to be taken into account, such as formal agreements and declarations, the existence of liaison offices, regular meetings between secretariats and the particular arrangements of working groups and steering committees (Koops 2017).

An important aspect of cooperation on any of these levels of interorganisational interaction is the role of autonomy. As the conceptualisation of international organisations has indicated, the constructivist understanding highlights that organisations possess their own autonomy, albeit limited and dependent on the delegation of autonomy by states and the degree of their expertise (Barnett and Finnemore 2004; Reinalda and Verbeek 1998). When cooperating with others, an organisation has to give up autonomy, especially decision-making autonomy and authority over its resources and tasks (Biermann 2008b, 2015, Koops 2012). However, despite the loss of autonomy and authority, organisations enter into interorganisational relations with others on the premise of certain motives and objectives. Motives to cooperate, either formally or informally and either ad hoc and short-term or long-term, vary from autonomy concerns to relative gains and from functional overlap to resource dependence. Haugevik (2007) distinguishes between material and ideational motives. While organisational survival, neutralising competition and resource dependence are understood as material motives, ideational motives include legitimisation, shared values and organisational learning. An incentive for organisations to give up autonomy and authority to a certain extent, to enter a cooperative relationship with other organisations, is to make use of the cooperation partner's vital resources which the organisation itself might lack (Biermann and Harsch 2017). These resources can include military assets and capabilities as well as planning and operational structures. Organisations might seek cooperation to survive and remain relevant on the international level. Cooperation facilitates the usage of resources that enable organisational survival, that is, the exchange and sharing of essential resources. Another reason to enter interorganisational cooperation is the search for greater legitimacy of actions. This is usually the case when cooperating with the UN because it authorises and thus legitimises crisis management operations through UN Security Council mandates (Haugevik 2007). Concerning the EU and NATO, autonomy concerns have shaped their interaction in particular with reference to the loss of autonomy with an increasing overlap of responsibilities and the decision-making over the use of the alliance's military capabilities (Biermann 2015).

Gehring and Faude (2014; Faude 2015) argue that interorganisational interaction creates opportunities for organisational adaptation and organisational change, whilst Biermann (2009) refers to organisational transformation. Due to their own dynamics and autonomy, both member states and organisations can exercise influence on organisational adaptation. Organisational adaptation implies that the governance activities of both organisations gradually become accommodated and adapted to the respective other. The more interactions and exchanges take place and the higher the functional and membership overlaps, the more likely both international organisations become more accommodating to facilitate further exchanges and cooperation. Organisational adaptation leads to diverging outcomes depending on the power distributions among the organisations in the structural network. Power distribution can either be symmetric or asymmetric. In this context, power of an organisation denotes 'its ability to retain, or expand, its capability to pursue its policies within the area of functional overlap' (Gehring and Faude 2014: 479). Under an asymmetric power distribution, a so-called 'sectoral specialisation' (Gehring and Faude 2014: 479) of the organisations is most likely to occur because the weaker organisations have to withdraw their governance activities from the concerned policy domain. In case of a symmetric power distribution, the organisations have to coordinate their governance activities in the particular policy area. Herein, multiple members, that is, those states that are members in more than one international organisation within the same interorganisational network, play a crucial role as they have to negotiate the institutional arrangements within both organisations to avoid conflicts and malfunctions of the regulatory bodies. Under symmetric power distribution, co-governance and a division of labour are more likely to occur than role specification of either organisation. More specifically, organisational adaptation 'under symmetrical power relations is likely to produce institutionalised schemes of permanent co-governance instead of clear-cut sectoral separation' (Gehring and Faude 2014: 481).

In accordance with these findings, Gehring and Faude (2014: 482) observe that organisational adaptation 'gives rise to an institutionalised division of labour among the elemental institutions of an institutional complex'. In his analysis, Faude (2015: 304–305) defines interorganisational division of labour as

> a set of rules, which defines the tasks and responsibilities of competing organisations within a wider system of interorganisational coordination or cooperation. This set of rules includes generalised expectations about how each organisation should perform their tasks within the area of functional overlap. It therefore serves as a mechanism for containing interorganisational competition and dissolving opportunities for forum-shopping in areas of functional overlap.[2]

This division of labour results in deeper cooperation of the organisations in which they become so-called 'interlocking institutions' (Biermann 2009; Gehring and Faude 2014; Schleich 2014). This is especially the case when a high level of functional overlap between organisations is recorded. A division of labour should not be taken for granted, however, because it is not automatically triggered by functional overlap, but it can emerge from complimentary organisational adaptation processes. In order to occur and be used effectively, the respective international organisations need to agree on a specific division of labour and the allocation of the responsibilities, tasks and governance areas for each actor (Faude 2015).

Several categorisations and approaches to typologies have already been developed drawing on the extent and design of networks of international organisations, the power distribution and the degree of division of labour between overlapping organisations. Gehring and Oberthür (2009) propose a typology composed of seven dimensions: functional interdependence, interaction and/or membership overlap, intentionality of action, ability to influence another organisation, quality of effect, response and policy domains. This attempt to develop a typology helps to understand the process of interactions of international organisations and how it affects organisational adaptation and change. However, it does not provide much detail about the scope and type of interactions. Young (1999) distinguishes between functional interplay and political interplay. Functional interplay is related to functional overlap and occurs when the organisations are geophysically or socioeconomically linked. Political interplay is created on purpose by the concerned organisations in order to set up links in pursuit of specific goals, which can either be collective or individual. Loewen (2006) adds to this categorisation two additional types: horizontal interplay and vertical interplay. While horizontal interplay takes place on the same level of similar types of organisations including interactions on the interregional level, such as the interplay between the EU and African Union, vertical interplay is based on 'cross-scale interactions' (Loewen 2006: 2) between different types of international organisations, such as the EU and the WTO. Biermann (2008a, 2015) distinguishes first between three categories of interorganisational cooperation – information sharing, coordination of policies and joint actions and decision-making – and then between different intensity levels of interorganisational interaction – absent, minimal, moderate and strong. Interorganisational cooperation can thus also be ad hoc and short-term or formalised, structured and long-term. In his conceptualisation, Dijkstra (2017) refers to four different dimensions of interorganisational interaction: level of formalisation, intensity of interaction (frequency and extent), symmetry of participating organisations (whether are seen as equal partners) and degree of standardisation (agreed procedures and structures).

Based on the existing literature and the conceptualisation of interorganisational cooperation, a set of features emerge that help to depict the importance of member states. Table 2.1 provides an overview of the most important features: density of network, functional overlap, level of formalisation, frequency of interactions, intensity of interactions and membership overlap. These help to explain the relationship, including its emergence and maintenance, and how the organisations' interactions affect their respective internal and bureaucratic structures. What is more, in each of these dimensions, member states play a central role considering that they build the foundation of international organisations, are the key decision-makers particularly in foreign, security and defence affairs and have the ability to trigger functional overlap and domain similarity. The existing literature on interorganisational relations has often overlooked the relevance of membership, although member states, especially in security and defence, essentially shape and sometimes even control international organisations.

Table 2.1 Features of interorganisational interaction

Features	Description
Density of network	Density illustrates the number of international organisations in a network of organisations, that is, in the network of international security organisations. It is assumed that the more links exist in a network, the less conflicts occur (Dorussen and Ward 2008; Keck and Sikkink 1998). A higher degree of density can be created by member states who establish new institutions in the same policy area with overlapping tasks.
Functional overlap	Functional overlap indicates the overlap of policy areas that are covered by the international organisations in the same network. The more functional overlaps exist, the more links exist and the more interactions and exchanges take place. This dimension also includes geographical scope, that is, the geographical area covered by an international organisation in regard to both membership and activity. Functional overlap can be triggered intentionally or it can occur unintendedly (Faude 2015). Functional overlap is primarily triggered by member states or, alternatively, by international bureaucracies.
Formalisation	This is similar to the level of institutionalisation. It includes how formal or informal relationships of organisations are. Formal agreements, such as declarations, contracts or pacts, are indicators of high level of formalisation. Ad hoc cooperation without agreements as the foundation are considered as low level of formalisation.
Frequency of interactions	Frequency indicates the number of interactions and interplays between international organisations. Interactions include formal and informal exchanges and meetings as well as joint actions and exercises. The higher the level of formalisation, the higher the frequency of interactions. Two or more international organisations may even set up formal arenas for interactions, such as joint councils. Frequent interactions can lead to organisational adaptation to accommodate each other's structures and procedures.
Intensity	According to Biermann (2015), four levels of intensity of interorganisational interactions can be distinguished: (1) absent, (2) minimal, (3) moderate and (4) strong. This encompasses the dimensions of frequency and formalisation and adds the character and form (that is, ad hoc, short-term, structured, long-term, etc.) of interactions. The higher the intensity of interactions, the more convergence of values, norms and procedures may occur. Moderate and strong intensity levels can lead to a division of labour to avoid competition.
Membership overlap	This shows the number of states that are members in more than one international security organisations. As the building blocks of organisations, membership overlap is crucial to identify channels of interactions. Membership overlap affects organisational adaptation and enhances cooperation and interactions.

Theorising the role of member states

Member states play vital roles in shaping the institutional design and form of interactions between organisations. However, research on the actual role of member states in interorganisational cooperation is shallow. Rather little attention has so far been paid to membership and states' positioning within international organisations to explain the dynamics, interactions and relations between international organisations. Member states, especially those with membership in multiple international organisations, pursue specific strategies and thus have the ability to shape interorganisational relations through different channels and on multiple levels while they also possess the capacity to behave differently in the respective organisations. In areas of high politics in international relations, Koops (2017: 198–199) identifies the following responsibilities, powers and duties of member states: approval for negotiations, approval for the formation of contractual relationships between organisations and subunits, providing key resources, veto power which allows states to obstruct deeper cooperation, facilitating interorganisational coherence and facilitating cooperation across organisations to limit duplication. This range of identified tasks and responsibilities has triggered questions about the role of member states as well as their abilities, positions and responsibilities in interorganisational cooperation. Derived from their foreign and security policy orientations, historical experiences, domestic politics, resources and capabilities, member states formulate their preferences towards interorganisational relations. In accordance with the overall argument of this book, member states apply political strategies to shape the exchanges and interactions between organisations in the same policy domain and therefore play a crucial role in explaining the contemporary state of EU–NATO cooperation.

Membership and political strategies

In general, membership is central to interorganisational relations. Scholars of interorganisationalism point out that member states are the prime building blocks of international organisations and provide essential resources and capabilities, which makes membership, and membership overlap, a fundamental component of interorganisational cooperation (Gehring and Faude 2014; Gehring and Oberthür 2009; Hofmann 2009; Koops 2017). Two types of membership have been identified by Magliveras (2011). Original members are those states that take the initiative to create an international organisation and who have the right over its determination, purpose and design. Subsequent members are those states that join at a later stage and their membership is granted based on the discretion of original members and depending on the organisation's admission clauses. Gehring and Oberthür (2009) distinguish between two additional categories of membership: multiple members and single members. This distinction contributes significantly to developing the typology of member states in interorganisational relations because it helps to identify the specific position of certain states and to define the political strategies available to them.

Single members are those states which are members in only one organisation and who might not be directly affected by functional overlap of organisations. They do not have the ability to exert influence immediately because they are not involved in the decision-making process of those organisations of which they are not members. While states that join several international organisations with overlapping mandates have numerous advantages, single member states can also influence interorganisational cooperation. For example, they make use of the strategy of hostage-taking, which occurs when single members 'use their membership to obstruct the relationship between both institutions, holding them hostage in pursuit of national interests' (Hofmann 2009: 46). This has happened, for example, in the cases of Turkey in NATO and Cyprus in the EU.

Multiple members refer to those states that are members of two or more international organisations in the same policy area, which provides them with the advantage of being able to choose one organisation over another. They 'transmit influence from one institution to another' (Gehring and Oberthür 2009: 150) and play key roles in exerting influence on both organisations as well as their interactions with each other. Functional overlap can be established on purpose 'to challenge the regulatory dominance of an existing one (...), or if they seek to shift regulatory activities from one to another [organisation]' (Gehring and Faude 2014: 474). Even though these states have the ability to shape and influence an organisation's direction, multiple member states might also have a clear preference for one organisation over another. This enables them to trigger regime-shifting, that is, the change of organisational structures (Alter and Meunier 2009; Gehring and Faude 2014), as well as to take blocking and obstructive roles by using the strategy of turf battles. When using this strategy, multiple members 'advocate policies that shape the capability and mandate of one institution – often at the expense of the other' (Hofmann 2009: 47). One example in the EU–NATO relationship is the distinction between those states which prefer the EU, the so-called Europeanists, and those Atlanticist states that favour NATO (Cornish and Edwards 2001).

As members of international organisations, states can apply political strategies to shape interorganisational interaction according to their preferences. Political strategies are valuable tools to shape the design, functioning and execution of interorganisational cooperation and to 'explain whether, when and how both organisations manage to execute their mandates' (Hofmann 2019: 884). The most prominent strategies that have been recorded in the EU–NATO relationship are forum-shopping, regime-shifting, hostage-taking and brokering (Alter and Meunier 2009; Hofmann 2009, 2019). Forum-shopping, as a widely studied strategy, refers to the situation when a member state chooses one organisation over another to put a particular issue on the agenda because it is convinced that it will receive more gains in this organisation than in another (Gehring and Oberthür 2009). Due to the increasing network density of international organisations, the likelihood for states to select the appropriate governance structures and international organisations according to their interests has increased significantly, which has enabled states to make use of forum-shopping more frequently (Alter and Meunier 2009; Drezner 2009; Hofmann 2019). Yet, forum-shopping can also be considered as a new form of free-riding because it increasingly allows multiple members to pursue national interests instead of collective goals, which causes greater fragmentation and less optimal results for both international organisation and other member states (Faude 2015). In addition to forum-shopping, hostage-taking and regime-shifting, another option is brokering. In this case, states 'do not necessarily appreciate both IOs [international organisations] in equal terms, but they want them to work according to their mandates' and therefore seek to mediate among the organisations (Hofmann 2019: 886). Brokers act as bridges whereby they create 'links between actors that would remain otherwise unconnected' and therefore, it is 'this network position, and not the actors' attributes or interests' that define its role as broker in interorganisational relations (Goddard 2009: 250). While actors that opt for brokering can create ties, they can also break these ties which affects an organisation's external relations. The use of political strategies is decisive for the characterisation and categorisation of states in the context of interorganisational relations because they significantly influence the design, intensity and formalisation of interorganisational cooperation.

In addition to the distinction between original and subsequent members and between single and multiple members as well as the use of political strategies, states can take different roles, such as the role of linking-pin actors. These are actors that link sub-networks with larger interorganisational networks. In this position, they can enable the exchange of information, trigger regime shifts and increase functional overlap (Doreian and Fujimoto 2004). States also have the capability to delegate authority to international organisations so that these fulfil their mandates and tasks, including to take decisions and to engage in external relations with other actors on states' behalf. Overall, states take specific roles and positions and make use of strategies depending on their preferences and national orientation, resources and the international context.

Foreign and security policy orientation

In the analysis of states' rationales, preferences and behaviour in interorganisational cooperation, the debate around foreign and security policy orientation has emerged with regard to the concept of strategic culture. In the context of EU–NATO cooperation, foreign and security policy orientation considers member states' specific characteristics, norms, histories, operational experiences and national caveats that shape their system of beliefs, norms and values in conjunction with its own specific experiences. These factors form states' very own foreign and security policy orientation, which shape their policy preferences in foreign, security and defence affairs (Aras and Gorener 2010). In the study of member states' roles, influence and behaviour in interorganisational interaction, identity plays an essential part in understanding the motivations, interests and objectives of both states and international organisations who develop their own identities (Poopuu 2015). In the context of EU–NATO relations, member states have often been categorised into the camp of Atlanticists, those preferring a NATO-led approach to crisis management and security issues, and the camp of Europeanists, those in favour of EU response to crises and conflicts (Cornish and Edwards 2001). Alternatively, they have been distinguished between those with a tendency of military engagement in contrast to those states that seek to avoid or are restricted concerning the use of force. Yet, more factors than the preference for either the EU or NATO shape a state's foreign and security policy orientation.

The concept of foreign and security policy orientation is related to the notion of strategic culture, which entails both political and operational elements that define a county's approach to security and defence affairs. Different understandings of strategic culture exist that also inform the conceptualisation of foreign and security policy orientation. According to Gray (1999: 51), strategic culture is comprised of 'socially transmitted ideas, attitudes, traditions, habits [...], and preferred methods of operation that are more or less specific to a particular geographically based security community that has had a necessarily unique historical experience'. Strategic behaviour is thus not only formed by attitudes, habits and ideational factors but also by geography, military history and operational experience, technological advancement in warfare and a state's international relationships (Bloomfield 2012; Lord 1985). Central for this understanding is the distinction between the declared policy and the actual rationales and aims of a state (Biehl, Giegerich and Jonas 2013; Lock 2010). In contrast, Johnston (1995) takes a broader approach to strategic culture by referring to military culture and history, organisational culture and political-military culture. He defines strategic culture as 'an integrated "system of symbols (e.g., argumentation structures, languages, analogies, metaphors) which acts to establish pervasive and long-lasting strategic preferences by formulating concepts of the role and efficacy of military force in interstate political affairs [...]"' and further assumes that it is 'an ideational milieu which limits behavioural choices' (Johnston 1995: 46). Hence, it is not only rooted in historical experiences and strategic preferences but also seen as the result of recent practices and experiences.

Derived from the debates on strategic culture, states have their own distinct foreign and security policy orientation, while international security organisations have also developed their own foreign, security and defence policies. A state's foreign and security policy orientation is consequently shaped by its worldviews, interests, ideologies, historical experiences and domestic politics. External factors such as a state's geographical location and the strategic environment, that is, the existing security challenges and threats, play additional roles for making choices about behaviour and responses that influence a state's foreign and security policy orientation. These policies and orientations are formulated in official documents in the form of white papers or national security and defence strategies, which are published by national ministries but also by international organisations such as the EU and NATO (see Appendix B). NATO introduces regular strategic concepts that summarise its main challenges and threats and outline the Alliance's responses (NATO 1991, 2010). Similarly, with the development of CFSP and CSDP, the EU followed suit by launching the ESS in 2003 and the subsequent EUGS in 2016, which outline a list of risks and threats to Europe and how the EU seeks to approach them (EU 2003, 2016). The debate on the EU's strategic culture has been particularly contested and hotly debated during the development of its foreign, security and defence policies (Matláry 2006; Zyla 2011). In contrast to national white papers and strategies, however, the security strategies by the EU and NATO 'can both be conceptualised as outcomes of the bargaining and negotiation processes of nationally held strategic beliefs, values, norms and ideas of security' (Zyla 2011: 672). This refers to the understanding that the EU and NATO's foreign, security and defence strategies and policies are the result of their member states' agreed commonalities and the lowest common denominator of their preferences, strategies and threat perceptions.

For the understanding of an actor's foreign and security policy orientation, the notion of identity plays a relevant part in international politics as it constructs an actor's interests and goals (Guzzini 2003; Hopf 1998). The theoretical framework of interorganisational relations treats organisations and member states as equal actors and argues that their interests, interactions and behaviour are shaped by their self-perception as well as by their positioning within existing networks. Consequentially, not only states but also other international actors, including international organisations, possess their own identities (Wendt 1994). Wendt (1999) proposed and developed four categories of identity: personal/corporate, type, role and collective identity. Personal identity refers to states' identity and corporate to those of international organisations. Their identities are 'constituted by the self-organising, homeostatic structures that make actors distinct entities' (Wendt 1999: 224). Type identity refers to a group of actors that share some characteristics that make up their identity, which might include language, skills, experience and knowledge. This assumption relates to the understanding that identity serves as a 'collective phenomenon' which 'denotes a fundamental and consequential *sameness* among members of a group or category' (Brubaker and Cooper 2000: 7). Role identity implies the existence of the Other and identity helps to formulate an actor's beliefs and behaviour by distinguishing between the Self and Other. Through the existence of the Other, actors take specific roles accompanied by their self-perception and distinction from the Other (Poopuu 2015).

Identities of states and international organisations as well as foreign and security policy orientations have been formed over the course of time through the historical, cultural, social and political experiences of states. These orientations and identities are not fixed and therefore subject to change triggered by specific events and external factors. For example, NATO's identity has changed as it adapted to the new security environments, especially after its identity crisis with the end of the Cold War and the diminishing of the Soviet Union as its main threat (Flockhart 2015). Furthermore, the practice of member states in NATO to second staff from their defence and foreign affairs ministries to posts within the Alliance further shapes its identity. This contributes to the learning and socialisation process of member states' foreign and security policy orientation and the alignment with NATO's objectives, responsibilities and mandates. Such a learning process also takes place when the seconded staff return to their national ministries.

According to the conceptualisation of interorganisational cooperation, each member state as well as the international organisations possess their own distinctive identities. A state's foreign and security policy orientation is influenced by its national identity, which further rests on the country's historical experiences, legal and constitutional frameworks, geopolitical location, resources and capabilities. As the next section outlines, states from each category within the typology distinguish themselves from the others by formulating common positions, attitudes and policy preferences, whereby they possess elements of a shared identity. In addition, the international organisations of which they are members also acquire their own identities, which overlap with those of their member states. Taking into account the notion of identity and that both states and organisations develop their own identities through their self-perception and the distinction from the Other helps to categorise each of the states to a type of member state in interorganisational interaction and enables to identify their shared characteristics.

Typology of member states in interorganisational relations

Drawing on the theoretical framework of interorganisational relations, the conceptualisation of membership and the identification of political strategies and orientation, member states in interorganisational relations can be categorised as: (1) advocates, (2) blockers, (3) balancers and (4) neutrals (see Table 2.2 for an overview). These four categories provide the basis of the typology of member states in interorganisational cooperation. The use of the labels for each category attaches a name to the phenomenon and to the shared characteristics of a certain group of states. These labels can be seen as concepts or abstract frames that help to organise, name and give meaning to their characteristics and features (Berenskoetter 2017: 154).

Table 2.2 Typology of member states in interorganisational interaction

Type of member state	Description
Advocate	In favour of interorganisational interactions; promotes cooperation and interplay with other organisations in a network through membership or functional overlap; most likely to be a multiple member.
Blocker	Not in favour of interorganisational interactions; makes use of veto rights to prevent deeper cooperation; takes this position based on particular national interests or conflicts with other organisations in the network; can be single or multiple member.
Balancer	No explicit preference for a particular international organisation but attempts to balance between them; seeks equilibrium between organisations and acknowledges the strengths of each in order to achieve a division of labour.
Neutral	Neither advocates nor blocks interorganisational interactions; takes this position based on particular national interests or restraints; can be either a multiple or single member state.

Advocates refer to those member states that are multiple members and those that prefer a functioning and effective relationship between overlapping international organisations. They promote enhanced cooperation among international organisations in the same network by creating ties either through the benefit of their own multiple memberships or through increasing functional overlap, such as exchanges and joint actions in the same issue area. They can also serve as bridges between two or more international organisations due to their embeddedness in international networks and the maintenance of bilateral and minilateral relations. Among multiple member states, it is significant to identify the most powerful states or leading governments in interorganisational cooperation. Koops (2017: 201) labels these powerful member states 'interorganisational hegemon', which seek to heavily influence interorganisational cooperation. Advocates also have the ability to influence policies, preferences and interests of international organisations and can therefore serve as vital contact points in interorganisational relations due to their resources and capabilities.

In contrast, *blockers* of interorganisational interaction do not favour cooperation of international organisations because of particular national interests and therefore block or veto efforts to strengthening interorganisational relations. This role can be taken by both single and multiple member states. Blockers are especially able to obstruct interorganisational interaction by making use of strategies such as hostage-taking and turf battles (Hofmann 2009). For example, Turkey and Cyprus block each other's memberships in the respective other organisations and thereby also block EU–NATO cooperation in military crisis management to a certain extent. France also serves as a case example because of its disintegration from NATO's military command structure and its role as main driver of the EU's CSDP. One key aspect is that blockers are not against interorganisational relations *per se*, however, they obstruct the progressive development, design and formalisation of closer cooperation in accordance with their preferred outcomes and foreign and security policy orientations.

Balancers characterises those member states that aim to balance their own practices and policies concerning the choice of international organisation for their action. They also seek to balance between international organisations internally within the organisations and among other members. By trying to find an equilibrium between international organisations in the same network, balancers seek to moderate and mediate between them and their member states. These states have no explicit preference for one organisation over another (Hofmann 2019). Instead, they acknowledge and value the benefits of each international organisation and aim to make full use of each organisation's comparative advantage. These member states are therefore in favour of co-governance of international organisations in which a specific division of labour is clearly defined and regulated. In addition, balancers often take the position of brokers or mediators in interorganisational relations and seek to connect all actors in the network to maintain a balance among the other actors (cf. Goddard 2009).

Neutrals are neither active, or even proactive, nor obstructive states in interorganisational interaction. They are neutral and sometimes even disengaged because of particular national interests or constraints, for example, concerning the use of force. Neutrals can be either single or multiple member states. But it is suggested that single members are more likely to take this role to facilitate cooperation without their own involvement. In this regard, neutrals are silent supporters of interorganisational relations by neither blocking nor actively promoting interorganisational cooperation. These states should, however, not be confused with those neutral states that are militarily neutral states in general and whose neutrality primarily refers to military non-alignment. Neutrals often lack the resources and capabilities, in addition to multiple membership, to be more actively engaged in interorganisational cooperation.

As outlined in the introductory chapter, the categorisation of states into the typology is not a straightforward process. The categorisation of member states in the typology of member states in interorganisational relations rests upon a set of selection criteria. This list of selection criteria includes the attitude towards interorganisational interaction and cooperation among international organisations (positive, negative, balanced, indifferent), the level of active promotion of closer interorganisational cooperation (absent, low, medium, high), states' view on division of labour that varies between negative to positive and also includes the option of specific which will be elaborated in the empirical chapters, the level of engagement in negotiations (absent, low, medium, high) and material contributions to the international organisations and their operations (absent, low, medium, high). Additional aspects such as domestic politics, bilateral and minilateral partnerships, resources and capabilities, foreign and security policy orientation, and historical experiences, including operational experiences and legal caveats, are relevant to identify and categorise a member state to advocates, blockers, balancers or neutrals of interorganisational relations.

During the categorisation process based on the examination of member states' national security strategies and defence papers, a shift of attention has become evident for some member states, for instance, a shift of focus from one organisation to two organisations in the same policy area with the recognition of their equal importance. Such developments and shifts occur on the domestic level. While foreign and security policy orientations do not change abruptly, the domestic political context can change over time, such as the shaping and formation of interests and the preferences of political parties, which can heavily influence states' attitudes, practices and behaviour (Putnam 1988). For example, Hofmann (2017) finds that French political parties have diverging views on the Atlantic Alliance and its value for the country's security and defence, and therefore have different preferences regarding the purpose and transformation of NATO depending on their policy preference. Consequently, member states' choices for an international organisation depend on the interactions, preferences and decision-making power on the domestic level. The formation and shaping of member states' interests and preferences for the design, framework and intensity of interorganisational interaction is furthermore closely linked to the debate of identity of both states and international organisations.

While the four categories present ideal types, each member state has its own national attributes, interests and preferences that influence their positions in both international organisations and interorganisational cooperation. Throughout their memberships, states can shift between types and could therefore be categorised into more than one type based on the extent to which they match the characteristics of each type. In this sense, some states present themselves as boundary or fluid cases or 'swing states' (Rodt 2017: 139–140). This means that they possess characteristics of more than one type and cannot necessarily be clearly grouped into one of the above types. The possibility to shift types particularly implies the need for caution in the analysis of states' behaviour, while it also provides more flexibility and comprehensiveness in understanding states' preferences and decisions in interorganisational cooperation. With the help of the review of official documents published by member states, the analysis of the interviews and the examination of the secondary data, each member state will be categorised into one type according to how they meet the set of criteria.

Conclusions

This chapter has discussed different theoretical and conceptual approaches to the study of international organisations and cooperation in international politics and developed the theoretical framework of interorganisational relations. The theoretical framework's core characteristic is its ability to generalise the relations and interactions between international security organisations on different levels, particularly on the member state, bureaucratic and inter-secretariat levels. It helps to explain the influence of one organisation on another in the same policy area, the increase of functional overlaps and the motivation to trigger and enhance cooperation among security organisations. As elaborated in this chapter, the main features and indicators of interorganisational interaction include the density of network, functional overlap, formalisation, frequency of interactions, intensity and membership overlap (see Table 2.1). According to these features, different constellations of interorganisational cooperation can occur. What is more, member states play a central role in each dimension as they are the building blocks of international organisations, possess the decision-making power particularly in foreign and security policy and they provide the necessary resources, linkages and capabilities for organisations to maintain interorganisational relations.

Membership is thus a decisive factor in analysing the relationships and interactions between overlapping organisations in the area of foreign and security policy. While it can be distinguished between single and multiple members as well as between original and subsequent members, this book has introduced a new typology of member states in interorganisational cooperation. States take specific positions to influence, support or obstruct relations between international organisations. Consequently, the newly developed typology consists of four types of member states, namely advocates, blockers, balancers and neutrals (see Table 2.2). Member states have the ability to influence the intensity, functional overlaps and frequency of the external relations of international organisations, including their relationships with those organisations in the same network. They can draw on a range of political strategies to shape interorganisational relations, such as brokering, forum-shopping and hostage-taking. Taking into consideration states' foreign and security policy orientation and positioning in international organisations, member states can be categorised in the typology on the basis of their national security policies, positions towards the particular international organisations and security identities, which translate into their policy preferences, attitudes and behaviour vis-à-vis interorganisational cooperation. Both the theoretical framework of interorganisational relations and the typology of member states are applied to examine the relationship between the EU and NATO and to identify the opportunities, challenges and dysfunctions of their cooperation.

Notes

1 Translation by the author; original quote:

> Ein funktionaler Überlappungsbereich internationaler Organisationen liegt dann vor, wenn zwischen zwei oder mehr IOs Überschneidungen hinsichtlich der Mitgliedschaft und der inhaltlichen Regelungsbereiche vorliegen.

2 Translation by the author; original quote:

> Bei einer inter-organisationalen Arbeitsteilung handelt es sich um einen Regelsatz, der die Aufgaben der konkurrierenden Organisationen innerhalb eines breiteren Systems inter-organisationaler Koordination oder Kooperation definiert. Dieser Regelsatz beinhaltet generalisierte Erwartungen darüber, wie die einzelnen Organisationen ihre Aufgaben im funktionalen Überlappungsbereich ausüben sollen. Er fungiert daher als Mechanismus zur Eindämmung inter-organisationalen Wettbewerbs und zur Schließung von Möglichkeiten zu Forum-Shopping in funktionalen Überlappungsbereichen.

References

Adler, Emanuel (2008) 'The spread of security communities: Communities of practice, self-restraint, and NATO's post-Cold War transformation', *European Journal of International Relations*, 14(2): 195–230.

Adler, Emanuel and Michael Barnett (1998) *Security Communities*, Cambridge: Cambridge University Press.

Adler, Emanuel and Patricia Greve (2009) 'When security community meets balance of power: Overlapping regional mechanisms of security governance', *Review of International Studies*, 35(S1): 59–84.

Aldrich, Howard E. and David A. Whetten (1981) 'Organization sets, action sets, and networks: Making the most of simplicity'. *In*: Nystrom, Paul and William Starbuck (eds) *Handbook of Organisational Design*, Oxford: Oxford University Press, 385–408.

Alter, Karen J. and Sophie Meunier (2009) 'The politics of international regime complexity', *Perspectives on Politics, Symposium*, 7(1): 13–24.

Alter, Karen J. and Kal Raustiala (2018) 'The rise of international regime complexity', *Annual Review of International Law and Social Science*, 14(1): 329–349.

Aras, Bülent and Aylin Gorener (2010) 'National role conceptions and foreign policy orientation: The ideational bases of the Justice and Development Party's foreign policy activism in the Middle East', *Journal of Balkan and Near Eastern Studies*, 12(1): 73–92.

Archer, Clive (2001) *International Organisations*, 3rd edition, London and New York: Routledge.

Axelrod, Robert (2006) *The Evolution of Cooperation*, New York: Basic Books, Perseus Books Group.

Bailes, Alyson J.K. and Andrew Cottey (2006) 'Regional security cooperation in the early 21st century'. *In*: *SIPRI Yearbook 2006: Armaments, Disarmament, and International Security*, Stockholm: SIPRI, 195–223.

Barnett, Michael and Martha Finnemore (1999) 'The politics, power, and pathologies of international organisations', *International Organisation*, 53(4): 699–732.

Barnett, Michael and Martha Finnemore (2004) *Rules for the World: International Organisations in Global Politics*, Ithaca; London: Cornell University Press.

Bauer, Michael W. and Jörn Ege (2016) 'Bureaucratic autonomy of international organisations' secretariats', *Journal of European Public Policy*, 23(7): 1019–1037.

Berenskoetter, Felix (2017) 'Approaches to concept analysis', *Millennium: Journal of International Studies,* 45(2): 151–173.

Biehl, Heiko, Bastian Giegerich and Alexandra Jonas (2013) *Strategic Cultures in Europe: Security and Defence Policies Across the Continent*, Wiesbaden: Springer VS.

Biermann, Rafael (2008a) 'Towards a theory of inter-organisational networking: The Euro-Atlantic security institutions interacting', *The Review of International Organisations*, 3(2): 151–177.

Biermann, Rafael (2008b) Rivalry Among International Organisations. Paper presented at Konferenz Internationale Beziehungen und Organisationsforschung: Stand und Perspektiven, Munich, 18–19 September 2008.

Biermann, Rafael (2009): 'Interorganisationalism in theory and practice', *Studia Dilomatica. The Brussels Journal of International Relations*, 62(3): 7–12.

Biermann, Rafael (2015) 'Designing cooperation among international organisations: The quest for autonomy, the dual-consensus rule, and cooperation failure', *Journal of International Organisation Studies*, 6(2): 45–66.

Biermann, Rafael (2017) 'The role of international bureaucracies'. *In*: Biermann, Rafael and Joachim A. Koops, (eds) *Palgrave Handbook of Inter-Organizational Relations in World Politics*, New York, Basingstoke: Palgrave Macmillan, 243–270.

Biermann, Rafael and Michael Harsch (2017) 'Resource dependence theory'. *In*: Biermann, Rafael and Joachim A. Koops (eds) *Palgrave Handbook of Inter-Organizational Relations in World Politics*, New York, Basingstoke: Palgrave Macmillan, 135–156.

Biermann, Rafael and Joachim A. Koops (2017) *Palgrave Handbook of Interorganisational Relations in World Politics*, New York, Basingstoke: Palgrave Macmillan.

Bloomfield, Alan (2012) 'Time to move on: Reconceptualising the strategic culture debate', *Contemporary Security Policy*, 33(3): 437–461.

Brubaker, Rogers and Frederick Cooper (2000): 'Beyond "identity"', *Theory and Society*, 29(1): 1–47.

Checkel, Jeffrey R. (2005) 'International institutions and socialisation in Europe: Introduction and framework', *International Organisation*, 59(4): 801–826.

Cornish, Paul and Geoffrey Edwards (2001) 'Beyond the EU/NATO dichotomy: The beginnings of a European strategic culture', *International Affairs*, 77(3): 587–603.

de Wijk, Rob (2004) 'The reform of ESDP and EU-NATO cooperation', *The International Spectator*, 1: 71–82.

Dijkstra, Hylke (2017) 'The rational design of relations between international organisations'. *In*: Biermann, Rafael and Joachim A. Koops (eds) *Palgrave Handbook of Inter-Organisational Relations in World Politics*, New York, Basingstoke: Palgrave Macmillan, 97–112.

DiMaggio, Paul M. and Walter W. Powell (1983) 'The iron cage revisited: Institutional isomorphism and collective rationality in organisational fields', *American Sociological Review*, 48(2): 147–160.

Doreian, Patrick and Kayo Fujimoto (2004) 'Identifying linking-pin organisations in inter-organisational networks', *Computational & Mathematical Organization Theory*, 10(1): 45–68.

Dorussen, Han and Hugh Ward (2008) 'Intergovernmental organisations and the Kantian Peace: A network perspective', *Journal of Conflict Resolution*, 52(2): 189–212.

Drezner, Daniel W. (2009) 'The power and peril of international regime complexity', *Perspectives on Politics, Symposium*, 7(1): 65–70.

Duffield, John S. (2013) 'Alliances'. *In*: Williams, Paul D. (ed): *Security Studies: An Introduction, 2nd edition*, Abingdon, New York: Routledge, 339–354.

Duke, Simon (2008) 'The future of EU–NATO relations: A case of mutual irrelevance through competition?' *Journal of European Integration*, 30(1): 27–43.

European Union (2003) *European Security Strategy: A Secure Europe in a Better World*, Brussels: European Union.

European Union (2016) *Shared Vision, Common Action: A Stronger Europe – A Global Strategy for the European Union's Foreign and Security Policy*, Brussels: European Union.

Faude, Sebastian (2015) 'Zur Dynamik inter-organisationaler Beziehungen: Wie aus Konkurrenz Arbeitsteilung entsteht', *Politische Vierteljahresschrift*, 49: 294–321.

Flockhart, Trine (2015) 'Understanding NATO through constructivist thinking'. *In*: Webber, Mark and Adrian Hyde-Price (eds) *Theorising NATO*, Abingdon: Routledge, 141–160.

Gebhard, Carmen and Simon J. Smith (2015) 'The two faces of EU-NATO cooperation: Counter-piracy operations off the Somali coast', *Cooperation and Conflict*, 50(1): 107–127.

Gehring, Thomas and Benjamin Faude (2014) 'A theory of emerging order within international complexes: How competition among regulatory international institutions leads to institutional adaptation and division of labour', *Review of International Organisations*, 9(4): 471–498.

Gehring, Thomas and Sebastian Oberthür (2004) 'Exploring regime interaction: A framework of analysis'. *In*: Underdal, Arild and Oran R. Young (eds) *Regime Consequences: Methodological Challenges and Research Strategies*, Dordrecht: Kluwer, 247–269.

Gehring, Thomas and Sebastian Oberthür (2009) 'The causal mechanisms of interaction between international institutions', *European Journal of International Relations*, 15(1): 125–156.

Goddard, Stacie E. (2009) 'Brokering change: Networks and entrepreneurs in international politics', *International Theory*, 1(2): 249–281.

Græger, Nina (2016) 'European security as practice: EU-NATO communities of practice in the making?' *European Security*, 25(4): 478–501.

Græger, Nina (2017) 'Grasping the everyday and extraordinary in EU-NATO relations: The added value of practice approaches', *European Security*, 26(3): 340–358.

Græger, Nina and Kristin M. Haugevik (2011) 'The EU's performance with and within NATO: Assessing objectives, outcomes and organisational practices', *European Integration*, 33(6): 743–757.

Gray, Colin S. (1999) 'Strategic culture as context: The first generation of theory strikes back', *Review of International Studies*, 25(1): 49–69.

Greve, Patricia (2018) 'Ontological security, the struggle for recognition, and the maintenance of security communities', *Journal of International Relations and Developmnent*, 21(4): 858–882.

Guzzini, Stefano (2003) 'Constructivism and the role of institutions in international relations', *Columbia International Affairs Online*, 3: 1–23.

Haas, Ernst B. (1982) 'Words can hurt you; or, who said what to whom about regimes', *International Organisation*, 36(2): 207–243.

Hafner-Burton, Emilie M., Miles Kahler and Alexander H. Montgomery (2009) 'Network analysis for international relations', *International Organisation*, 63(3): 559–592.

Haugevik, Kristin M. (2007) 'New partners, new possibilities: The evolution of inter-organisational security cooperation in international peace operations', *NUPI Series: Security in Practice*, 6: 3–31.

Hofmann, Stephanie C. (2009) 'Overlapping institutions in the realm of international security: The case of NATO and ESDP', *Perspectives on Politics*, 7(1): 45–51.

Hofmann, Stephanie C. (2017) 'Party preferences and institutional transformation: Revisiting France's relationship with NATO (and the common wisdom on Gaullism)', *Journal of Strategic Studies*, 40(4): 505–531.

Hofmann, Stephanie C. (2019) 'The politics of overlapping organisations: Hostage-taking, forum-shopping and brokering', *Journal of European Public Policy*, 26(6): 883–905.

Hopf, Tedd (1998) 'The promise of constructivism in international relations theory', *International Security*, 23(1): 171–200.

Howorth, Jolyon and John T.S. Keeler (2003) *Defending Europe: The EU, NATO and the Quest for European Autonomy*. New York, Basingstoke: Palgrave Macmillan.

Johnston, Alastair Iain (1995) 'Thinking about strategic culture', *International Security*, 19(4): 32–64.

Johnston, Alastair Iain (2001) 'Treating international institutions as social environments', *International Studies Quarterly*, 45(4): 487–515.

Jones, Seth G. (2007) *The Rise of European Security Cooperation*. Cambridge: Cambridge University Press.

Jönsson, Christer (1986): 'Interorganisation theory and international organisation', *International Studies Quarterly*, 30(1): 39–57.

Jönsson, Christer (2017) 'IR paradigms and international organisation: Situating the research programme within the discipline. *In*: Biermann, Rafael and Joachim A. Koops (eds) *Palgrave Handbook of Inter–Organisational Relations in World Politics*, New York, Basingstoke: Palgrave Macmillan, 49–66.

Juncos, Ana E. and Karolina Pomorska (2006) 'Playing the Brussels game: Strategic socialisation in the CFSP Council Working Groups', *European Integration Online Papers*, 10(11): 1–17.

Jungcurt, Stefan (2006) A Framework for Analysing Interplay Between International Institutions. Draft Version of the Paper Presented at the Workshop in Political Theory and Policy Analysis, Indiana University on 11 September 2006.

Kagan, Robert (2003) *Of Power and Paradise: America and Europe in the New World Order*, New York: Alfred A. Knopf/Random House Publisher.

Keck, Margret E. and Kathryn Sikkink (1998) *Activities Beyond Borders: Advocacy Networks in International Politics*, Ithaca: Cornell University Press.

Koops, Joachim A. (2007) Towards Effective and Integrative Inter-Organisationalism, DGAP Bericht: From Conflict to Regional Stability: Linking Security and Development, New Faces Conference, Madrid, 5–7 November 2007, 23–32.

Koops, Joachim A. (2012) 'Inter-organisational approaches'. *In*: Jørgensen, Knud Erik and Katie Verlin Laatikainen (eds) *Routledge Handbook on the European Union and International Institutions*, London and New York: Routledge, 71–85.

Koops, Joachim A. (2017) 'Inter-organisationalism in international relations: A multilevel framework of analysis'. *In*: Biermann, Rafael and Joachim A. Koops (eds) *Palgrave Handbook of Inter-Organisational Relations in World Politics*, New York, Basingstoke: Palgrave Macmillan, 189–216.

Krasner, Stephen D. (1982) 'Structural causes and regime consequences: Regimes as intervening variables', *International Organisation*, 36(2): 185–205.

Lipson, Michael (2017) 'Organisation theory and cooperation and conflict among international organisations'. *In*: Biermann, Rafael and Joachim A. Koops (eds) *Palgrave Handbook of Inter-Organisational Relations in World Politics*, New York, Basingstoke: Palgrave Macmillan, 67–96.

Lock, Edward (2010) 'Refining strategic culture: Return of the second generation', *Review of International Studies*, 36(3): 685–708.

Loewen, Howard (2006) 'Towards a dynamic model of the interplay between international institutions', *GIGA Working Paper*, 17: 1–27.

Lord, Carnes (1985): 'American strategic culture', *Comparative Strategy*, 5(3): 269–293.

Magliveras, Konstantinos D. (2011) 'Membership in international organisations'. *In*: Klabbers, Jan and Asa Wallendahl (eds) *Research Handbook on the Law of International Organisations*, Cheltenham and Northampton: Edward Elgar Publishing, 84–107.

Major, Claudia and Christian Mölling (2009) 'More than wishful thinking? The EU, UN, NATO and the comprehensive approach to military crisis management', *Studia Diplomatica*, 62(3): 21–28.

Maoz, Zeev (2012) 'How network analysis can inform the study of international relations', *Conflict Management and Peace Science*, 29(3): 247–256.

Matláry, Janne Haaland (2006) 'When soft power turns hard: Is an EU strategic culture possible?' *Security Dialogue*, 37(1): 105–121.

Mearsheimer, John J. (1994) 'The false promise of international institutions', *International Security*, 19(3): 5–49.

Missiroli, Antonio (2002) 'EU–NATO cooperation in crisis management: No Turkish delight for ESDP', *Security Dialogue*, 33(1): 9–26.

Müller, Harald (2012) 'Security cooperation'. *In*: Carlsnaes, Walter, Thomas Risse-Kappen and Beth A. Simmons (eds) *Handbook of International Relations,* 2nd edition, London: SAGE, 607–634.

NATO (1991) *The Alliance's New Strategic Concept*, Brussels: NATO.

NATO (2010) *Active Engagement, Modern Defence: Strategic Concept for the Defence and Security of Members of the North Atlantic Treaty Organisation*, Brussels: NATO.

Ojanen, Hanna (2006) 'The EU and NATO: Two competing models for a common defence policy', *Journal of Common Market Studies*, 44(1): 57–76.

Poopuu, Birgit (2015) 'Telling and acting identity: The discursive construction of the EU's common security and defence policy identity', *Journal of Language and Politics*, 14(1): 134–153.

Putnam, Robert D. (1988) 'Diplomacy and domestic politics: The logic of two-level games', *International Organisation*, 42(3): 427–460.

Raustiala, Kal and David G. Victor (2004) 'The regime complex for plant genetic resources', *International Organisation*, 58(2): 277–309.

Reichard, Martin (2006) *The EU-NATO Relationship: A Legal and Political Perspective,* Abingdon: Routledge.

Reinalda, Bob and Bertjan Verbeek (1998) *Autonomous Policy Making by International Organisations,* London and New York: Routledge.

Rodt, Annemarie Peen (2017) 'Member states policy towards EU military operations'. *In*: Hadfield, Amelia et al. (eds) *Foreign Policies of EU Member States: Continuity and Europeanisation,* Abingdon: Routledge, 131–147.

Schleich, Caja (2014) 'NATO and EU in conflict regulation: Interlocking institutions and division of labour', *Journal of Transatlantic Studies,* 12(2): 182–205.

Scott, Richard W. (1994) 'Conceptualizing organizational fields: Linking organisations and societal systems'. *In*: Derlien, H., U. Gerhardt and Fritz W. Scharpf (eds) *Systems Rationality and Partial Interests,* Baden-Baden: Nomos Verlagsgesellschaft, 203–221.

Sloan, Stanley R. (2003) *NATO, the European Union, and the Atlantic Community: The Transatlantic Bargain Reconsidered,* Lanham, Boulder, New York, Oxford: Rowman & Littlefield Publishers Inc.

Smith, Simon J. (2011) 'EU-NATO cooperation: A case of institutional fatigue?' *European Security,* 20(2) 243–264.

Varwick, Johannes (2006) 'European Union and NATO: Partnership, competition or rivalry?' *Kieler Analysen zur Sicherheitspolitik,* 18: 1–22.

Waltz, Kenneth N. (1959) *Man, the State, and War: A Theoretical Analysis,* New York: Columbia University Press.

Wendt, Alexander (1987) 'The agent-structure problem in international relations theory', *International Organisation,* 41(3): 335–370.

Wendt, Alexander (1994) 'Collective identity formation and the international state', *American Political Science Review,* 88(2): 384–396.

Wendt, Alexander (1999) *Social Theory of International Politics.* Cambridge: Cambridge University Press.

Wooten, Melissa E. and Timothy Sacco (2017) 'Configurations in inter-organisational cooperation: From dyads to organisational fields'. *In*: Biermann, Rafael and Joachim A. Koops (eds) *Palgrave Handbook of Inter-Organisational Relations in World Politics,* New York, Basingstoke: Palgrave Macmillan, 289–302.

Young, Oran R. (1999) *Governance in World Affairs,* Ithaca: Cornell University Press.

Zyla, Benjamin (2011) 'Overlap or opposition? EU and NATO's strategic (sub-) culture', *Contemporary Security Policy,* 32(3): 667–687.

3 Advocates

The UK, the US, BeNeLux, the Baltics and Central and Eastern European States

As states take different positions in the interorganisational relationship between the EU and NATO, advocates play a key role in promoting closer cooperation and intensified interactions. This chapter presents an overview of advocates' engagement and provides an analysis of this group of states in EU–NATO cooperation. It also examines some selected member states from this group in more depth to illustrate advocates' ability and extent to engage and promote the relationship between the EU and NATO in practice.

States in this group serve as promoters and drivers of cooperation between organisations and are enthusiastic about becoming more engaged. The majority of member states in the EU and NATO are generally in favour of some kind of cooperation and maintaining a good relationship with the respective other organisation. This was highlighted in the most recent developments and the process leading to the 2016 Joint Declaration between the Presidents of the EU and the NATO Secretary General (EU Official 2). Advocates stand out especially due to their proactive and supportive behaviour, interconnectedness with other members and their contributions to EU–NATO interoperability. In addition, member states' affiliation with the group of advocates is shaped by their domestic politics, that is, the extent to which political parties on the domestic level support interorganisational cooperation, their view on each organisation and how changes in government influence the country's foreign and security policy orientation. One country that is particularly prominent is the UK. Its withdrawal from the EU, which was finalised in 2020, however, limits its abilities to continue as the main transatlantic bridge. Moments of external rupture and changes in domestic politics can therefore trigger states to swing and shift (cf. Rodt 2017), and the ability to do so has been taken into account for this analysis.

Through the examination of national security strategies and defence papers, member states have been categorised into the group of advocates based on their supportive attitude towards EU–NATO cooperation. According to the criteria set out for categorising states in the typology of member states in interorganisational relations, advocates generally score high in most criteria. This means that advocates demonstrate positive attitudes towards interorganisational cooperation, have a rather positive view on

DOI: 10.4324/9781003170068-3

division of labour with clear tasks for each organisation, show higher levels of promotion and higher levels of engagement in negotiations and make significant contributions of troops and resources in relation to their individual positioning and their own resources in total. Subsequently, the following states can be considered as advocates: Albania, Belgium, Bulgaria, Canada, Croatia, Czech Republic, Estonia, Hungary, Latvia, Lithuania, Luxembourg, Montenegro, the Netherlands, Norway, North Macedonia, Poland, Romania, Slovakia, Slovenia, the UK and the US. While all of these states are located in the group of advocates, some have been more engaged and active in supporting EU–NATO cooperation than others, and therefore receive greater attention throughout this chapter.

Advocates share a certain set of specific characteristics which enables them to drive the efforts towards closer cooperation even further. However, these characteristics and the peculiarity of each member state varies in the degree of actively promoting EU–NATO cooperation due to the diverging national interests and preferences. Some of the states in this group have not necessarily been labelled as advocates from the beginning of the EU–NATO relationship or from their accession to these organisations. Advocates of the interorganisational relationship between the EU and NATO are very active members in both organisations and have sufficient or even outstanding military resources, which they can use to convince and persuade other member states to follow their approach. They are eager to support each organisation's strengths in security and defence affairs, seek to facilitate further cooperation and follow a defined strategy for the future of the EU–NATO relationship.

This chapter is divided into three sections. First, the shared characteristics are outlined and their attributes are described with more details. Then the group of advocates is examined in relation to the perception and use of their own membership to promote and enhance cooperation between the EU and NATO. With a focus on advocates' operational involvements, this chapter considers advocates' behaviour and positioning as well as their contributions towards military capabilities, interoperability and division of labour in the EU–NATO interorganisational relationship.

Shared characteristics of advocates

Advocates share a common set of characteristics and features (see Table 3.1), which they express to varying degrees and for diverging reasons, including national interests and preferences, historical pathways or bilateral relations and partnerships. As outlined in the theoretical framework, the widely accepted objective is the facilitation of interorganisational relations and, more specifically, the enhancement and strengthening of the EU–NATO relationship. They take different approaches to express their position in the EU–NATO relationship and to advocate further cooperation. This section explores these shared characteristics and analyses advocates' behaviour, activities and contributions in greater detail.

Table 3.1 Overview of advocates' characteristics

Shared characteristics	Advocates and their membership	Contributions to the capabilities	View on division of labour interoperability
• Active participation in the formalisation process of cooperation • Key actors and drivers in this process • Maintain close cooperation with other member states in both organisations	• Well-networked and maintenance of minilateral frameworks • Represented in many groups within and between both organisations • Overall good relations with all member states • If making trouble, then without decisive implications • Cooperation with member states outside the interorganisational relationship	• Possess vital resources and military capabilities • Engaged in capability development projects in both organisations • Aim at convincing other member states to improve and develop military capabilities • Seek to avoid (unnecessary) duplication • High levels of military expenditure	• Promote and actively engage in achieving interoperability among all states and organisations • Internal and external consultations on interoperability • Favour division of labour to support each organisation's strengths • Prefer a division of labour to avoid duplication and overlap of activities

Concerning their membership, advocates belong to both old and new member states, and to both original states and subsequent states as well as to multiple and single member states (Gehring and Oberthür 2009; Magliveras 2011). Multiple members are more likely to play a proactive role in supporting closer cooperation and enhanced interaction because their multiple membership status allows to effectively promote interorganisational cooperation equally in both organisations. Bilateral and minilateral relations with other member states have significant relevance because they create ties through which advocates are able to persuade other states and foster coalitions, in particular those usually aligned with advocates in other policy areas. For example, if something is at stake in another policy area, enthusiasts of interorganisational relations can then use the leverage to influence the voting behaviour and to form coalition groups among member states. This approach is known to be a common practice in negotiations and decision-making scenarios, especially in the last stages of finding agreements (UK Official 2). Single member states among the group of advocates are also able to take over positions as drivers. However, they need to have strong and stable bilateral agreements and partnerships with the respective other organisation either through NATO's PfP programme or with the EU through an FPA as well as bilateral ties. Single members have made wide use of both programmes and agreements to avoid isolation and, instead, to strengthen closer EU–NATO cooperation, for instance in crisis management.

Original member states were involved in the creation of the two organisations, which does not necessarily mean that they are enthusiastic about EU–NATO cooperation, since the original purpose, when the two organisations were established, differed from what they have evolved into over the past decades. They nevertheless see benefits of enhanced cooperation and a closer relationship to economise their military assets, capabilities and other relevant resources. In addition, for many advocates, both old and new, cooperation between the EU and the Atlantic Alliance seems 'natural' given the high degree of membership overlap (British Officials 2; Romanian Official 1). For new member states, especially the Central and Eastern European states, one of the main objectives after gaining independence from the Soviet Union was to integrate into the European security architecture by joining the EU and NATO. Therefore, they participated and contributed to EU and NATO operations even prior to their accessions and were already much in favour of closer cooperation to use their single set of forces more effectively and efficiently. Despite their more Atlanticists foreign and security policy orientation, the choice between the EU and NATO as well as the partnership with the US has been actively avoided to prevent any duplication (Pomorska 2017; Weiss 2015).

A shared recognition among advocates is the need for actively promoting the EU–NATO relationship among other member states, especially those with less optimistic outlooks. One way of doing so is in consultations and minilateral negotiations. Some advocates are more involved in these activities, primarily those with more resources and capabilities. This can also be done through the maintenance of a wide network of partnerships and continuity of good relations with the majority of members in both organisations. In this regard, advocates take the position of boundary-role actors, which means that they have close and overlapping ties with other states that enable organisations and states to connect (Jönsson 1986). Another way to show their enthusiasm of this relationship and to push for deeper cooperation is through trade-offs and conditionality. As pointed out by one national representative, advocates make use of their resources to persuade fellow member states and to promise them advantages in other policy domains (British Officials 2).

The depiction and overview of these shared characteristics helps to analyse advocates' role and efforts. While some drivers of this relationship are 'silent followers', those that align with some of the bigger, older, more powerful and resourceful member states, such as the UK and the US, others are more proactive and thereby play a more significant role, which will receive greater attention in this analysis. Examples of how some more proactive member states behave within the institutionalisation process, maintain relations with other states in both organisations and how they contribute to closing the capabilities gap and increasing interoperability serve to illustrate the active engagement of advocates in EU–NATO cooperation.

Making use of their membership

As outlined in the shared characteristics, advocates can be both multiple and single member states, old and new member states as well as small and large member states, making them a homogenous group in membership terms. Due to the overall membership overlap of 22 states (until 2020), advocates are likely to be multiple members, which enables them to promote the EU–NATO relationship equally and more proactively among other states in both organisations. Concerning their relations with other states, advocates are generally well connected and engaged in bilateral and minilateral security and defence cooperation within and outside the frameworks of the EU and NATO. Membership and the positioning of states in international organisations is highly significant for gaining access to vital resources and being able to participate in decision-making. Being equipped with both allows to exert influence on relevant decisions concerning the organisations' external relations (Dorussen and Ward 2008). Advocates make use of their multiple memberships, alongside the possession of other important resources, to manage their network of social connections and are embedded and lead a number of groups of interests with like-minded states. Yet, while some drivers are deeply embedded in international organisations and in international networks with other actors, such as third states, non-governmental organisations and international institutions, other advocates maintain fewer bilateral and minilateral connections.

In the course of developing the European foreign, security and defence policies and European military capabilities, states have often taken sides in either the Europeanist camp, those states pleading for the idea of developing autonomous European military capabilities independent from NATO, or the Atlanticist camp, those states seeking future engagement of NATO and the US in European security. The latter are not in favour of developing autonomous European capabilities and structures unless these do not undermine but support the Atlantic Alliance (Larrabee 2004; Stahl et al. 2004). The majority of advocates can be categorised in the camp of Atlanticists because they rely on NATO for national and European defence, aim to strengthen the Atlantic Alliance and favour the US presence in Europe (Estonia 2011; Poland 2014; UK 2010). More importantly, they do not fundamentally oppose the development of European military capabilities as they regard them as an added value to NATO.

The United Kingdom

The UK is an example of an old but not original, big and multiple member state, which maintains a wide network with ample linkages which it uses to actively promote not only its national interests but also its position on the EU–NATO relationship. It has also been labelled as the leader of the Atlanticist camp in European security and defence affairs (Dunne 2004; Howorth 2000). Britain maintains one of the most extensive networks of bilateral, minilateral and multilateral connections, not only in Europe but also globally. Accordingly, Bailes (1995: 85–86) characterises the philosophy of the British defence policy as 'active, global, multinational and intergovernmental'. The UK is not only member of key international and regional organisations, such as the EU, NATO, OSCE, the Council of Europe as well as its permanent seat in the United Nations Security Council (UNSC), but it also draws on its long list of bilateral cooperation partners with key strategic states in the transatlantic space. Among these, however, only some countries qualify as 'worthy partners' (O'Donnell 2011: 425), including France, Germany, Turkey, Estonia, Denmark and Norway alongside the US (UK 2003, 2010).

In addition to its contributions to civil and military operations under the frameworks of the EU and NATO, Britain also participates in coalitions of the willing with its security and defence cooperation partners. This shows that the UK has become 'a "networked" foreign policy actor' (Whitman 2016: 44), making it worthy of the label as a 'globally significant player' (Whitman and Tonra 2017: 43), since it has evolved as a country with a 'sense of responsibility for international security policy' (Cornish 2013: 371). Drawing on its 2010 Strategic Defence and Security Review, bilateral and minilateral cooperation receive significant relevance in its foreign, security and defence policy: 'building new models of practical bilateral cooperation with those countries whose defence and security posture is closest to our own or with whom we cooperate in multinational operations' (UK 2010: 59). The UK sees these bilateral and minilateral relations as advantageous for its own position because they enable to shape its cooperation partners' view on the EU–NATO relationship. This became evident in the developments leading to the Saint-Malo Declaration in 1998 as well as in the process resulting in the 2003 Berlin Plus arrangements. Throughout its memberships, the UK has applied forum-shopping strategies rooted in its memberships in numerous multilateral forums and organisations. It has also utilised its networks to persuade and convince other member states of the importance of EU–NATO cooperation in security and defence (Rodt 2017).

Within the EU–NATO relationship, the UK has played a significant part in building the bridge between the two organisations and their members as well as between Europe and North America in converging security and defence interests. It does so through participating in minilateral groups with key partners. While multilateral frameworks, such as the EU and NATO as a whole, have their advantages, the UK has been frustrated by the lack of efficiency. Britain is aligned with the so-called Friends of Europe within the Atlantic Alliance, which consists of France, Germany, the US, the Netherlands, Italy, Belgium, Spain and also Slovakia, which recently joined this group of interest (NATO Official 1). These like-minded member states see a clear advantage in strengthening the European pillar in NATO. Alongside Germany, France, Italy and the US, the UK regularly meets as the so-called Quint to consult on security issues. These meetings take place in an informal setting among the military representatives specifically before official meetings of the EUMC and the NAC (German Officials 2). Although the UK, France and Germany pursue divergent security and defence policies and strategies, possess different military assets and capabilities and take different positions on the EU–NATO relationship, they form the Big Three, also known as E3. These three states contribute the largest financial share for military operations under CSDP and they are perceived as the most influential EU member states in security and defence. With the UK's withdrawal from the EU, the E3 has gained more significance that allows the UK to coordinate with its European counterparts and allows to shape European security post-Brexit (cf. Billon-Galland, Raines and Whitman 2020). While the future of the E3 depends on the developments in the transatlantic relationship, it also shapes the EU–NATO relationship in which Britain tries to maintain a special position.

Besides the minilateral formats, the UK builds upon its extensive bilateral connections. The most prominent bilateral relationship is the special partnership with the US. Both countries share values of liberal democracy and free-market capitalism and maintain close economic, political and social links. In addition, they are both founding members of NATO and possess permanent seats in the UNSC. In the US perspective, the UK has been a key ally in European geopolitics and in the European integration process because as a mediator and bridge between Europe and the US, 'the UK has played a central part both in US engagement in Europe's geopolitics and in the development of the EU' (Oliver and Williams 2016: 553). The UK and the US have aligned parts of their policies in security and defence, which is reflected in their joint efforts and engagements in military interventions, for example, in Afghanistan and Iraq, despite subsequently hitting rock bottom in their special relationship. They maintain close cooperation in the military domain, including intelligence and information sharing, increasing interoperability and on nuclear warfare. Their bilateral cooperation in information sharing has been of significance in the development of the 2002 Security of Information Agreement. Due to their already established practices, the two countries were able to facilitate and support the negotiations between the EU and NATO and promoted the advantages as well as the necessity of such an agreement. British efforts and approaches to European integration have also been in favour of the US policies, including the UK's promotion of acquiring military capabilities among its European partners (Marsh and Rees 2012; Oliver and Williams 2016). The UK–US special relationship is highly relevant and significant for the EU–NATO relationship as both countries seek to motivate NATO and EU countries to increase their defence spending for maintaining peace and security in Europe and beyond the Euro-Atlantic borders. They make the biggest contributions coming from either side of the Atlantic, and both acknowledge that Europe would not be able to manage peace, security and stability within and on its borders without US military capabilities through NATO (UK Official 1). Notwithstanding, Brexit also has implications for the UK–US special relationship and the disability for the US to shape the EU's foreign, security and defence policies through the UK.

The UK's most important bilateral security and defence cooperation within Europe is the one with France. Traditionally, however, Britain and France represent the two poles in European security and defence in which the UK leads the camp of Atlanticists and France heads the camp of Europeanists. Although the two countries pursue diverging strategic goals concerning international security and prefer different international organisations for their actions – NATO is seen as the UK's cornerstone for security and defence and takes a pre-eminent position in its strategic culture (British Official 1), and France has always favoured developing autonomous European military capabilities through the EU (French Official 2) – the two countries have converged their policies and attitudes towards the EU and NATO over time. Their relationship is based on a series of agreements as well as shared positions in security and defence, including two key agreements namely the Saint-Malo Declaration in 1998 and the Lancaster House Treaties in 2010 (UK 2010). Their overlapping perceptions of their international status, similar conceptions of their national interests and their emphasis on the willingness concerning the use of force for interventions make them important partners, even beyond Brexit, contributing to enhanced EU–NATO cooperation.

The British–Franco Summit in Saint-Malo in December 1998 marks a significant milestone for the EU–NATO relationship. In fact, the summit was initiated by then Prime Minister Tony Blair, under whose government a shift towards European integration in security and defence was recorded. The two countries discussed the idea to create a European capability for autonomous action and to improve its readiness to be able to respond to international crises as well as to strengthen the transatlantic link. Yet, they had different objectives because, 'whereas Britain saw capability development as a means to strengthen the transatlantic relationship; France perceived it as a means to strengthen the EU as a foreign and security policy actor' (Simón 2017: 71). Blair emphasised that the EU would take over some security-related activities, but the defence dimension would remain solely in NATO's realm (Biscop 1999; Dryburgh 2010; Dyson 2011; Miskimmon 2004). The UK set one key conditionality to find an agreement: the EU would be able to acquire autonomous military capabilities and develop a security and defence policy, albeit limited to crisis management and the Petersberg Tasks. However, this could only occur in close cooperation and consultation with NATO. The UK thereby sought to trigger reforms and to increase the military capabilities among member states to support both NATO and the EU (O'Donnell 2011). Resulting from the Saint-Malo Summit and the subsequent declaration, EU member states furthered the development of the European security and defence policy at the European Council meetings in Cologne and Helsinki in 1999 and at the same time, the EU High Representative and the NATO Secretary General began to meet informally and more periodically.

With the formalisation of the British–Franco cooperation, their policy preferences have gradually converged in two ways. Firstly, France has aligned with the UK's attitude towards international security organisations and subsequently re-joined NATO's integrated military command structures in 2009, and secondly, both countries have gradually converged over their defence instruments and means primarily due to their overlapping ambitions and their similar experiences in military operations (Ostermann 2015; Pannier 2017; Pannier and Schmitt 2014). The Franco–British security and defence cooperation has therefore enabled the UK to promote its view on international security organisations and on the EU–NATO relationship among French policymakers and successfully convinced its strategic partner to accept and follow its policy preferences. Their bilateral agreements have concurrently strengthened EU–NATO cooperation in military crisis management because of the development of defence capabilities, the convergence of ambitions and the increased interoperability of armed forces. In addition, Britain eventually accepted the institutional developments as well as the inclusion of a defence dimension within CSDP. This highlighted the change in its domestic policy and shows how it has 'swung back and forth between more or less pro-EU positions' (Rodt 2017: 139). On the other side, the UK was also active in defining the ESDI within the Atlantic Alliance. It originally perceived the ESDI to be an opportunity to strengthen the military capabilities among other European member states and due to its long-lasting special relationship with the US, it acted as 'interlocutor' between Europe and North America (Rees 1996: 232).

Both the EU and NATO have also benefited from the UK's bilateral engagement with other members beyond its relations with France and the US. For example, British officials under the Blair government were heavily involved in the procedures that resulted in the agreement on the Berlin Plus arrangements between the EU and the Alliance. They vocalised their concerns as well as the opportunities of cooperation on military capabilities. Eventually, they were able to convince the Turkish officials to agree to the arrangements, who were initially opposed to such arrangements on sharing NATO's military assets and capabilities. British officials held bilateral negotiations with Turkey as well as with both organisations in order to overcome any oppositions and disagreements, which allowed the signing of the agreement of the Berlin Plus arrangements (Missiroli 2002). In the same year, the UK was able to broker a compromise between NATO and the EU – more specifically with those states that participated in the so-called Chocolate Summit in Tervuren, including Belgium, France, Germany and Luxembourg – which later led to the establishment of the permanent EU liaison cells at NATO's SHAPE and in the EU Military Staff (Duke 2008). The UK has therefore provoked an important step towards the establishment of formal relations between the EU and NATO. It played a significant part particularly in the early beginnings in enabling the institutionalisation and formalisation of the EU–NATO relationship while, based on its pragmatic approach, more actively promoting the necessity for cooperation among member states in both arenas. Consequently, the UK has acted as a boundary-role actor (cf. Jönsson 1986) as it connects states and international actors despite their diverging policy preferences. Drawing on its wide network of bilateral relationships and its embeddedness in multilateral security cooperation frameworks inside and outside NATO and the EU, the UK plays an important role in advocating their approaches to security and defence as well as their cooperation efforts in crisis management.

The Baltics and Central and Eastern Europe

Countries in the Baltics and Central and Eastern Europe claim similar positions to the UK, though not as strongly. The Baltic states – Estonia, Latvia and Lithuania – present one group among advocates that strikes out in the EU–NATO relationship. Despite their slightly varying attitudes towards NATO and the EU, the Baltics form a group of like-minded states concerning their view on the EU–NATO relationship. Their primary reason for membership in both NATO and the EU was to avoid the historical events of the twentieth century and to avoid isolation in the post-Cold War era as well as to find a source of power to counter Russia. They see NATO as the cornerstone for their territorial defence and the security of their sovereignty when backed by the US (Estonia 2010, 2011; Latvia 2008; Lithuania 2017). In fact, some of them perceive themselves as 'Atlanticists from within' the CSDP (Tromer 2006: 364). The EU, in contrast, is regarded as an important actor for soft security issues, including economic and environmental security. To avoid any duplications, advocates from the Baltics seek to ensure close coordination between the EU and NATO (Rikveilis 2013; Salu and Männik 2013; Šešelgytė 2013).

Although the Baltics only joined both organisations in 2004, they have built up an extensive network of connections with other member states. Most notably, they connect the Central and Eastern European countries with the Nordics and other states in the Baltic Sea region, such as Germany. While most of the military cooperation between the Baltics and Nordics takes place through NATO, they have been invited to participate in the NORDEFCO, which focuses on the harmonisation of security and defence policies as well as on the development of defence capabilities (Bajarūnas 2014; Tromer 2006; von Voss et al. 2013). Because of their multiple memberships, which is not the case among the Nordic countries, the Baltics are able to promote their positions and viewpoints of EU–NATO cooperation inside these two organisations as well as through their external relations. Concerning the EU–NATO relationship, the Nordics take diverging positions, but through interactions with the Baltics they have become increasingly supportive of the interorganisational cooperation between the Union and the Atlantic Alliance (Herolf 2006; Tiilikainen 2006; Tromer 2006). Similarly, the Baltics are well connected with Central and

Eastern European countries based on their shared historical experiences and geographical proximity to Russia, which has been a common security concern to all states in Eastern Europe. In addition, they seek to increase cooperation with older member states from Western Europe, such as Germany and the Netherlands. This has been highlighted by their participation in and contribution to EU Battlegroups and the NATO Response Force in which, for example, Lithuania has participated in both rapid response forces with some of the Nordic countries, Germany, the Netherlands, Poland, and the UK (EEAS 2015). As small and new members, they prefer to collaborate with old members in rapid response forces to increase the level of interoperability with important actors and to converge their security interests.

In contrast to the Baltics, some Central and Eastern European states, such as the Czech Republic, were not exactly sure what to do with their membership after having joined NATO between 1999 and 2004 and the EU in 2004 (Weiss 2015), but they were nevertheless supportive of any developments within both organisations. For example, with the recognition of the need for EU–NATO cooperation, the Czech Republic has more recently served as one of the drivers of EU initiatives, such as the MPCC and PESCO, as it regards significant contributions to NATO and thus to strengthening Euro-Atlantic security and defence. As expressed by one national representative, the country even claims that 'the closer the cooperation, the better' (Czech Official 1). Eastern European and Baltic states as countries of the former Soviet Union sought to join the EU, the WEU and NATO and, subsequently, debates on how to harmonise the accessions and enlargement processes within these organisations arose (Flockhart 1996). The Central and Eastern European countries and the Baltics applied for membership with similar intentions. All of them wanted to become part of the club and gain greater stability and prosperity as well as security vis-à-vis Russia. Relating thereto, this group among the advocates also belongs to the camp of Atlanticists since they favour any actions for collective defence through NATO (Pomorska 2017; Tromer 2006). Sometimes this group of states is also referred to as 'New Atlanticists' or 'New Europe' (Šešelgytė 2013: 225). Their Atlanticist tradition, including the strong partnership with the US as one of their most important allies, has long been emphasised in their national security and defence strategies (Czech Republic 2012; Latvia 2008; Poland 2007). In the more recent national security and defence strategies and updated national defence reviews, the EU did not only receive more attention in regard to cooperative security and crisis management, but also the cooperation between the EU and NATO has become an increasingly important factor (see, for example, Czech Republic 2015; Poland 2014, 2017; Slovenia 2010). As stated by one Romanian official, both the EU and NATO are key for its national security and it thus does not come to a surprise that 'there is a natural need to have the EU and NATO work together and to synchronise' (Romanian Official 1). The importance and need for their cooperation have also been confirmed by officials from Poland and the Czech Republic (Polish Official 1; Czech Official 1).

All of the Central and Eastern European and Baltic countries avoided having to make a decision between the EU and NATO and therefore opted for preferring the formalisation of the relationship. Some countries acknowledge that an 'increased overlapping membership would facilitate both cooperation and convergence' (Missiroli 2004: 130–131), which would enable them to become members in both organisations without discriminating the other. Hence, especially the Baltics states 'see their main function as ensuring coordination between the [CSDP] and NATO' (Tromer 2006: 364; also see Tiilikainen 2006). Among the Central and Eastern European states among the advocates there are two exceptions: Montenegro and North Macedonia. Both are single members and joined NATO recently in 2017 and 2019, respectively. They can be considered as 'silent advocates' because of their recent accessions to the Alliance while also being EU candidate countries, thus seeking to join the Union in the future. Generally, the new member states particularly put an emphasis on achieving complementarity, maintaining sustainable cooperation and the prevention of any duplication of both command structures and capabilities since they had to find their positions in both the EU and NATO and their interorganisational cooperation (Abukevicius 2015; Jankowski 2015; Kiukucans 2015; Pomorska 2017; Šešelgytė 2013).

BeNeLux and the United States

Belgium, the Netherlands and Luxembourg – often referred to as BeNeLux – present an interesting group of states among advocates. Despite their geographical proximity, historical ties and similar membership processes, that is, all three are founding members of both the EU and NATO – their foreign and security policies differ slightly. The Netherlands is a keen Atlanticist, while Belgium and Luxembourg belong to the Europeanist camps (Biscop 2013; Noll and Moelker 2013). Nevertheless, Belgium's pro-European and pro-EU stance on foreign, security and defence affairs is not to be set in contrast to its advocative role and its promotion of closer EU–NATO cooperation. Instead, it pursues to push for enhanced cooperation based on pragmatical terms with a focus on its limited capabilities and resources (cf. Biscop 2013). Both Belgium and the Netherlands particularly use their bilateral and minilateral networks and belong to the Friends of Europe group in which they informally negotiate and seek to find consensus with their fellow member states. The BeNeLux countries are considered to be among the 'silent followers' in the group of advocates. They take a pragmatic view on the EU–NATO relationship and their own membership on both organisations. All three countries therefore seek to build bridges based on pragmatism and practical cooperation (Dutch Official 1 2018).

Among the advocates is also the US, a close partner of the UK in security and defence affairs as well as the prime ally for most Central and Eastern European and Baltic states. Although it has shown initial signs of scepticism towards the project of developing European security and defence policies and capabilities with the capacity to carry out autonomous actions, it has nevertheless been a contributor to the formalisation process. It welcomed the decisions taken at the Franco–British Saint-Malo Summit as it also saw this as an enhancement of European capabilities to support and strengthen the Atlantic Alliance. Moreover, it was much in favour of the development of European self-responsibility in the security and defence realm, and thus actively supported the ESDI under the Clinton administration. As a condition, from the point of view of the US government, the ESDP would have to be closely tied to NATO (Hunter 2002; Larrabee 2004; Touzovskaia 2006). In addition, in her renowned speech at the NAC on 8 December 1998, then Secretary of State Madeleine Albright confirmed the US government's support and stated that the ESDI provides an initiative for better burden sharing because it 'allows there to be a partnership that does not in any way undercut NATO' (Albright 1998). But she also set out three conditions, which were known as the famous 'three Ds': no decoupling, no duplication and no discrimination. Accordingly, 'any initiative must avoid pre-empting Alliance decision-making by delinking ESDI from NATO, avoid duplicating existing efforts and avoid discrimination against non-EU members' (Albright cited in Hunter 2002: 33– 34). Under these conditions, which were reassured by the UK throughout the development process of European capabilities and capacity, the US finally gave the 'political green light' (Howorth 2000: 380) and actively supported and promoted the necessity of a close relationship, as it saw a clear benefit for the Atlantic Alliance.

Over time, the US position on European security and especially on the EU–NATO relationship has changed with shifts in its domestic politics, showing some signs of a 'swing state' (Rodt 2017). The US has for long been labelled as a 'European power', though with its unilateral foreign policy starting under George W. Bush's presidency (2001–2009) and peaking under Donald Trump's presidency (2017–2021), it is increasingly becoming a 'power in Europe' (Hamilton 2019). Its view on transatlantic security cooperation and its own role within NATO has also changed. Security cooperation with European partners and the EU was widely perceived as positive and as an added value to American national security under the presidencies of Bill Clinton (1993–2001), George W. Bush and Barack Obama (2009–2017). Trump's 'America First' approach, the great power competition with China and Russia, continuous rebuke of key European allies and the distaste for multilateral organisations – even calling NATO 'obsolete' and dismissing the EU altogether – also had implications on the US's own position in the Atlantic Alliance as well as in the EU–NATO relationship. For example, the US commitment to Article 5 has been put into question and its increasingly transactional approach raised concerns about American reliability and future security guarantee, especially in France and Germany (Kaufman 2017; Schreer 2019). The election of Joe Biden as the new president in 2020 triggered a widespread relief in the Euro-Atlantic area and a US return to supporting the EU–NATO relationship is expected, though less attention to Europe in the US foreign and security policy and some divergences in the transatlantic security relationship will likely remain (cf. Lesser 2020).

Contributions to military capabilities, interoperability and division of labour

The gaps between the EU and NATO in terms of military capabilities, procurement and technology as well as leadership have been highlighted from the early beginnings of their interorganisational interaction (Sperling 2004; Yost 2000). Advocates see the benefits of a homogenous and common approach towards filling this gap in a balanced way to achieve higher levels of complementarity and interoperability. Like all member states, advocates face pressures from lacking capabilities and reduced numbers of armed forces, which are double-hatted due to states' multiple memberships, as well as from low levels of interoperability especially among European states. This has gained even more relevance in the course of declining defence budgets. Since the group of advocates is not a homogenous group in terms of their foreign and security policy orientation, political and historical constraints concerning the use of force, which also condition the procurement of military assets and capabilities, pose additional challenges to overcoming the capabilities gap between the EU and NATO. Nevertheless, none of the member states in this group face heavy national constraints and, instead, these states have a tendency of a lenient attitude towards the use of force in peacekeeping, interventions and crisis management operations. Advocates have demonstrated their preferences for engagement through active participation in military campaigns through multilateral forums, such as NATO and the EU, and utilised both forums to promote a defined division of labour while ensuring interoperability and complementarity.

Advocates belong to those countries with the highest military expenditures and increased investments in acquiring and developing military capabilities. At the 2002 Prague Summit, NATO set itself the defence spending target of 2% of GDP, within which 20% of the total amount shall be allocated to equipment, investment and research and development. This pledge has been reaffirmed at past NATO Summits, most prominently at the 2014 Wales Summit. As shown in Figure 3.1, only four states met this target in 2016 (Estonia, Poland, the UK, the US), but advocates' defence budgets have since increased and in 2020, eight member states among the advocates in fact met the 2% of GDP target. New member states have particularly caught up with some of the older ones since gaining membership, such as Romania with an increase from 1.44% to 2.38% and Croatia with an increase from 1.38% to 1.87% (NATO 2020; SIPRI 2020). Since all of the top five states, except for the US and the UK since Brexit, are multiple members they also contribute a big share of their military budget to the EU and CSDP. For example, in 2015, the military contribution of the UK amounted to 20.8% of the EU's overall military expenditure and in 2012, and it was the only EU member state that met the capability objectives of the EDA as it was able to make significant

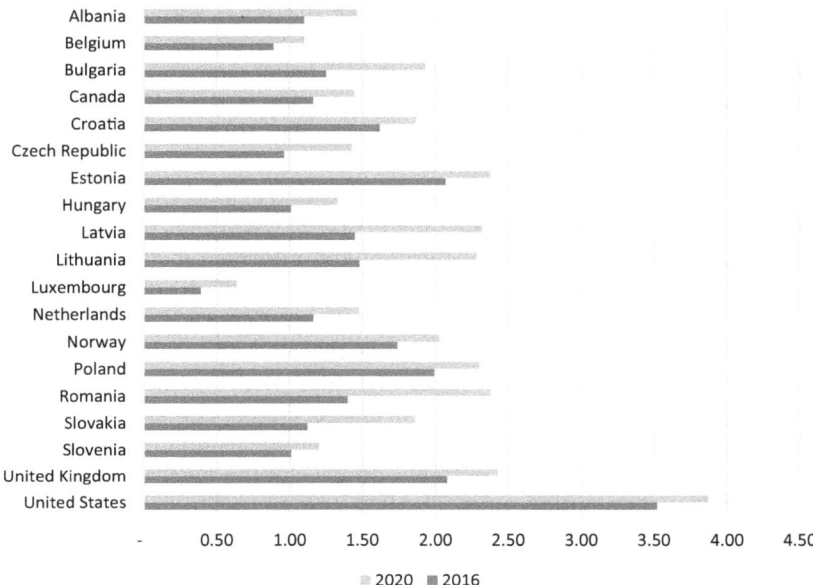

Figure 3.1 Defence expenditure as a share of GDP, 2016 and 2020.

improvements and procurements (Biscop 2012; SIPRI 2015). Brexit will therefore have a significant impact on the defence budget for EU operations and instruments in the future.

In the debates on developing a European military capacity and a security and defence policy, it has often been stressed that the UK concentrated rather on the acquisition of military capabilities instead of institutional structures, which has been emphasised by France (British Officials 2; French Official 2). Britain was initially reluctant towards the creation of CSDP in the debates leading to the Treaty of Maastricht and also opposed the creation of new institutional structures due to fears over duplicating NATO. Yet, throughout the 1990s and early 2000s the UK played a fundamental role not only in contributing towards developing the structures of the ESDP but, more importantly, in shaping the institutional design of the EU–NATO relationship. From the early stages, it advocated for formal contacts between the EU and the Alliance. It acted as a watchdog to ensure the avoidance of any duplication and competition on the one hand and to guarantee complementarity with NATO's command and institutional structures on the other hand. For example, it promoted the idea of establishing and strengthening ESDI, which the UK regarded as a NATO project, while it also vocalised its endorsement for developing stronger European military capabilities in general during the mid-1990s (Giegerich 2007; Howorth 2000; Rees 1996). According to one

NATO official, in bilateral talks between the UK and France, the former even agreed to lift its veto on the merger of the WEU with the EU to secure NATO's relevance and to trigger exchanges between the two organisations (NATO Official 2). This illustrates the British belief in pragmatism concerning security and defence organisations in Europe, that is, the UK seeks pragmatic solutions especially to economic and personnel constraints (Cornish 2013; Ostermann 2015).

With their accession to the EU and NATO and against the backdrop of the changing security environment in the post-Cold War era, particularly small and new member states have modernised and reformed their capabilities and armed forces towards role specialisation. Most of their armed forces were not able to interoperate with other armed forces. These had previously put an emphasis on territorial defence, which was not required ensuing their accession to the EU and NATO and subsequently, some of these small member states focused on the specialisation of their armed forces. For example, Hungary focused on engineering squads, Romania specialised in mountain light infantry and the Czech Republic concentrated on developing nuclear, biological and chemical decontamination units. The Baltics even had to develop new armed forces almost from scratch (Missiroli 2004). In contrast, original members record a greater variety of assets and capabilities, which gives them a higher level of authority among member states. Their armed forces have been reformed towards more flexibility, endurance and sustainability with the ability to conduct expeditionary operations (UK 2003). In addition to their higher levels of military expenditure, the UK and the US, alongside France, are the only nuclear powers in the Euro-Atlantic community. Military power based on the possession of crucial resources including military and civilian assets, equipment and capabilities and a high number of armed forces allows advocates to influence the EU–NATO relationship because they are able to allocate certain resources to either or both organisations according to their preferences and the needs for conducting operations. They can also make use of this military power for bargaining purposes and to set certain conditions vis-à-vis other member states to convince and persuade them for a benefit in other policy areas (British Officials 2).

Another divide that has been identified in the EU–NATO relationship concerns the development and procurement of vital capabilities. This is linked to the question of resource allocation to EU-led and NATO-led military operations faced by all member states due to their single set of forces at their disposal, which is commonly emphasised especially by small member states (Czech Official 1; Romanian Official 1; Slovak Official 1). Declining defence budgets and the resource allocation problem trigger multinational and interorganisational capability procurement projects. Both organisations have launched programmes and initiatives to improve and acquire capabilities, such as NATO's DCI and Smart Defence as well as the EU's launch of the EDA to coordinate and promote defence industry collaborations and to stimulate research and development. With the 2009 Lisbon Treaty, the EU also initiated a set of procurement mechanisms including PESCO, EDF and CARD, which were eventually launched in November 2017. These are initiatives through which EU member states seek to deepen defence cooperation and to combine capability acquisition through clusters of states. Both organisations, with the DCI and Smart Defence as well as the EDA, emphasise the importance of complementarity of their capability initiatives and projects to increase further efficiency and interoperability (Biscop 2017; EU 2003; NATO 2010).

The actual procurement of military capabilities is the responsibility of member states however. To resolve capabilities shortages, advocates have been actively engaged in cooperative efforts and capability development projects. The benefits of joint procurement as well as pooling and sharing are primarily economic but also political. They allow greater economies of scale which, in turn, lead to considerable efficiency and savings as well as the ability to invest in more advanced capabilities and weapon systems, which increases the interoperability of armed forces. Because European states usually prefer to acquire their military capabilities from their national defence industries, the interoperability between both organisations becomes even more complex. To overcome this problem, member states have launched bilateral and minilateral initiatives for the joint procurement of armament and other capabilities. Politically, joint procurements also stimulate the convergence of priorities and security threats, and thus facilitate a common response to such threats (Keohane 2002; von Voss et al. 2013). Some member states, notably the UK, are active in promoting greater burden sharing and capability improvements among European partners (O'Donnell 2011). Advocates furthermore widely agree that in the development of structures and capabilities any (unnecessary) duplications between the EU and NATO need to be avoided (British Officials 2; Czech Official 1; Romanian Official 1; Slovak Official 1). Both organisations should instead make use of their capabilities to orchestrate their responses and approaches to common security threats, for example, hybrid warfare (Jankowski 2015; Keohane 2002).

Examples of minilateral armaments cooperation and joint procurement initiatives include the cooperation among the Visegrád countries. They seek to acquire capabilities together and form an EU Battlegroup to improve their interoperability within as well as outside this group (Törő 2011). NORDEFCO and the BeNeLux group illustrate two other examples. NORDEFCO also invited the Baltics to participate in its procurement activities to address shortages in their military capabilities. The Nordic states have been cooperating on defence capabilities even before states like Finland and Sweden joined the EU and have a successful record of joint efforts, such as in tactical air transport and the set-up of a joint command and control system. Some of the Nordics and Baltics have also formed EU Battlegroups and cooperate within NATO's Response Force. Similarly, the BeNeLux countries have especially concentrated on launching joint procurements in the area of naval capabilities and air policing. Yet, most of these occur on a case-by-case basis and further formalisation would enhance joint procurements and increased interoperability (von Voss et al. 2013).

Taking into account the military expenditure and hardware, it becomes evident that NATO has a clearly defined leader within NATO – the US – whereas the EU lacks such as clear leadership. The possession and development of vital military capabilities and civilian resources gives states certain reputation and authority. Accompanied with operational experiences in crisis management and out-of-area deployments, such powerful states also have a more forceful voice. Through its military power and record of military deployments globally, the US has gained a specific reputation among its European allies. Most Central and Eastern European and Baltic states as well as the Netherlands see their relationship with the US as highly relevant for their national security. They therefore rely on US security guarantees and presence in European security and in EU–NATO cooperation (Eilstrup-Sangiovanni 2014; Noll and Moelker 2013; Tromer 2006). Yet, the US has recently been faced with resistance from its European allies and because of the changes on its domestic level, it showed signs of lacking abilities to effectively take the lead within NATO. The EU, in contrast, faces a leadership problem since there is not a single member state that is able to take the lead in CFSP and CSDP. Within the EU there is an emphasis on the equality of its member states but, as stated by one Czech Official, 'all are equal, but some are more equal' in the context of the EU's foreign, security and defence policy (Czech Official 1). Therefore, France, Germany and the UK have formed an 'informal EU foreign policy *directoire*' (Whitman and Tonra 2017: 42). While the UK would have had leadership potential due to its military resources, track record of deployments and its widely connected diplomatic service, it abandoned its leadership role in CFSP and CSDP and in the EU altogether with its decision to leave the Union.

Drawing on their military resources and capabilities, advocates regularly partake and contribute to EU-led and NATO-led military operations. In fact, some of these states have the highest share of contributions to EU and NATO military operations (see Appendix C). Among these states are Belgium, Canada, the Netherlands, the UK and the US, although the latter has not participated in any EU-led operations. The Baltics and Central and Eastern Europe states have also participated in many military operations, especially in the Western Balkans, (Operation Concordia in North Macedonia, SFOR and Operation Althea in Bosnia and Herzegovina and Kosovo Force (KFOR) in Kosovo) as well as in operations abroad, such as the EU Operation Artemis in the Democratic Republic of Congo and the ISAF and its successor Resolute Support Mission in Afghanistan (cf. Eilstrup-Sangiovanni 2014; Grevi, Helly and Keohane 2009). Moreover, in the case of the naval operations conducted by both the EU and NATO in the Gulf of Aden, the UK has played a key part. It has provided the operational headquarters in Northwood for both naval operations – EUNAVFOR Operation Atalanta (since 2008) and NATO

Operation Ocean Shield (2009–2016). A shared operational headquarters allows for smoother communication and exchange of information between the organisations involved, as well as the divergence of policy approaches and the efficient use of member states' capabilities. Providing the operational headquarters has allowed the UK to play a contributing act towards EU–NATO cooperation as it consented to the launch of EUNAVFOR Operation Atalanta despite its initial reservations (Gebhard and Smith 2015).

The issues of interoperability and division of labour are closely interlinked with capabilities and operational engagements. As drivers of the EU–NATO relationship, advocates aim to increase efficiency and improve interoperability among member states' armed forces, for which they favour defence standardisations. Interoperability is especially crucial in the areas of communication systems, command, information systems and sharing of intelligence, network structures and logistics (Bialos 2005; Sperling 2004; von Voss et al. 2013). While interoperability did not pose a drastic problem to NATO and the EU during the Balkan wars due to a clearly defined division of responsibilities, both organisations have struggled with it internally in more recent military operations. For example, Operation Enduring Freedom and ISAF in Afghanistan highlighted the limits of interoperability between the US and European armed forces (Binnendijk and Braw 2017). The introduction of joint capability development programmes in the EU and NATO seek to enhance their interoperability based on the harmonisation of capabilities and through the conduct of parallel and coordinated trainings and exercises, such as the Combined Training Initiative in NATO. This is, however, only achievable with certain contributions by member states.

According to their national security and defence strategies, the UK and the Baltics aim to improve interoperability of their armed forces and weaponry with other EU and NATO partners, particularly with the US. In its 2010 National Security Strategy and 2015 Strategic Defence and Security Review, the UK stresses the importance of interoperability especially in terms of information sharing and logistics with its key allies, the US, France and Germany (UK 2010, 2015). Through its bilateral cooperation with France based on the 2010 Lancaster House Treaties it ensures further interoperability, for instance, through the development of a Combined Joint Expeditionary Force (CJEF) and the joint usage of its aircraft carrier in addition to cooperation in satellite communications, cyber security, unmanned air systems and research and technology (UK 2010). Outside the NATO framework, Britain has also been cooperating with the US on information and intelligence sharing, which further enhances interoperability due to increased shared awareness. The continuation and added value for the interoperability between the EU and NATO has been frequently emphasised (UK 2015). Several minilateral groups in the EU–NATO relationship, such as the Baltic, Nordic and Visegrád countries, follow this example by conducting joint exercises and through their capability development projects (Törő 2011; Tromer 2006). The continuous search for opportunities to achieve greater interoperability on the member state level indicates advocates' engagement in extending the efficiency between the EU and NATO to avoid the duplication of capabilities and efforts.

Similar to interoperability, the issue of division of labour has received increased attention with closer cooperation between the EU and NATO (cf. Biscop 2021; Tardy 2021). While their responsibilities and tasks were clearly defined during the Cold War – NATO was in charge of collective defence and territorial security and the EU was primarily responsible for economic and political integration – this has changed with the evolving security environment. Advocates believe that a division of labour between the two organisations can lead to more consultations and reduces the capabilities and interoperability gaps. Based on clear mandates and well-defined sets of tasks and responsibilities, each organisation can develop and acquire the required capabilities. Member states nevertheless acknowledge that there will always be overlaps and duplications to a certain extent, but additional duplication should be avoided through a defined and negotiated division of tasks (Estonian Official 1; Polish Official 1; Romanian Official 1).

Some advocates share a common view on division of labour. The Baltics and Central and Eastern Europe see the EU and NATO as two different organisations that serve 'two parallel and complementary but essentially distinct goals' (Missiroli 2004: 132). They pursue a division of hard and soft security. Because of their close relations with the US and their interest in keeping the US involved in European security, they underline the importance of NATO's contribution to their territorial defence, especially vis-à-vis the underlying threat on the Eastern border. Yet, the line of division is ambiguous and blurred. As stated by a Polish official, there is 'no division of labour in geographical terms', but there should automatically be a division of labour concerning their mandates and responsibilities due to the availability of capabilities and resources (Polish Official 1). Furthermore, there is no division of tasks based on the intensity of conflicts since, for example, the EU-led training mission in Mali (EUTM Mali) has an intensity level compared to NATO-led operations. As expressed by some member states, NATO is and remains in charge of collective defence, whereas the EU should focus on military training and executive operations such as the ones in Bosnia and Mali (Czech Official 1; Estonian Official 1). Advocates promote this view in the debates and negotiations preceding the launch of new deployments or the extension of ongoing operations. For example, as mentioned by one British official, if a crisis emerges and states within groups of interests agree that action needs to be taken, partners in NATO are consulted first. They exchange their views and discuss whether the issue concerns one of NATO's core tasks and in a second stage, they consider whether and how the EU would be able to contribute (British Official 1). Consequently, the UK alongside Central and Eastern European states first look at options within NATO while concomitantly considering the EU's capabilities and toolbox. This allows for a division of labour in which both organisations can act according to their strengths and core tasks while ensuring complementarity at the same time.

Advocates thereby avoid the risk of competition between the EU and NATO and, instead, contribute to their practical cooperation in crisis management.

While advocates acknowledge the gaps and the challenges of interoperability and division of labour between the EU and NATO, they seek to overcome them by facilitating better communication and exchanges, improving their military capabilities and harmonising their efforts. By collaborating with other states for joint exercises as well as by partaking in similar groupings for EU Battlegroups and the NATO Response Force, they contribute to a higher degree of interoperability among member states. Advocates further agree on a specific division of labour to make full use of the capabilities, policies and practices of each organisation. Nevertheless, there is still not a clearly defined division of functions or geographical scope agreed by both organisations, which leads advocates to participate and contribute to EU and NATO operations on case-by-case decisions to support each organisation's advantages and strengths.

Conclusions

Advocates of the EU–NATO relationship form a group that seeks closer cooperation and enhanced interactions. They are generally characterised as proactive and supportive member states that are deeply embedded in the structures of both organisations and that contribute vital resources. Key features of advocates include their wide ranging network of bilateral and minilateral connections, higher levels of investments in military capabilities to contribute to both EU and NATO operations and active promotion of institutionalising interactions and enhancing cooperation. Alongside the UK, the Central and Eastern European states as well as the Baltics serve as the most prominent states that connect other member states within and between international organisations, and through their bargaining, conditionality and use of capabilities. With the help of vital military resources, such as the nuclear power of both the UK and the US, as well as their higher defence budgets, advocates utilise their military power to influence and direct the EU–NATO relationship by allocating calculatedly these resources. Advocates' shared awareness of the necessity for enhanced interoperability and their common idea on a division of labour allows them to act unitedly by promoting and disseminating this view outside their group of interests towards more sceptical member states. They do so in negotiations within both the EU and NATO while acting as a majority coalition group. Advocates overall drive the EU–NATO cooperation forward by making use of their resources, initiatives and ideas as well as networks of partnerships and continuous exchanges with fellow member states. They see more benefits than costs in the EU–NATO relationship which helps them to economise their military resources, increase their security and pursue their national security and defence interests more effectively.

With the changes on the domestic political level, both the UK and the US present special cases among advocates with signs of swing states. The US, on the one hand, experienced a change from a pro-transatlanticist (until the Obama administration) to a pro-American (under the Trump administration) foreign policy. With the election of Joe Biden as president, a transatlanticist and pro-European foreign policy outlook is expected that would also facilitate and support EU–NATO cooperation (cf. Lesser 2020). The UK, on the other hand, has been one of the major drivers and most prominent states among advocates of the EU–NATO relationship. The decision to leave the EU, however, has a significant impact on its role as transatlantic bridge and advocate. Because of its embeddedness in European security and its close ties with key European allies, especially France and Germany, the UK is likely to remain committed to a close EU–NATO relationship that will benefit its own security. However, with a loss of influence, it is likely to foster ties through NATO and minilateral frameworks (Dunn and Webber 2016).

References

Abukevicius, Margiris (2015) 'Refocusing CSDP: A Lithuanian perspective'. *In*: Fiott, Daniel (ed.) *The Common Security and Defence Policy: National Perspectives*, Brussels: Egmont – Royal Institute for International Relations, 89–90.

Albright, Madeleine K. (1998) *Speech and Press Conference Held at North Atlantic Council, NATO HQ in Brussels on 8 December 1998*, www.nato.int/docu/speech/1998/s981208x.htm (accessed on 21/12/2017).

Bailes, Alyson J.K. (1995) 'Sécurité européenne: le point de vue britannique', *Politique étrangère*, 1: 85–98.

Bajarūnas, Eitvydas (2014) 'Cooperation of Nordic-Baltic countries in the areas of security and defence', *Lithuanian Annual Strategic Review*, 11(1): 83–118.

Bialos, Jeffrey P. (2005) The United States, Europe and the Interoperability Gap, *The Internationa Spectator*, 40(2): 53–62.

Billon-Galland, Alice, Thomas Raines and Richard G. Whitman (2020) *The Future of the E3: Post-Brexit Cooperation Between the UK, France and Germany,* Chatham House Research Papers, London: Chatham House.

Binnendijk, Hans and Elizabeth Braw (2017) 'For NATO, true interoperability is no longer optional', *Defense One*, published on 18 December 2017, www.defenseone.com/ideas/2017/12/nato-true-interoperability-no-longer-optional/144650/ (accessed on 20/12/2017).

Biscop, Sven (1999) 'The UK's change of course: A new chance for the ESDI', *European Foreign Affairs Review*, 4(2): 253–268.

Biscop, Sven (2012) 'The UK and European defence: Leading of leaving?' *International Affairs*, 88(6): 1297–1313.

Biscop, Sven (2013) 'Belgium'. *In*: Biehl, Heiko et al. (eds) *Strategic Cultures in Europe: Security and Defence Policies Across the Continent*, Wiesbaden: Springer VS, 31–41.

Biscop, Sven (2017) Oratio Pro Pesco, *Egmont Papers*, 91: 1–13.

Biscop, Sven (2021) 'EU and NATO strategy: A compass, a concept, and a concordat', *Egmont Security Policy Brief*, 141: 1–8.

Cornish, Paul (2013) 'United Kingdom'. *In*: Biehl, Heiko et al. (eds) *Strategic Cultures in Europe: Security and Defence Policies Across the Continent*, Wiesbaden: Springer VS, 371–385.

Dorussen, Han and Hugh Ward (2008) 'Intergovernmental organisations and the Kantian Peace: A network perspective', *Journal of Conflict Resolution*, 52(2): 189–212.

Dryburgh, Lynne (2010) 'Blair's first government (1997–2001) and European security and defence policy: Seismic shift or adaptation', *British Journal of Politics and International Relations*, 12(2): 257–273.

Duke, Simon (2008) 'The future of EU–NATO relations: A case of mutual irrelevance through competition?' *Journal of European Integration*, 30(1): 27–43.

Dunn, David Hastings and Mark Webber (2016) 'The UK, the European Union and NATO: Brexit's unintended consequences', *Global Affairs*, 2(5): 471–480.

Dunne, Tim (2004) '"When the shooting starts": Atlanticism in British security strategy', *International Affairs*, 80(5): 893–909.

Dyson, Tom (2011) 'Defence policy under the labour government: Operational dynamism and strategic inertia', *British Journal of Politics and International Relations*, 13(2): 206–229.

EEAS (2015) *EUMC Report to PSC on the Outcome of BGCC 2/15*, COPS 321, CSDP/PSDC 568, EEAS (2015) 1466 ADD 1 REV 1 From 27 October 2015.

Eilstrup-Sangiovanni, Mette (2014) 'Europe's defence dilemma', *The International Spectator*, 49(2): 83–116.

European Union (2003) *European Security Strategy: A Secure Europe in a Better World*, Brussels: European Union.

Flockhart, Trine (1996) 'The dynamics of expansion: NATO, WEU, and EU', *European Security*, 5(2): 196–218.

Gebhard, Carmen and Simon J. Smith (2015) 'The two faces of EU-NATO cooperation: Counter-piracy operations off the Somali coast, *Cooperation and Conflict*, 50(1): 107–127.

Gehring, Thomas and Sebastian Oberthür (2009) 'The causal mechanisms of interaction between international institutions', *European Journal of International Relations*, 15(1): 125–156.

Giegerich, Bastian (2007) 'European positions and American responses: ESDP-NATO compatibility'. *In*: Casarini, Nicola and Costanza Musu (eds) *European Foreign Policy in an Evolving International System: The Road Towards Convergence*, Basingstoke: Palgrave Macmillan, 43–56.

Grevi, Giovanni, Damien Helly and Daniel Keohane (2009) *European Security and Defence Policy: The First Ten Years (1999–2009)*, Paris: European Union Institute for Security Studies (EUISS).

Hamilton, Daniel S. (2019) 'Piece of the puzzle: NATO and Euro-Atlantic architecture after the Cold War'. *In*: Hamilton, Daniel S. and Kristina Spohr (eds) *Open Door: NATO and Euro-Atlantic Security After the Cold War*, Washington DC: Brookings Institution Press, 3–56.

Herolf, Gunilla (2006) 'The Nordic countries and the EU-NATO relationship: Further comments'. *In*: Bailes, Alyson J.K., Gunilla Herolf and Bengt Sundelius (eds) *Nordic Countries and the European Security and Defence Policy*, Stockholm: SIPRI, 67–77.

Howorth, Jolyon (2000) 'Britain, NATO and CESDP: Fixed strategy, changing tactics', *European Foreign Affairs Review*, 5(3): 377–396.

Hunter, Robert E. (2002) *The European Security and Defence Policy: NATO's Companion or Competitor?* Santa Monica, Arlington: RAND.

Jankowski, Dominik P. (2015) 'Poland and the CSDP: From Wales to Warsaw with a strategic stopover in Brussels'. *In*: Fiott, Daniel (ed) *The Common Security and Defence Policy: National Perspectives.* Brussels: Egmont – Royal Institute for International Relations, 71–72.

Jönsson, Christer (1986): 'Interorganisation theory and international organisation', *International Studies Quarterly*, 30(1): 39–57.

Kaufman, Joyce P. (2017) 'The US perspective on NATO under Trump: Lessons of the past and prospects for the future', *International Affairs*, 93(2): 251–266.

Keohane, Daniel (2002) *The EU and Armaments Co-operation*, London: Centre for European Reform.

Kiukucans, Edgars (2015) 'Latvia and the CSDP'. *In*: Fiott, Daniel (ed.) *The Common Security and Defence Policy: National Perspectives*, Brussels: Egmont – Royal Institute of International Relations, 65–67.

Larrabee, F. Stephen (2004) 'ESDP and NATO: Assuring complementarity', *The International Spectator*, 39(1): 51–70.

Lesser, Ian (2020) 'Great optimism in the EU and NATO as Brussels looks to Biden', *The German Marshall Fund of the United States*, https://shar.es/aowSwC (accessed on 12/02/2021).

Magliveras, Konstantinos D. (2011) 'Membership in international organisations'. *In*: Klabbers, Jan and Asa Wallendahl (eds) *Research Handbook on the Law of International Organisations*, Cheltenham and Northampton: Edward Elgar Publishing, 84–107.

Marsh, Steve and Wyn Rees (2012) *The European Union in the Security of Europe: From Cold War to Terror War*, Abingdon: Routledge.

Miskimmon, Alister (2004) 'Continuity in the Face of Upheaval – British Strategic Culture and the Impact of the Blair Government', *European Security*, 13(3): 273–299.

Missiroli, Antonio (2002) 'EU–NATO cooperation in crisis management: No Turkish delight for ESDP', *Security Dialogue*, 33(1): 9–26.

Missiroli, Antonio (2004) 'Central European between the EU and NATO', *Survival*, 46(4): 121–136.

NATO (2010) *Active Engagement, Modern Defence: Strategic Concept for the Defence and Security of Members of the North Atlantic Treaty Organisation*, Brussels: NATO.

NATO (2020) *Defence Expenditure of NATO Countries (2013–2020)*, www.nato.int/cps/en/natohq/news_178975.htm (accessed on 15/02/2021).

Noll, Jörg and René Moelker (2013) 'Netherlands'. *In*: Biehl, Heiko et al. (eds) *Strategic Cultures in Europe: Security and Defence Policies Across the Continent*, Wiesbaden: Springer VS, 254–267.

O'Donnell, Clara Marina (2011) 'Britain's coalition government and EU defence cooperation: Undermining British interests', *International Affairs*, 87(2): 419–433.

Oliver, Tim and Michael John Williams (2016) 'Special relationships in flux: Brexit and the future of the US-EU and US-UK relationships', *International Affairs*, 92(3): 547–567.

Ostermann, Falk (2015) 'The end of ambivalence and the triumph of pragmatism? Franco-British defence cooperation and European and Atlantic defence policy traditions', *International Relations*, 29(3): 334–347.

Pannier, Alice (2017) 'From one exceptionalism to another: France's strategic relations with the United States and the United Kingdom in the post-Cold War era', *Journal of Strategic Studies*, 40(4): 475–504.

Pannier, Alice and Olivier Schmitt (2014) 'Institutionalised cooperation and policy convergence in European defence: Lessons from the relations between France, Germany and the UK', *European Security*, 23(3): 270–289.

Pomorska, Karolina (2017) 'Foreign policies of Eastern EU states'. *In*: Hadfield, Amelia et al. (eds) *Foreign Policies of EU Member States: Continuity and Europeanisation*, Abingdon: Routledge, 51–65.

Rees, Wyn G. (1996) 'Constructing a European defence identity: The perspective of Britain, France and Germany', *European Foreign Affairs Review*, 1(2): 231–246.

Rikveilis, Airis (2013) 'Latvia'. *In*: Biehl, Heiko et al. (eds) *Strategic Cultures in Europe: Security and Defence Policies Across the Continent*, Wiesbaden: Springer VS, 207–216.

Rodt, Annemarie Peen (2017) 'Member states policy towards EU military operations'. *In*: Hadfield, Amelia et al. (eds) *Foreign Policies of EU Member States: Continuity and Europeanisation*, Abingdon: Routledge, 131–147.

Salu, Kadi and Erik Männik (2013) 'Estonia'. *In*: Biehl, Heiko et al. (eds) *Strategic Cultures in Europe: Security and Defence Policies Across the Continent*, Wiesbaden: Springer VS, 99–112.

Schreer, Benjamin (2019) 'Trump, NATO, and the future of Europe's defence', *The RUSI Journal*, 164(1): 10–17.

Šešelgytė, Margarita (2013) 'Lithuania'. *In*: Biehl, Heiko et al. (eds) *Strategic Cultures in Europe: Security and Defence Policies Across the Continent*, Wiesbaden: Springer VS, 217–228.

Simón, Luis (2017) 'France and Germany: The European Union's "central" member states'. *In*: Hadfield, Amelia et al. (eds) *Foreign Policies of EU Member States: Continuity and Europeanisation*, Abingdon: Routledge, 66–82.

SIPRI (2015) *SIPRI Yearbook 2015: Armaments, Disarmament and International Security*, Oxford: Oxford University Press on behalf of SIPRI.

SIPRI (2020) *SIPRI Military Expenditure Data Base 1949–2019*. Stockholm: SIPRI.

Sperling, James (2004) 'Capabilities traps and gaps: Symptom or cause of a troubled transatlantic relationship', *Contemporary Security Policy*, 25(3): 452–478.

Stahl, Bernhard et al. (2004) 'Understanding the Atlanticist–Europeanist divide in the CFSP: Comparing Denmark, France, Germany and the Netherlands', *European Foreign Affairs Review*, 9(3): 417–442.

Tardy, Thierry (2021) 'For a new NATO-EU bargain', *Egmont Security Policy Brief*, 138: 1–5.

Tiilikainen, Teija (2006) 'The Nordic countries and the EU-NATO relationship'. *In*: Bailes, Alyson J.K., Gunilla Herolf and Bengt Sundelius (eds) *Nordic Countries and the European Security and Defence Policy*, Stockholm: SIPRI, 50–66.

Törő, Csaba (2011) 'Visegrad Cooperation Within NATO and CSDP', *V4 Papers*, No. 2.

Touzovskaia, Natalia (2006) 'EU-NATO relations: How close to "strategic partnership?"', *European Security*, 15(3): 235–258.

Tromer, Elzbieta (2006) 'Baltic perspectives on the European security and defence policy'. *In*: Bailes, Alyson J.K., Gunilla Herolf and Bengt Sundelius (eds) *Nordic Countries and the European Security and Defence Policy*, Stockholm: SIPRI, 364–391.

von Voss, Alicia et al. (2013) 'The state of defence cooperation in Europe', *SWP Working Paper*, 3: 1–14.

Weiss, Tomas (2015) 'Confused and divided: Czech foreign and security policy in the EU'. *In*: Fiott, Daniel (ed) *The Common Security and Defence Policy: National Perspectives*, Brussels: Egmont–Royal Institute for International Relations, 87–88.

Whitman, Richard G. (2016) 'The UK and EU foreign, security and defence policy after Brexit: Integrated, associated or detached?' *National Institute Economic Review*, 238(1): 43–50.

Whitman, Richard G. and Ben Tonra (2017) 'Western EU member states foreign policy geo-orientations: UK, Ireland and the Benelux'. *In*: Hadfield, Amelia et al. (eds) *Foreign Policies of EU Member States: Continuity and Europeanisation*, Abingdon: Routledge, 38–50.

Yost, David S. (2000) 'The NATO capabilities gap and the European Union', *Survival*, 42(4): 97–128.

4 Blockers

France, Cyprus, Greece, Ireland and Turkey

Among the main obstacles for the EU–NATO relationship is the political blockage enacted by particular member states. Some states have been frustrated with the state of the EU–NATO relationship and in turn, other states seek to actively slow down the progress and create obstructions in their own interests. States in the group of blockers are not *per se* blockers of EU–NATO cooperation as a whole, and neither would they actively block further enhancement and interactions based on disapproval. They nevertheless undertake actions that has stalled the relationship. Blockers, in this context, are those states that inhibit the process of closer cooperation. The majority among blockers do not automatically veto any further improvements or enhancements once the topic is on the agenda, neither do they intentionally obstruct any cooperative efforts during crisis management operations. Yet, there are certain signs which indicate that they feel being left out of the EU–NATO relationship, ultimately triggering frequent oppositions and obstructive behaviour. The reasons for hampering closer EU–NATO cooperation are determined by their national interests, foreign and security policy orientations and perceptions of each organisation and their interorganisational relationship. While there is greater fluctuation of who can be assigned to this group and because they exercise obstructing behaviour to varying degrees, states such as Cyprus, Greece and Turkey as well as France and Ireland are considered as blockers in the EU–NATO interorganisational relationship. Some of their efforts and behaviour, however, have also benefitted EU–NATO cooperation. Therefore, some of these states are not essentially fully-fledged blockers but can occasionally be considered as boundary cases.

What makes these states to be recognised as blockers is the extent to which they hamper interorganisational interactions. Blockers generally demonstrate less positive, and sometimes even negative, attitudes towards closer EU–NATO cooperation. They actively seek to obstruct the enhancement of interorganisational relations and even though they aim to be heavily engaged in the negotiations, they do so by slowing down closer cooperation in line with their own interests and benefits. Contributing to military operations and providing resources to the international organisations is thus a way of

DOI: 10.4324/9781003170068-4

increasing their influence in negotiations to realise their own preferences in regard to the scope of interorganisational cooperation.

This chapter depicts the behaviour and involvement of blockers in the EU–NATO relationship by first outlining the main characteristics shared by all states in this group. The subsequent examination of their membership in both the EU and NATO helps to investigate their hampering behaviour and positioning between both organisations. The final section examines blockers' approaches to the capabilities gap, interoperability and division of labour between the EU and NATO and determines how some of their initiatives have been counterproductive to advancing this interorganisational relationship.

Shared characteristics of blockers

States in the group of blockers share a common set of characteristics, which have changed over time and with the course of the development of EU–NATO cooperation (see Table 4.1). The individuality of national security strategies and approaches to international security organisations as well as the different natures of their positions in the relationship makes the identification of commonalities of blockers more complex. This section thus focuses on the generally shared features and characteristics by all states in the group of blockers.

Blockers comprise both single member states and multiple member states as well as original and subsequent members (Gehring and Oberthür 2009; Magliveras 2011). Each state in the group of blockers differs, however, in the nature of its membership. France is considered to be a big and original member state, which has regained its status among other powerful states such as the UK and the US (Bozo 2016). Turkey is of similar size though it is a single and subsequent member state. Greece and Ireland are small states, and Cyprus is even considered as a 'microstate' (Dobrescu et al. 2017: 83). While member states generally pursue specific objectives in organisations, blockers seek to make maximum benefits of their membership, which means their behaviour is interest-driven based on national advantages. Yet, some blockers also experience the disadvantages of their single membership (Tofte 2003). Their positioning in both the EU and NATO and the perception of their membership result in the use of specific strategies, such as hostage-taking, turf battles and forum-shopping (Hofmann 2009). These strategies are applied particularly in times when crucial issues are at stake, such as the launch of military operations, troop deployments, triggering or intensifying interorganisational cooperation, enlargement towards new member states or the widening of organisations' responsibilities and mandates.

Membership is a key factor for blockers since this is decisive for their approach to shaping the EU–NATO relationship, as only multiple membership allows involvement in both decision-making procedures in which states can express their concerns and oppositions. Blockers with multiple memberships seek to maintain a wide network of bilateral and minilateral relations within

Table 4.1 Overview of blockers' characteristics

Shared characteristics	Blockers and their membership	Contributions to capabilities	View on division of labour and interoperability
• Make use of their veto right in decisions on formalisation and institutionalisation • Not much in favour of strengthening cooperation • Agreement on interorganisational cooperation depends on issue area, scope and geographical location • Concerned about formalising interorganisational relations	• Among the 'troublemakers' • Might have inter-state clashes and disagreements with other member states • Signs of 'schizophrenic' behaviour in discussions • Ambivalent relations with organisations and member states • Maintain partnerships with member states outside the interorganisational relationship	• Possess vital resources and military capabilities • Use of resources and capabilities for bargaining • Pursuit of different capability development programmes in each organisation • Higher levels of military expenditure	• Low engagement in improving interoperability • Seek to strengthen their preferred organisation instead of striving for a division of labour • Interoperability only needed in cases of clear absence of required capabilities and resources

and between the two organisations to promote their views and initiatives (Pannier and Schmitt 2014). Single member states, in contrast, either seek to become multiple members by accessing the respective other organisation or seek to take advantage of their position by hostage-taking. They can exploit their situation to obstruct closer EU–NATO cooperation by making their own gains through the realisation of their national interests, such as better conditions and positioning of their own membership, and by blocking other member states from joining the organisations (Hofmann 2009, 2019).

While blockers have been engaged in the institutionalisation process of the EU–NATO cooperation, albeit with concessions and compromises, they also possess certain military and strategic resources. These include the possession of vital and inevitable military capabilities such as nuclear weapons (France), high levels of defence expenditures (France, Greece, Turkey) or well-trained and specialised armed forces (France, Turkey) (NATO 2017, 2020; The Military Balance 2017). In addition, their geographical location in the Euro-Atlantic space can be of detrimental value and strategic importance. Such is the case for Cyprus, Greece and Turkey with their location in the Mediterranean Sea region and their proximity to the Middle and Near East, Central Asia and the Black Sea region. These are areas which have recently received increased attention for the security activities of the EU and NATO (Economides 2013;

Müftüler-Baç 2000; Samokhvalov 2013). France's relations with its former African colonies can further be seen as a strategic asset due to the country's overseas engagements, which have resulted in the development of well-equipped and well-trained expeditionary armed forces. Yet, these relations also represent new challenges and threats, rising instabilities and also create growing divergences among member states in finding common responses (Charbonneau 2008).

The extent to which these member states have obstructed the enhancement of the EU–NATO relationship has changed over time. At times, blockers do not necessarily hamper or obstruct progress, however, their continuous actions, behaviour and policies inside and outside the EU–NATO framework have not always been beneficial and contributory. Blockers' domestic political context as well as their bilateral and minilateral relationships are influential for changes in their national foreign, security and defence policy orientations (cf. Hofmann 2017). States' domestic politics and external relations have therefore also shaped their attitudes and behaviour towards the EU–NATO interorganisational relationship. In one way or another, each of the states in the group of blockers has made use of obstructing strategies and of their veto rights that has led to labelling them as 'troublemakers' among member states in the EU and NATO. Each state has its own rationale for slowing down the interorganisational relations which will be analysed in this chapter in regard to their contributions to capability developments, division of labour and operational engagements.

Making use of their membership and political strategies

Membership in international organisations is vital for states to realise their national interests, to coordinate action and to shape policy preferences as well as for the benefits of collective action and the reduction of transaction costs. In contrast, membership can also produce competition and tensions among member states over resources, the level of influence they can exert on the policy outcomes, institutional developments and over filling key positions within the structure of international organisations (Abbott and Snidal 1998; Keohane and Martin 1995). Organisations often serve different purposes for individual member states depending on the organisation's functions and mandates. The high degree of functional overlap in the EU–NATO relationship has triggered states to reformulate their objectives. Member states might enter into a conflict of interest vis-à-vis the respective organisations, which leads to unpredictable behaviour. Consequently, the behaviour of some member states in this relationship has been characterised as 'schizophrenic' and 'paranoid' (EU Official 1; EU Official 4; NATO Official 2).

Blockers are among the 'troublemakers' in terms of using their membership because of their record of conflictual bilateral and multilateral relations with other member states, which have an overall impact on the relationship and the cooperative efforts between the EU and NATO. When representatives from the EU, NATO and member states' delegations were asked about what countries are most troublesome concerning the EU–NATO relationship, the two most common answers were France and Turkey in addition to the problematic triad between Cyprus, Greece and Turkey. According to German officials, especially Turkey has been labelled as the prime 'troublemaker' of this relationship (German Officials 2). Many states feel frustrated by this problem and solving the conflict between the three states has further been named as the major hurdle to improving EU–NATO cooperation (British Officials 2; Czech Official 1; Italian Official 1; NATO Officials 4; Polish Official 1; Slovak Official 1). Yet, the conflict has also been increasingly perceived as an 'alibi' for other member states to slow down cooperation efforts (Cypriot official 2) and in fact, 'the political obstacle goes beyond the Cyprus issue' (EU Official 4). This section therefore explores blockers' use of their membership and particularly their use of political strategies such as hostage-taking and forum-shopping. It also examines more in-depth the 'schizophrenic' behaviour of members in the group of blockers as well as the Cyprus issue, illustrating one example of inter-state tension and the application of hostage-taking strategies.

France: trapped between endorsement and obstruction

As a founding member of both NATO and the EU, France has pursued its strategy of detaching European security and defence from US dominance from the early beginnings. It has played an instrumental role in the development and institutional evolution of both organisations separately and their relationship. In collaboration with the UK, France was involved in creating NATO's integrated military structures and two of its key politicians – Jean Monnet and Robert Schuman – are considered to be the founding fathers of the European Community and among the main drivers of the European integration project (Bozo 2014, 2016). Since the end of the Second World War, France pursued four fundamental objectives, which have often put strains on the EU–NATO relationship: (1) its desire for French and European *grandeur*, that is, military autonomy and independence, (2) national ownership, military sovereignty and especially national control over its *force de frappe* (nuclear warfare), (3) regaining and maintaining its status as a great power among the UK, the US and Russia (then the Soviet Union) and (4) the rebalancing of US dominance in the international system and the establishment of a multipolar world order (France 2008, 2013; Irondelle and Mérand 2010; Pannier 2017; Simón 2017; Treacher 2011). France has taken its individual route in shaping the evolution of the EU–NATO relationship, which has been influenced by its national interests and policy preferences. It is known for its drive towards a stronger European security and defence policy which is much in favour of France's strategies and security culture. While the country has challenged the enhancement and institutionalisation of EU–NATO cooperation, it has shown two faces: its supportive role and its ability, though limited, to obstruct the process. This has been demonstrated particularly by its own approach to and membership in the two security organisations as well as its behaviour in negotiations with other member states.

The French foreign and security policy orientation position within the EU-NATO relationship is evidently shaped by two aspects, its relations with the Alliance and the US and its domestic politics. Over the course of time, France has had a special relationship with the Atlantic Alliance and with the US in European security. The disagreements with the UK and the US over the Suez crisis in 1966 led to the decision to withdraw from the Alliance's integrated military command structures under Charles de Gaulle's presidency. As a low-level supporter of NATO from the beginning, France was especially dissatisfied with US dominance in NATO as well as NATO's prevalence in Europe, which triggered its pursuit of a European defence capability (Bozo 2016; Cizel and von Hlatky 2014; Fortmann, Haglund and von Hlatky 2010; Pesme 2010; Rieker 2013). Despite its withdrawal, France kept its formal membership and thus its decision-making power in the NAC. While it was outside NATO's integrated military command structures, France sought to develop a European defence capacity and capability under the EU's umbrella in the 1990s and thereby obstructed the enhancement of cooperation.

France's approach to NATO, its relations with the US and its role in EU-NATO cooperation were also influenced by its domestic politics (Hofmann 2017). While France focused on the European integration project under the Socialist President François Mitterrand, the rapprochement with NATO as well as the relations between the EU and NATO moved to the centre of attention when the Republican Jacques Chirac assumed office in 1995. Although Chirac announced the continuation of the Gaullist tradition of autonomy, independence, sovereignty and the aim to establish a 'European power' (Bozo 2016: 151), relations with the US, the UK and NATO improved fundamentally. This was vital for triggering the 1998 Saint-Malo Summit and subsequent Declaration where British Prime Minister Tony Blair and French President Jacques Chirac signalled an important step towards the creation of a European security and defence capacity as well as strengthening relations between both organisations (Bozo 2016; Simón 2017). At first, France seemed to be in favour of normalising relations with the Alliance and enhancing the EU–NATO interorganisational relationship, particularly because it suggested the creation of joint committees (Flockhart 2014). Then, however, French officials opposed proposals by US Defence Secretary Cohen in 2000, which anticipated a 'reciprocal NATO-EU defence planning process' that sought to foster closer cooperation (Ratti 2014: 371). With the country's full reintegration into NATO's military structures under President Nicolas Sarkozy in 2009, France anticipated a normalisation of relations with the Alliance and the US under Barack Obama's presidency. Nevertheless, while it sought to normalise relations, 'the underlying motive to support full participation in NATO was primarily to restore French influence within the Alliance' (Cizel and von Hlatky 2014: 355).

France generally sees both the EU and NATO as tools to regain its power status and political rank on the international level and aspires to rebalance the international order, especially in regard to US predominance on the European continent (Hofmann and Kempin 2007; Perruche 2014). Its dissatisfaction with both a US-dominated alliance and a NATO-dominated Europe supported its objective to realise a European security and defence capacity to create a counterweight that would allow greater autonomy for Europe (Bozo 2016; Ratti 2014). The changed international security environment after the end of the Cold War triggered a rethinking of the French attitude towards NATO as well as the European integration project. It was faced with the choice between the creation of a European pillar within NATO, which later became known as the ESDI, and the development of an autonomous European defence policy in the form of CSDP (Boyer 1993; Bozo 2016; Irondelle and Mérand 2010). This dilemma has become evident in the case of the conflicts in the Western Balkans for example. While French policymakers initially hoped for a European solution to this European conflict, they soon had to realise that the EU's capabilities and capacity were not advanced enough, which led to France's first disappointment with the European integration project. Subsequently, as a sign of its pragmatic approach to remaining a powerful player, France accepted the need to move closer to the idea of ESDI and to collaborate with NATO and its allies despite the scepticism vocalised by former French President François Mitterrand (Bozo 2016; Hofmann and Kempin 2007; Pannier 2017; Rieker 2013).

Against the backdrop of France's overall ambitions, its focus on strategic autonomy, national ownership and sovereignty of its *force de frappe* has become obstructive and has led to the indecisiveness between the pursuit of its national objectives, pushing for the development of the EU as a security actor through enhancing its CSDP and favouring NATO because of the frustration with its fellow EU member states over their lack of capabilities, commitment and willingness (Bozo 2016; Muniz 2013; Pannier 2017). Yet, despite the rapprochement with NATO and improved relations with the US, French policymakers have still been perceived as paranoid about being 'patronised' by both the US and NATO, which they aim to counter by all means (NATO Official 2). Although the French return under Sarkozy did not come as a surprise (Bozo 2014; Fortmann, Haglund and von Hlatky 2010; Muniz 2013), it was nevertheless seen by some European partners as proof of the French ambivalence and even perceived as a potential 'death knell' for CSDP (Irondelle and Mérand 2010). Therefore, this behaviour has left European states and transatlantic partners in a state of limbo because France's behaviour has become increasingly unpredictable as well as contradictory.

Leaving partners and allies in confusion due to the behaviour of French representatives in the negotiation and decision-making forums of the EU and NATO as well as the state's shifting preferences and positions between the two organisations and towards their cooperation efforts, makes France a less predictable and unreliable partner in other member states' minds. As a consequence, this behaviour has been characterised as 'schizophrenic' by EU staff members and repeatedly also by a NATO representative, especially in regard to the behaviour of France, and also Turkey, during negotiations and decision-making procedures (EU Official 1; EU Official 4; NATO Official 2). In this sense, the term 'schizophrenic' is used to describe how a state would promote a specific initiative or project, including capability developments, training and interoperability plans, in one organisation that would be beneficial and contributory to both EU and NATO, but in the respective other organisation it would obstruct further developments of these initiatives and projects.

A concrete example for this is the positioning and behaviour of French officials in EU and NATO negotiations, which was put forward by one EU Official. It was observed that in one week, in one of the meetings of the EU to plan a potential takeover from NATO's KFOR, the French EU representative announced to withdraw the Gendarmerie Force. In the following week, however, the French defence minister claimed in a NATO meeting that the EU would not meet its commitments and would not be able to come up to its expectations (EU Official 1). This shows that, on the one hand, France seeks to act through the EU and CSDP in terms of crisis management, peacekeeping and post-conflict activities, and thus wants to strengthen European autonomy and the EU's defence capabilities. On the other hand, it desires to increase its global influence, and in this context, 'to restore French influence within the Alliance' (Cizel and von Hlatky 2014: 355). Multiple members who have recorded this particular French position were left confused and without a clear standpoint, which complicated negotiations as well as reliance on French decision-makers. Subsequently, some member states have perceived the French 'exceptionalism' as an underlying ambivalence as well as a grand pursuit of the country's national interests (British Officials 2; Romanian Official 1).

France's ambivalent behaviour towards EU–NATO cooperation has also been illustrated by its engagement in negotiations over formalising their relations which began in September 2000 between the joint meeting of the NAC and the interim PSC and which were concluded with the signing of the 2002 EU–NATO Declaration on ESDP. Throughout the negotiations, several member states wanted to make changes and modifications, especially to the wording. Among these were notably France alongside Greece and Turkey. France was not very pleased with the wide scope of cooperation that the two organisations agreed upon in the first draft because it feared that NATO would again take the dominant position and thereby restrict the further development of CSDP. The main objective of French policymakers was to 'protect the EU from being eaten by NATO' (NATO Official 2). This shows that despite the rapprochement with NATO, France maintained its original scepticism and caution about strengthening EU–NATO cooperation, which has been indicated throughout the negotiation process. In the wake of the 2003 Berlin Plus arrangements, France further defended its position by disagreeing on wordings of the arrangements and by opposing NATO's predominance in European security. Among the reasons were the disagreements between France and the US over the 2003 intervention in Iraq and the French initiative of establishing autonomous European headquarters as discussed at the so-called Chocolate Summit in Tervuren in the same year (Flockhart 2014; Ratti 2014).

Furthermore, France only wanted to enhance cooperation if it proves to be truly necessary, depending on the international and European security environment. Whereas some member states prefer EU–NATO cooperation and the EU's referral to NATO's military assets as normal practice, it takes a more cautious approach and sees it rather as an exception (French Official 2; NATO Official 2). The agreement on the Berlin Plus arrangements was originally perceived as a downgrade of the capacities and capabilities of CSDP and thus a strengthening primarily of NATO. Yet, it did not veto the arrangements because it understood it as a pragmatic step towards enhancing the EU's role as an international security provider because of the widening of the toolbox for crisis management operations. With these arrangements France also accepted the need for NATO's military assets and capabilities and desired to exert influence from within (Ratti 2014; Rieker 2013).

Despite having fully reintegrated and becoming a more active member in NATO, France continuously demonstrates its desire to develop independent and autonomous European security and defence capacities. This ambition as well as the debate about European strategic autonomy gained more traction when Emmanuel Macron came into office in 2017. While the notion of European strategic autonomy, alternatively called strategic sovereignty, is hotly debated although no common understanding exists by European states, Macron claims that 'Europeans must be able to protect themselves together. They must be able to decide and act on their own when necessary' (Macron 2020). Although his objective is to pursue European strategic autonomy through the EU as its preferred security forum, Macron also made clear in his infamous Sorbonne speech that 'in the area of defence, our aim needs to be ensuring Europe's autonomous operating capabilities, in complement to NATO' (Macron 2017). Macron's persistence on strategic autonomy has, however, also sparked controversies and criticism among European EU and NATO member states. Particularly Central and Eastern European states, who see the US military presence and NATO dominance as crucial elements for their national and European security and defence, voiced their criticism. Both the US and NATO fear that Macron's desire for European strategic autonomy would undermine the Alliance as a whole (Ringsmose and Webber 2020). Pushing further for strategic autonomy and creating new dividing lines among member states in both organisations furthermore demonstrate France's ambiguity towards the EU–NATO relationship.

The enduring problem of the Cyprus–Greece–Turkey triangle

Developments in the EU–NATO relationship have been profoundly hallmarked by the tensions between Cyprus, Greece and Turkey as the so-called Cyprus issue, which has been named as the biggest and most difficult political obstacle for the EU–NATO relationship, especially for institutionalising cooperation and exchanging information (EU Officials 3, 4; NATO Officials 1, 2). Three distinctive implications stem from these tensions for the development of the EU–NATO relationship: (1) the double veto on membership, (2) the impact on security exchanges and (3) Turkey's tensions with the EU and its member states.

Among these three states, only Greece is a multiple member state as it joined NATO in 1952 and the EU in 1981. Turkey joined NATO in the same year and gained official EU candidate status in 2005 but had already been an associate member state of the WEU since 1992. Accession talks with the EU have been partially stalled due to tensions, however. Cyprus joined the EU in 2004 and does not maintain formalised relations with the Alliance. Although both Greece and Turkey cannot be labelled as original members, they are seen as old members which have been involved in the institutional evolutions of these organisations and have therefore been able to exert influence on the early developments of the EU–NATO relationship. With the Cypriote accession to the EU as well as Turkey's quest to become a regional power in the Mediterranean Sea, bilateral relations and policy preferences have changed and tensions increased, which ultimately affected the evolution of EU–NATO cooperation.

Greece and Turkey have both struggled for regional influence due to their conflictual neighbourhood in the Mediterranean and Aegean Sea as well as their proximity to the Middle East, but took different approaches while pursuing parallel objectives[1]. The Turkish invasion of the Cypriot island in 1974 has not only spurred new tensions between the two countries but also affected their behaviour in international organisations and the dynamics in interorganisational interactions (Binder 2012; Larrabee 2012). In the early phases of rapprochement, neither Greece nor Turkey actively opposed the furthering of EU–NATO cooperation. Both valued the importance of their memberships and perceive the EU and NATO as essential international platforms to counterbalance each other (Tsakonas 2008; Tsakonas and Tournikiotis 2003). Especially with the improvement of their bilateral relationship in 1999, which was triggered by the events after the Ocalan affair and the so-called 'earthquake diplomacy' between their governments (Larrabee 2012: 473), Greece lifted its veto on Turkey's bid for accession to the EU and even strongly supported its candidacy. It saw a Europeanised Turkey beneficial for its own security interests and vice versa, and Turkey regarded EU membership as a further step towards acquiring a Western identity (Bilgin 2003; Larrabee 2012; Nestoras 2015; Tsakonas and Tournikiotis 2003). This had a positive effect on the EU–NATO relationship since a crucial hurdle was minimised that allowed to establish interorganisational meetings and exchanges.

Despite the evolving relations between Greece and Turkey, new obstacles had to be overcome. Turkey's exclusion from and Cyprus's inclusion in the enlargement agenda at the 1997 Luxembourg Summit of the European Council reflected Turkey's behaviour vis-à-vis the EU–NATO relationship (Ulusoy 2016). This inclusion–exclusion gap between Cyprus, Greece and Turkey created a double veto. Because Turkey had already applied for membership to the European Economic Community in the late 1980s and had become an associate member of the WEU in 1992, it sought to fully integrate into the EU through membership, but Greece initially obstructed this enterprise. With Cyprus's accession and the ongoing territorial dispute over the Cypriot island with Turkey, an additional veto player emerged to block Turkey's bid for EU membership (Ker-Lindsay 2007; Larrabee 2012; Dursun-Özkanca 2019; Tsakonas 2008). As a consequence, Turkey would veto against Cyprus's bid for NATO accession, including participation in the PfP programme. This does not only affect Cyprus itself but also the provisions of the institutionalisation process and the practical efforts of EU–NATO cooperation (Coskun 2013; Ker-Lindsay 2010; Samokhvalov 2013; Ulusoy 2016). What is more, Turkey's use of veto is also a way of signalling its discontent with its relations with the EU and specifically with the EDA in the sense that it is not allowed to participate in the Agency's activities. This use of its veto power has been labelled as 'strategic non-cooperation' (Dursun-Özkanca 2019: 66), which deliberately blocks further EU–NATO cooperation. Nevertheless, although all conflicting parties continue peace talks and maintain political dialogue, no agreement has been reached and therefore the conflict remains a key impediment for the EU–NATO relationship.

Moreover, this double veto has caused a 'participation problem' (Biermann 2015: 53) for the EU–NATO relationship because of the lack of a formal security or partnership agreement between Cyprus and NATO. As a consequence, Cyprus does not partake in any negotiations that involve sensitive information and operational issues, for example, in operations under the Berlin Plus framework. The country is thus excluded from this essential aspect of EU–NATO cooperation (Cypriot Officials 1 and 2; NATO Official 2). The second element of this participation problem is the intricate relationship between the EU and Turkey. Although Turkey had already been a WEU member state, it was not included in the EU's CSDP and felt discriminated as a non-EU European NATO member state (Dedeoğlu 2017; Hanbay 2011). Non-EU European NATO allies, including Norway and Turkey, have been particularly suspicious about the EU's plan to develop a European security and defene policy and autonomous military capabilities. In the negotiations between the EU and NATO over the Berlin Plus arrangements, Turkey was concerned that the EU would use NATO's military assets and capabilities against a NATO member, that is, against itself, and therefore strongly sought to be involved in EU decision-making on CSDP, which it was denied however (Tofte 2003).

The Cyprus issue also has profound consequences and implications for exchanges, information sharing and formalisation process in the EU–NATO relationship (Dursun-Özkanca 2019). In the negotiations of the Berlin Plus arrangements, Turkey put a lot of emphasis on the wording of the arrangements. Within NATO, Turkey also pushed to clarify the role of non-EU NATO members and therefore promoted the inclusion of NATO's right of first refusal (Acikmese and Triantaphyllou 2012). In fact, the country proved to be a troublemaker and a stumbling block because it once again felt marginalised, and it thus threatened to use its veto power in case it would not receive any reassurances and concessions (German Official 1). When the agreement between the EU and NATO was drafted, Cyprus was in the accession process but had not been a member of the EU. Therefore, in the document of the Berlin Plus arrangements, it says 'as things stand at present', referring to the agreements made between the EU and NATO counting for the state of affairs in 2003, that is, before Cyprus's EU accession (NATO Official 2). With the changed circumstances in 2004, however, the original agreements lost their validity. In this context, Turkey actively tried to 'push Cyprus out of the game and initiated conditions on the NATO side' by using and promoting this particular wording (NATO Official 2). Furthermore, in regard to Cyprus's planned accession to the EU and 'in order to further assuage Turkish security concerns, the country would not take part in EU-led military operations using NATO assets once it had become a member of the EU' (Reichard 2006: 287). This would reassure Turkey and give it the opportunity to participate and contribute, although it in fact demanded to have decision-making power concerning EU-led operations under Berlin Plus.

The negotiations on the Interim Security Arrangements and the subsequent Security of Information Agreement between the EU and NATO proceeded in a similar way. Several member states, especially Turkey and the US, were cautious about setting up arrangements for the exchange of classified information and intelligence. The EU did not possess any internal regulations concerning the management and exchange of information prior to the development of its CSDP, whereas NATO retains a long tradition of maintaining a security of its information and intelligence (Reichard 2006). In addition, Turkey sought to limit the access to classified information and intelligence to some states. Consequently, in the Security of Information Agreement, it states that

> classified information (…) may be disclosed or released to states which are members of NATO, and to other States which are members of the EU and have subscribed to the "Partnership for Peace" framework document and, in that context, have a valid security agreement with NATO.
>
> (EU 2003: Art. 5)

This was specifically targeted at Cyprus in the context of the country's accession to the EU (NATO Officials 2, 4).

The relationship between the EU and Turkey as well as Turkey's unilateral foreign policy actions within NATO have also experienced a number of ruptures, especially under the Turkish government led by Recep Tayyip

Erdoğan as Prime Minister (2003–2014) and as President (since 2014), which have led to a gridlock of the accession process (Dedeoğlu 2017; Dursun-Özkanca 2019). Differences over human rights, the rule of law and democratic institutions as well as the diverging foreign and security policy orientations of both sides have furthermore shaped their bilateral relations but also Turkey's attitude towards the EU–NATO relationship. The decreasing ability to shape the EU's decisions on foreign, security and defence matters, and particularly the dwindling possibility to become a full member, triggered a disconnect between Turkey and its Western partners, which has also been perceived as obstructive for the EU–NATO relationship among member states (NATO Officials 4).

Turkey's membership in the EU would bring about a number of benefits and challenges for CSDP: (1) it has well-trained armed forces and possesses the second largest military capabilities in NATO, (2) it is a long-standing ally in NATO which would further contribute to interoperability, improved coordination and closer cooperation between the two organisations and (3) its geostrategic location between Europe and Central Asia, the Middle East, the Caucasus and the Black Sea as well its relations with neighbouring states (Bilgin 2003; Müftüler-Baç 2003; Tangör 2012). With Turkey's accession, however, new tensions and sensitive issues would also be added to the EU's agenda. Especially the country's proximity to conflictual regions, its poor record of democracy and human rights and the ongoing territorial dispute with Cyprus constitute the main problems and challenges (Müftüler-Baç 2000). Hence, the EU set conditions which, in case of fulfilment, would allow to open new chapters in the accession process and would allow Turkey to eventually join the Union and become integrated into its security and defence dimension. These conditions include the establishment of amicable relations with both Cyprus and Greece and other EU member states including Austria and Germany, as well as solving ongoing territorial disputes. Although Turkey received candidate status in 2005 and signed the FPA in 2006 allowing it to participate in EU-led crisis management operations without any decision-making powers (Müftüler-Baç 2003; Tsakonas 2008), the lack of agreements with Cyprus do not allow EU–NATO cooperation to progress further.

In recent years, Turkey's ambition of becoming a regional power in the Mediterranean and Middle East, its unilateral foreign policy actions, for example, in Syria and Nagorno-Karabakh both in 2019 and 2020 and the naval confrontations in the Mediterranean Sea with Greece and France in 2020 triggered tensions within NATO that cause additional challenges for EU–NATO cooperation. NATO members found it increasingly difficult to collaborate with Turkey and to find a common strategy to dealing with shared threats in the region. Turkey's autonomous approach and unilateral actions therefore risk greater friction within NATO that influence the Alliance's ability to cooperate and coordinate efforts with the EU (Got 2020). New incentives and initiatives will thus need to be found for all sides, the EU, NATO and Turkey, in order to reinstall trust, shared awareness and common ground.

Ireland's neutrality as obstruction

Ireland's obstructive behaviour is set in contrast to both France and the Cyprus–Greece–Turkey triad. As a militarily neutral country, it has a strong preference for the peaceful settlement of international tensions and disputes, and therefore puts greater emphasis on a non-military approach to crisis management. Despite its membership in the EU, it is outspokenly in favour of international peacekeeping by the UN and would only participate in EU-led actions if a UN option is not available (Keohane 2013). Ireland shows characteristics of a blocker due to its own exceptionalism, which has occasionally put strains on advancing EU–NATO cooperation. While it is not against EU–NATO cooperation *per se*, it is generally sceptical towards closer defence cooperation in general. The 'Irish exceptionalism' is constituted of its geostrategic location in the EU's periphery, the absence of a clear external security and defence strategy as well as the marginal level of defence expenditure in addition to the constitutional constraints on international military engagements and the strong adherence to international law (Keohane 2013; Tonra 2012). Because the EU needs to take into consideration all of its member states' preferences and interests when negotiating with the Alliance, Irish's constraints add to the slow progress of cooperation efforts. For example, one representative noticed that 'Ireland is also generally sceptical about EU–NATO cooperation' (Estonian Official 1), which has been perceived as hampering by other member states. Moreover, although Ireland is declared to be militarily neutral, it cannot be said to be completely neutral towards the EU–NATO relationship. Ireland's scepticism has been understood as 'a move towards Cyprus and Turkey', meaning it took over a hesitant and less supportive position (Slovak Official 1).

In addition, Ireland's relations with NATO need to be understood in terms of its own independence from the UK and its disassociation with great powers. After the Second World War, Ireland was inclined to join NATO and in fact, it hoped that the Alliance would get involved in solving the Northern Ireland conflict to end of partition so that it would be able become a member state. Because this did not occur and Ireland was not able to join due to partition, any initiatives proposed by the UK in regard to NATO and the EU–NATO relationship are consequentially perceived with caution (Cottey 2018). This shows that its feelings of scepticism and restraint can also lead to obstructive behaviour for enhancing cooperative efforts. In contrast to France and the Cyprus–Greece–Turkey triad, however, Ireland presents an exceptional case because its reserved attitude towards defence cooperation and military operations only makes a minor contribution to decelerating closer EU–NATO cooperation.

Contributions to military capabilities, interoperability and division of labour

Military capabilities and resources are vital for blockers' bargaining activities and resemble their leverage towards other member states. Some of the blockers possess significant capabilities and resources which are relevant for the EU–NATO relationship. While they acknowledge the existing capabilities gap, blockers also play an important part in contributing to these gaps due the selective use of their national assets and capabilities as well as their contributions to EU and NATO operations (Sperling 2004). This relates to the perception of their membership in the respective organisations in addition to their national interests and preferred forum to respond to international crises. Blockers vary in regard to their capabilities, participation and view on division of labour between the EU and NATO. France takes a staunch position on preserving military independence and autonomy over its nuclear weapons, Greece prefers to contribute its capabilities to the EU in order to exert influence vis-à-vis Turkey and Turkey itself is among NATO's biggest military powers with regional power ambitions (Bilgin 2003; Bozo 2016; Dobrescu et al. 2017; Nestoras 2015). Cyprus's historical link to the Non-Alignment Movement still shapes its approach to operational engagement and capability development (Samokhvalov 2013). Ireland, in contrast, demands UN authorisation for military operations conducted by the EU and NATO and its military neutrality disallows the country from participation in territorial defence engagement, which is among NATO's core tasks (Cottey 2018; Keohane 2013).

France, Greece and Turkey are among those states which possess well-trained armed forces, a high degree of advanced and sophisticated military capabilities and a long record of operational experience. Among the blockers (see Figure 4.1), France, Greece and Turkey nevertheless belong to those countries within NATO which meet, or are close to reaching, the 2% defence pledge. Cyprus and Ireland, in contrast, maintain low levels of defence expenditures with 1.4% and 0.3% of GDP, respectively (NATO 2020; SIPRI 2020). One of the main drivers for maintaining high levels of military expenditure for Greece and Turkey, and partially Cyprus, relates to the Cyprus issue and the still existing threat perception of each another. Notably, Greece preserves a high level of defence spending in comparison to other

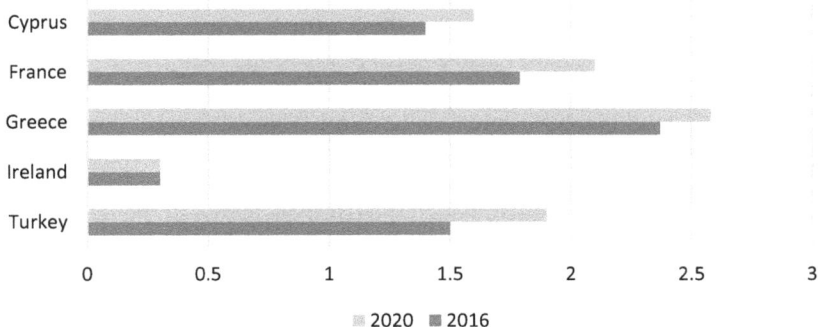

Figure 4.1 Defence expenditure as a share of GDP, 2016 and 2020.

European states despite the severe impact of the 2008 economic and financial crisis on its economy and despite its limited record of contributions to EU and NATO operations. Although perceived threats from Turkey can no longer be counted as a justification, both its participation and contributions in multilateral crisis management operations and frameworks are only marginal (Dempsey 2012; Eilstrup-Sangiovanni 2014). In contrast, Ireland's low level of military expenditure reflects its overall positioning on security and defence issues, its military neutrality and the emphasis on the peaceful (non-military) settlement of conflicts (Keohane 2013; Sweeney 2016), which has been perceived as an additional hindrance to EU–NATO cooperation (NATO Official 5).

France is considered to be one of the main leaders in Europe, alongside Germany and the UK, in terms of developing and contributing to European security and defence capabilities and particularly to CSDP. Due to its exclusion from NATO's integrated military structures until 2009 and its preference for European strategic autonomy, it has continuously promoted the importance of backing up CSDP with sufficient and adequate military assets and capabilities. Since de Gaulle's presidency, France has been an advocate of *Europe de la défense* encompassing European autonomous decision-making over security and defence matters and the acquisition of military capabilities by EU member states (Andréani 2002; French Officials 1, 2). This created a constant struggle with its fellow EU member states over acquiring and developing more advanced and sophisticated capabilities. Its ambition of European autonomous capabilities and the further enhancement of CSDP has not always been well perceived within the EU. As a consequence, France has become increasingly frustrated with its European partners, particularly with those states that actually possess the financial resources to procure more capabilities and make greater contributions to EU security and defence, most notably Germany (Cizel and von Hlatky 2014; Irondelle and Mérand 2010; Muniz 2013).

To overcome the lacking capabilities, France has been involved in a number of bilateral and multilateral initiatives to advance and develop joint capabilities. With its prime cooperation partners, it is involved in defence cooperation with the UK based on the 1998 Saint-Malo Declaration and the 2010 Lancaster House Treaties as well as with Germany and Poland in the so-called Weimar Triangle (France 2012; Pannier and Schmitt 2014; von Voss, Major and Mölling 2013; UK 2010). In the EU context, France has taken the lead in the capability development debate and 'bears by far the heaviest CSDP-specific defence burden relative to "average benefits received", whereas the remaining large countries all contribute less than their "fair" share of troops given the average benefits received' (Eilstrup-Sangiovanni 2014: 96). As the driver of military capabilities as well as operational engagements in the EU framework, France has been at the forefront of promoting and developing PESCO as well as other initiatives, such as the EDF and CARD, which all seek to contribute to strengthening the EU's security and defence capabilities and capacities (Biscop 2017). Moreover, France launched the European Intervention Initiative (EI2) following Macron's infamous Sorbonne speech in 2017. Although its concrete outlook is still unclear, the EI2 comprises a selected group of states and is aimed at bolstering European defence and security through a voluntary and collaborative framework outside the EU. It strives to strengthen the EU's role as a security and defence actor while also contributing to NATO (Sweeney and Winn 2020). Interestingly, although France has always pushed for an increase of contributions to the CSDP among its allies and partners, its own contributions of military force to NATO surmount the ones to EU-led operations. This raises questions about France's actual preferences and intentions behind its own participation and contributions as well as about its pragmatic approach to both security and crisis management (Eilstrup-Sangiovanni 2014; Irondelle and Mérand 2010). What is more, due to the persistence on European autonomy and the independence of its *force de frappe*, France has also posed an obstacle especially in terms of cooperation with other European partners as well as within the EU and NATO, which ultimately affect their cooperation. By advancing the idea of autonomous European defence capabilities, it neglects the interests and objectives of other member states and also of the two organisations themselves. This has led to tensions among states with consequences on the interorganisational level. Nevertheless, closer EU–NATO cooperation and moving towards an equal partnership would not be possible without France and its military capabilities and resources (German Officials 2; Romanian Official 1).

Military capabilities and assets allow member states to shape strategic decisions. Turkey makes use of its capabilities as a leverage for its political interests since its geostrategic location and bilateral relations are of significance for both the EU and NATO. For example, it 'serves as a buffer between Europe, the West and the Middle East' (NATO Officials 4), which is especially crucial for the conduct of military and civilian operations and the establishment of bases for operational activities in the proximity of conflictual areas. Because of the transformation of its armed forces, it has not only become one of the most powerful allies in the region but also one that seeks a comprehensive approach to crisis management by combining civilian and military components (Turkey 2011b). Turkey seeks to play an increasingly influential role in the Mediterranean Sea, Black Sea region and the Middle East, which are areas of NATO's strategic interest. Therefore, it utilises its capabilities and resources to receive more power by influencing the Alliance's decisions (Oğuzlu 2013). As observed in the case of Cyprus bid for participating in NATO's PfP programme, the country successfully mobilised its capabilities and resources to express its concerns and opposing views, which was translated into a veto. Yet, the military coup in July 2016 had negative impacts on the structure and composition of Turkey's military and armed forces because of the detainment of over 80,000 state employees and the reduction of serving officers by 10% (NATO Officials 4; The Military Balance 2017).

Interoperability, division of labour and member states' contributions to operations are closely linked to the debates on military expenditures and capabilities and present key areas in which blockers' preferences become visible concerning practical EU–NATO cooperation in operations. Although blockers seek to make their armed forces and military capabilities more efficient and sustainable, their contributions to improving interoperability and their attitude towards division of labour represent additional obstacles. A higher degree of participation and contributions to operations allows member states to have greater influence on and involvement in the planning process of operations. Contributions to interoperability also shape their view on the preferred division of labour and the allocation of responsibilities.

Generally, blockers agree on the necessity of interoperability for effective operational cooperation and therefore seek to increase the effectiveness and performance of their own armed forces through possibilities of collaboration, cooperation and coordination. National interests still prevail and internal obstacles have also proven to be challenging for achieving higher levels of interoperability. Among blockers there is a divergence between single and multiple member states concerning their attitude to division of labour and complementarity. While single members evidently favour the organisation in which they have membership, multiple members apply forum-shopping as they prefer one over the other organisation by providing more support and resources to the institutional and capability developments of their preferred organisation.

Under the presidency of Nicolas Sarkozy, interoperability was one of the main drivers for re-joining NATO's integrated military command structures (Irondelle and Mérand 2010). Despite its exclusion, France participated in the NATO's military operations, for instance in resolving the conflicts in the Balkans such as in Bosnia and Herzegovina, Kosovo and North Macedonia. However, the French government and armed forces were increasingly confronted with the lack of coordination and cooperation capacities with their NATO allies, which hampered their diplomatic effectiveness and military capabilities. It also had to acknowledge the incapability of the EU and its newly created security and defence policies. Despite the drive for European defence autonomy, France therefore acknowledged the significance of NATO and the importance of collaboration and interoperability. These problems had not been solved in such a short period of time and therefore re-occurred during the NATO-led ISAF operation in Afghanistan in the early 2000s (EU Official 1).

Problems have been recorded within and between NATO and the EU when both organisations conducted military operations in the same theatre (Bialos 2005; Sperling 2004). While France seeks to increase interoperability through the joint procurement of defence capabilities on the European level, it promoted parallel and coordinated trainings and military exercises between the EU and NATO on the interorganisational level (French Official 2). Simultaneously, however, it tried to maintain and even improve its own military and political ranks in both organisations as well as globally. In this respect, interoperability is seen as an objective as long as it serves France greater influence and a stronger position (Irondelle and Schmitt 2013; Simón 2017). Moreover, in the context of interoperability, the 2013 French White Paper on Security and Defence nevertheless emphasises the preservation of sovereignty as well as the ability to act independently and in any desired framework (France 2013). This clearly shows that France pursues two parallel objectives. On the one hand, it desires more efficient coordination and practices of interoperability and on the other hand, it favours strong European defence capacities in which it plays the dominant role.

Participation and contributions to military operations, exercises and trainings are ways of influencing the degree of interoperability between the EU and NATO. States' contributions to EU-led missions and operations are generally marginal compared to those of NATO operations and even UN missions. Some states are nevertheless eager to make the highest contributions to CSDP operations to pursue certain objectives and strategic goals. The level of participation and contributions varies among blockers and range from maximum engagement and even being at the forefront of launching new operations (France) to minimal involvement (Ireland, Cyprus) (see Appendix C). France has been the initiator of the majority of CSDP military operations, especially of those conducted on the African continent such as Operation Artemis in the Democratic Republic of Congo, EUFOR DR Congo, EUFOR Chad/CAR in Chad and the Central African Republic, EUTM Somalia and EUTM Mali. It has furthermore acted as a framework nation and provided the operational headquarters, for example, in EUFOR Operation Artemis and EUFOR Chad/CAR (Grevi, Helly and Keohane 2009). Despite its withdrawal from the Alliance's integrated military command structures, it participated in NATO-led operations during the 1990s and early 2000s, for example, in SFOR in Bosnia and Herzegovina, KFOR in Kosovo, Operation Essential Harvest as well as subsequent military operations in North Macedonia, ISAF in Afghanistan, Operation Unified Protector in Libya and Operation Sea Guardian in the Mediterranean Sea. In the case of initiating the no-fly zone in Libya, France was even one of the lead nations alongside the UK (Eilstrup-Sangiovanni 2014). France's eagerness to launch and conduct EU operations highlights its preference for EU over NATO as it seeks to increase the EU's role as an international security actor and because it finds the EU's toolbox and comprehensive approach more suitable for serving its national interests, for example, in the Sahel and Sub-Saharan Africa (Gegout 2009). According to a French official, the EU is 'more capable and suitable due to its existing policies and funds' (French Official 2). Additionally, it does not want NATO to get involved in areas such as capability and capacity building because it finds that this is part of the EU's territory and only wants the two to cooperate in those areas where it is regarded to be fruitful and necessary because of lacking capabilities on the EU's side (French Officials 1, 2).

For Greece, participating in CSDP and NATO operations serves a specific national objective. Although Greece has so far been engaged in every EU and NATO operation and despite being among those states with the highest military expenditure, 'its participation has been negligible' and therefore, 'it is not using its soldiers to boost either EU or NATO operations', nor does it enhance EU–NATO cooperation (Dempsey 2012). From the beginning, it has contributed to NATO operations, such as KFOR, ISAF and Operation Ocean Shield as well as in EU-led operations in the Western Balkans (Concordia, Althea) and in Africa (Artemis, DR Congo, Chad/CAR, Atalanta and Mali). Yet, Greece has neither taken over as framework nor as lead nation, and instead, it has deployed only marginal numbers of troops, assets and capabilities (Eilstrup-Sangiovanni 2014; Grevi, Helly and Keohane 2009). As a consequence, Greece's rationale behind participating in EU-led operations is to secure its own position in the EU vis-à-vis Turkey. It favours the EU for its national security interests because supporting the EU's security role helps to realise its national interests especially in the Mediterranean Sea and to restrict Turkey's regional power ambitions. Within NATO its participation therefore needs to be understood in parallel to Turkey's participation and contributions (Tsakonas and Tournikiotis 2003).

Turkey thus shares some of Greece's views on interoperability and contributing to EU and NATO operations. In the early stages of CSDP and in the beginning of EU–NATO relations, cooperation was seen as part of Turkey's strategy to join the EU (NATO Officials 4) and interoperability was perceived as a necessity for functional cooperation in military operations in cases of operational and geographical overlaps. While it sought to fully join and integrate into the EU, participating in CSDP operations seemed an effective way to facilitate the path to accession (Bilgin 2003). However, the pursuit of its national interests and regional power ambitions have also triggered divergences in NATO and with the EU. These translated into problems in EU–NATO cooperation, particularly in operations, making both interoperability and division of labour more difficult. Moreover, the triangular conflict between Cyprus, Greece and Turkey poses an additional obstacle to achieving interoperability and compatibility between the EU and NATO. Added barriers and challenges include the communication problem, the search for circumventing the disclosure of information problem and the particularities of cooperation inside and outside the Berlin Plus framework (Acikmese and Triantaphyllou 2012; Çağlar and Akdemir 2017).

In contrast to France, Greece and Turkey, both Cyprus and Ireland have made marginal contributions to EU and NATO operations. Because of the double veto and the intricate situation with Turkey, Cyprus is the only state among blockers that has only participated in EU-led operations. Its general foreign and security policy orientation is also reflected in its operational engagement, that is, Cyprus only participates in UN-mandated peacekeeping operations under the EU framework. In addition, it is interested in the security of its national borders by contributing to the EU's maritime security operations in the Mediterranean Sea (Samokhvalov 2013). Interestingly, Ireland has participated in a number of NATO operations, such as in the

Western Balkans (SFOR, KFOR) and Afghanistan (ISAF) despite its stated military neutrality. Nevertheless, its strong focus on non-military crisis resolution as well as its general scepticism towards military alliances and the EU–NATO relationship have been perceived as hampering for practical cooperation in crisis management operations (Estonian Official 1; Slovak Official 1).

Conclusions

Blockers play a particular part in the EU–NATO relationship because they frequently pose new obstacles and challenges to improving and enhancing cooperation. While blockers are not labelled as those who completely obstruct or oppose this interorganisational cooperation, these states interrupt its enhancement intentionally as well as unintentionally through their rhetorics and behaviour. States in this group are regularly named as the 'troublemakers' within the EU, NATO and their relationship. Although they do not always act homogeneously, their input and contributions as well as their approach to formalising the relations are the result of a series of compromises, concessions and bargaining outcomes. Some achievements of the EU–NATO relationship can be considered as the lowest common denominator based on the demands, expectations and policies of individual member states, especially of blockers. They have overall made use of political strategies, especially of hostage-taking and turf battles, that is, in terms of blocking each other's accession in the case of Cyprus and Turkey or when negotiating over the deployment of troops and the distribution of military capabilities for crisis management operations.

The Cyprus issue still illustrates a critical juncture that has had severe implications for the current state of the EU–NATO relationship, but it cannot be counted as the only obstacle to enhancing cooperation. In fact, the triad of Cyprus, Greece and Turkey remains a hurdle and only a solution of this conflict can bring positive implications for EU–NATO cooperation. Nevertheless, this has been used as an alibi or shield for many other member states when seeking to slow down cooperative efforts. The individual behaviour of specific states, particularly France and Turkey as well as the attitudes by Cyprus and Ireland have served as additional obstructing factors. France's behaviour is most prominent among the blockers. It has shifted its positions over time from a strong stance on European autonomous defence capacity and capabilities to a rapprochement with NATO leading to its reintegration, and from constituting to a major challenge for EU–NATO cooperation to a facilitator albeit with reservations. The renewed emphasis on European strategic autonomy and its complex bilateral relationship with the US in the European security context remain an obstacle. Similarly, Turkey's regional power ambitions, tensions with EU and NATO allies including Germany, France and Greece and outreach to states that have been classically labelled as NATO's adversaries, especially Russia and Iran, contribute to the lack of coherence and cooperation among member states and both organisations.

Overall, these states have impeded efforts to enhancing interorganisational cooperation while not fully opposing the EU–NATO relationship.

Note

1 For a detailed description and overview of the Greek–Turkish conflict, see, for example, Cemp 1980.

References

Abbott, Kenneth W. and Duncan Snidal (1998) 'Why states act through formal international organisations', *The Journal of Conflict Resolution*, 42(1): 3–32.

Acikmese, Sinem Akgul and Dimitrios Triantaphyllou (2012) 'The NATO-EU-Turkey trilogy: The impact of the Cyprus conundrum', *Southeast European and Black Sea Studies*, 12(4): 555–573.

Andréani, Gilles (2002): 'Europe de la Défense: y a-t-il encore une ambition française?' *Politique étrangère*, 4(67): 983–1000.

Bialos, Jeffrey P. (2005) 'The United States, Europe and the interoperability gap', *The International Spectator*, 40(2): 53–62.

Biermann, Rafael (2015) 'Designing cooperation among international organisations: The quest for autonomy, the dual-consensus rule, and cooperation failure', *Journal of International Organisation Studies*, 6(2): 45–66.

Bilgin, Pinar (2003) 'The "peculiarity" of Turkey's position on EU-NATO military/security cooperation: A rejoinder to Missiroli', *Security Dialogue*, 34(4): 345–349.

Binder, David (2012) 'Greece, Turkey, and NATO', *Mediterranean Quarterly*, 23(2): 95–106.

Biscop, Sven (2017) 'European defence: What's in the CARDs for PESCO?' *Egmont Security Policy Brief*, 91: 1–6.

Boyer, Yves (1993) 'France's new choices in security policy', *SAIS Review*, 13: 89–102.

Bozo, Frédéric (2014): 'Explaining France's NATO "normalisation" under Nicolas Sarkozy (2007–2012)', *Journal of Transatlantic Studies*, 12(4): 379–391.

Bozo, Frédéric (2016) *French Foreign Policy Since 1945: An Introduction*, New York: Bergham Books.

Çağlar, İsmail and Kevser Hülya Akdemir (2017) 'Turkey and the North Atlantic Treaty Organisation'. *In*: Toperich, Sasha and Aylin Ünver Noi (eds) *Turkey and Transatlantic Relations*, Washington DC: Centre for Transatlantic Relations, 35–48.

Cemp, Glend D. (1980) Greek-Turkish Conflict over Cyprus, Political Science Quarterly, 95(1): 43–70.

Charbonneau, Bruno (2008) 'Dreams of empire: France, Europe, and the new interventionism in Africa', *Modern & Contemporary France*, 16(3): 279–295.

Cizel, Annick and Stéfanie von Hlatky (2014) 'From exceptional to special? A reassessment of France-NATO relations since reintegration', *Journal of Transatlantic Studies*, 12(4): 353–366.

Coskun, Bezen Balamir (2013) 'Turkey'. *In*: Biehl, Heiko et al. (eds) *Strategic Cultures in Europe: Security and Defence Policies Across the Continent*, Wiesbaden: Springer VS, 359–370.

Cottey, Andrew (2018) 'Ireland and NATO: A distinctively low-profile partnership'. *In*: Cottey, Andrew (ed.) *The European Neutrals and NATO: Non-alignment, Partnership, Membership?* London: Palgrave Macmillan, 151–179.

Dedeoğlu, Beril (2017) 'Turkey and the European Union: Neither a marriage nor a separation on the horizon'. *In*: Toperich, Sasha and Aylin Ünver Noi (ed.) *Turkey and Transatlantic Relations*, Washington DC: Centre for Transatlantic Relations, 103–116.

Dempsey, Judy (2012) EU and NATO Look on at Greece's Pampered Armed Forces, *Carnegie Europe*, published on 27 August 2012, http://carnegieeurope.eu/strategiceurope/?fa=49185 (accessed on 29/03/2018).

Dobrescu, Madalina et al. (2017) 'Southern Europe: Portugal, Spain, Italy, Malta, Greece, Cyprus'. *In*: Hadfield, Amelia et al. (eds) *Foreign Policies of EU Member States: Continuity and Europeanisation*, Abingdon: Routledge, 83–98.

Dursun-Özkanca, Oya (2019) *Turkey-West Relations: The Politics of Intra-Alliance Opposition*, Cambridge: Cambridge University Press.

Economides, Spyros (2013) 'Greece'. *In*: Biehl, Heiko et al. (eds) *Strategic Cultures in Europe: Security and Defence Policies Across the Continent*, Wiesbaden: Springer VS, 153–164.

Eilstrup-Sangiovanni, Mette (2014) 'Europe's defence dilemma', *The International Spectator*, 49(2): 83–116.

European Union (2003) 'Agreement between the European Union and the North Atlantic Treaty Organisation on the Security of Information', *Official Journal of the EU*, L80/36.

Flockhart, Trine (2014) 'NATO and EU: A "strategic partnership" or a practice of "muddling through"?' *In*: Odgaard, Liselotte (ed.) *Strategy in NATO: Preparing for an Imperfect World*, Basingstoke, New York: Palgrave Macmillan, 75–89.

Fortmann, Michel, David Haglund and Stéfanie von Hlatky (2010) 'Introduction: France's 'return' to NATO: Implications for transatlantic relations', *European Security*, 19(1): 1–10.

Gegout, Catherine (2009) 'EU conflict management in Africa: The limits of an international actor', *Ethnopolitics*, 8(3–4): 403–415.

Gehring, Thomas and Sebastian Oberthür (2009) 'The causal mechanisms of interaction between international institutions', *European Journal of International Relations*, 15(1): 125–156.

Got, Antoine (2020) 'Turkey's crisis with the West: How a new low in relations risks paralysing NATO', *War on the Rocks*, published on 19 November 2020, https://warontherocks.com/2020/11/turkeys-crisis-with-the-west-how-a-new-low-in-relations-risks-paralyzing-nato/ (accessed on 23/02/2021).

Grevi, Giovanni, Damien Helly and Daniel Keohane (2009) *European Security and Defence Policy: The First Ten Years (1999–2009)*, Paris: European Union Institute for Security Studies (EUISS).

Hanbay, Seyda (2011) 'Involvement of non-EU European NATO members in CSDP: The Turkish case', *Baltic Journal of Law & Politics*, 4(1): 1–26.

Hofmann, Stephanie C. (2009) 'Overlapping institutions in the realm of international security: The case of NATO and ESDP', *Perspectives on Politics*, 7(1): 45–51.

Hofmann, Stephanie C. (2017) 'Party preferences and institutional transformation: Revisiting France's relationship with NATO (and the common wisdom on Gaullism)', *Journal of Strategic Studies*, 40(4): 505–531.

Hofmann, Stephanie C. (2019) 'The politics of overlapping organisations: Hostage-taking, forum-shopping and brokering', *Journal of European Public Policy*, 26(6): 883–905.

Hofmann, Stephanie C. and Ronja Kempin (2007) 'France and the transatlantic relationship: Love me, love me not', *SWP Working Paper*, 2: 1–7.

Irondelle, Bastien and Frédéric Mérand (2010) 'France's return to NATO: The death knell for ESDP?' *European Security*, 19(1): 29–43.

Irondelle, Bastien and Olivier Schmitt (2013) 'France'. *In*: Biehl, Heiko et al. (eds) *Strategic Cultures in Europe: Security and Defence Policies Across the Continent*, Wiesbaden: Springer VS, 125–138.

Keohane, Daniel (2013) 'Ireland'. *In*: Biehl, Heiko et al. (eds) *Strategic Cultures in Europe: Security and Defence Policies Across the Continent*, Wiesbaden: Springer VS, 181–192.

Keohane, Robert O. and Lisa M. Martin (1995): 'The promise of institutionalist theory', *International Security*, 20(1): 39–51.

Ker-Lindsay, James (2007) 'The politics of Greece and Cyprus towards Turkey's EU accession', *Turkish Studies*, 8(1): 71–83.

Ker-Lindsay, James (2010) 'Shifting alignments: The external orientation of Cyprus since independence', *The Cyprus Review*, 22(2): 67–74.

Larrabee, F. Stephen (2012) 'Greek-Turkish relations in an era of regional and global change', *Southeast European and Black Sea Studies*, 12(4): 471–479.

Macron, Emmanuel (2017) *Speech on New Initiative for Europe*. Speech Held on 26 September 2017 at Sorbonne University, www.elysee.fr/emmanuel-macron/2017/09/26/president-macron-gives-speech-on-new-initiative-for-europe.en (accessed on 22/02/2021).

Macron, Emmanuel (2020) *Speech on the Defence and Deterrence Strategy*. Speech Held on 7 February 2020 at the Military College, www.elysee.fr/en/emmanuel-macron/2020/02/07/speech-of-the-president-of-the-republic-on-the-defense-and-deterrence-strategy (accessed on 22/02/2021).

Magliveras, Konstantinos D. (2011) 'Membership in international organisations'. *In*: Klabbers, Jan and Asa Wallendahl (eds) *Research Handbook on the Law of International Organisations*, Cheltenham and Northampton: Edward Elgar Publishing, 84–107.

Müftüler-Baç, Meltem (2000) 'Turkey's role in the EU's security and foreign policies', *Security Dialogue*, 31(4): 489–502.

Müftüler-Baç, Meltem (2003) 'Turkey's accession to the European Union: Institutional and security challenges', *Perspectives*, Autumn issue: 29–43.

Muniz, Manuel (2013) 'France: The frustrated leader'. *In*: Santopinto, Federico and Megan Price (eds) *National Visions of EU Defence Policy: Common Denominators and Misunderstandings*. Brussels: CEPS/GRIP/COST, 6–26.

NATO (2017) *Defence Expenditure of NATO Countries (2009–2016)*, NATO Press Release, Communiqué No. PR/CP(2017)045 (March 2017).

NATO (2020) *Defence Expenditure of NATO Countries (2013–2020)*, www.nato.int/cps/en/natohq/news_178975.htm (accessed on 15/02/2021).

Nestoras, Antonios (2015): 'The view from Europe's borders: Greece and the CSDP as a security provider'. *In*: Fiott, Daniel (ed) *The Common Security and Defence Policy: National Perspectives*, Brussels: Egmont – Royal Institute for International Relations, 61–64.

Oğuzlu, Tarik (2013) 'Making sense of Turkey's rising power status: What does Turkey's approach within NATO tell us?' *Turkish Studies*, 14(4): 774–796.

Pannier, Alice (2017) 'From one exceptionalism to another: France's strategic relations with the United States and the United Kingdom in the post-Cold War era', *Journal of Strategic Studies*, 40(4): 475–504.

Pannier, Alice and Olivier Schmitt (2014) 'Institutionalised cooperation and policy convergence in European defence: lessons from the relations between France, Germany and the UK', *European Security*, 23(3): 270–289.

Perruche, Jean-Paul (2014) 'From exception to facilitator: What place for France in the EU/NATO partnership in the post-Cold War global world?' *Journal of Transatlantic Studies*, 12(4): 432–442.

Pesme, Frédéric (2010) 'France's "return" to NATO: Implications for its defence policy', *European Security*, 19(1): 45–60.

Ratti, Luca (2014) 'Stepping up to reintegration: French security policy between transatlantic and European defence during and after the Cold War', *Journal of Transatlantic Studies*, 12(4): 367–378.

Reichard, Martin (2006) *The EU-NATO Relationship: A Legal and Political Perspective,* Abingdon: Routledge.

Rieker, Pernille (2013) 'The French return to NATO: Reintegration in practice, not in principle', *European Security*, 22(3): 376–394.

Ringsmose, Jens and Mark Webber (2020) Hedging their bets? The case for a European pillar in NATO, *Defence Studies*, 20(4): 295–317.

Samokhvalov, Vsevolod (2013) 'Cyprus'. *In*: Biehl, Heiko et al. (eds) *Strategic Cultures in Europe: Security and Defence Policies Across the Continent*, Wiesbaden: Springer VS, 55–68.

Simón, Luis (2017) 'France and Germany: The European Union's "central" Member States'. In: Amelia Hadfield et al. (eds) *Foreign Policies of EU Member States: Continuity and Europeanisation*, Abingdon: Routledge, 66–82.

SIPRI (2020) *SIPRI Military Expenditure Data Base 1949–2019*. Stockholm: SIPRI.

Sperling, James (2004) 'Capabilities traps and gaps: Symptom or cause of a troubled transatlantic relationship', *Contemporary Security Policy*, 25(3): 452–478.

Sweeney, Daniel (2016) 'Ireland, the Lisbon Referendums, and the ongoing debate on European security', *The Global Studies Journal*, 9(1): 43–54.

Sweeney, Simon and Neil Winn (2020) 'EU security and defence cooperation in times of dissent: Analysing PESCO, the European Defence Fund and the European Intervention Initiative (EI2) in the shadow of Brexit', *Defence Studies*, 20(3): 224–249.

Tangör, Burak (2012) 'Turkey's role in European security governance', *Central European Journal of International and Security Studies*, 6(3–4): 219–243.

The Military Balance (2017) *The Military Balance Volume 117*, London: International Institute for Strategic Studies (IISS).

Tofte, Sunniva (2003) 'Non-EU NATO members and the issue of discrimination'. *In*: Howorth, Jolyon and John T.S. Keeler (eds) *Defending Europe: The EU, NATO and the Quest for European Autonomy*, Basingstoke: Palgrave Macmillan, 135–156.

Tonra, Ben (2012) *Global Citizen and European Republic: Irish Foreign Policy in Transition*, Manchester: Manchester University Press.

Treacher, Adrian (2011) 'France and transatlantic relations'. *In*: Dorman, Andrew M. and Joyce P. Kaufman (eds) *The Future of Transatlantic Relations: Perceptions, Policy and Practice*, Stanford: Stanford University Press, 95–112.

Tsakonas, Panayotis (2008) 'From "perverse" to "promising" institutionalism? NATO, EU and the Greek-Turkish conflict'. *In*: Bourantonis, Dimitris et al. (eds) *Multilateralism and Security Institutions in an Era of Globalisation*, Abingdon: Routledge, 223–251.

Tsakonas, Panayotis and Antonis Tournikiotis (2003) 'Greece's elusive quest for security providers: The "expectations-reality gap"', *Security Dialogue*, 34(3): 301–314.

Ulusoy, Kivanç (2016) 'The Cyprus conflict: Turkey's strategic dilemma', *Journal of Balkan and Near Eastern Studies*, 18(4): 393–406.

von Voss, Alicia, Claudia Major and Christian Mölling (2013) 'The State of Defence Cooperation in Europe', *SWP Working Paper*, 3: 1–14.

5 Balancers

Germany, Italy, Portugal and Spain

The primary objective of member states in the group of balancers is to strike the balance between the EU and NATO in their own foreign and security policy and between the other member states. Balancers bring forward a broad set of skills and tools, which they apply to mediate between the different positions within the EU–NATO relationship. Since some of these states are said to have no concrete strategy in their foreign, security and defence policy, they float with the current and act responsively instead of proactively (Dyson 2014; Muniz 2013). Their strategy is precisely to serve as a balancing act between the Europeanist and Atlanticist camps and to mitigate between the security interests of the North and the South as well as the East and the West of both organisations' geographical membership scope. Balancers take more flexible and adjustable positions because they are in favour of cooperation between the EU and NATO as a whole but might also seek to slow down specific initiatives and projects. States such as Germany, Italy, Portugal and Spain are considered to be balancers who all aim to create an equilibrium of the diverse positions and viewpoints within the EU–NATO membership. Among these balancers, some are more vocal about their positions, whereas others remain less outspoken among other like-minded states.

While their attitude towards EU–NATO cooperation is generally positive, they show traces of medium to low levels of active promotion of enhanced cooperation and their level of engagement in negotiations is of medium intensity. This further relates to their mediocre contributions and possession of resources allocated as well as their national constraints, or viewpoints, regarding the use of force. The following analysis shows how balancers take the middle way by epitomising the mediators in the EU–NATO interorganisational relationship and how they simultaneously pursue their own interests and objectives. The overview of their shared characteristics provides the foundation for the subsequent analysis of balancers' involvement in EU–NATO cooperation through the use of their own memberships and partnerships with fellow member states. This is followed by the examination of their military capabilities and contributions to EU and NATO military operations as well as their view on interoperability and division of labour, which is concluded by the outline of balancers' positioning in the EU–NATO relationship.

DOI: 10.4324/9781003170068-5

Shared characteristics of balancers

Throughout their actions and behaviours, balancers pursue the aim of balancing other member states' positions, especially among those traditionally belonging to either the Atlanticist or Europeanist camp, and seek to mitigate among states with conflicting positions about deepening EU–NATO cooperation. Alternative labels for balancers, or at least for some specific members in this group, have been used in the scholarly literature such as '*Mittellage*'[1] or 'middle ground' (Simón 2017; Zimmer 1997), 'balancing act' and 'third way' (Faleg 2013) and 'mediator' (Algieri 2011; Zyla 2012). Despite their general support for the EU–NATO relationship, these states are nevertheless considered as balancers due to their pursuit of an equitable approach to EU–NATO cooperation. Balancers, however, depict the following set of characteristics to varying levels and at different points in time (see Table 5.1).

Concerning their membership, balancers are multiple member states and are deeply rooted in the institutional structures of both the EU and NATO

Table 5.1 Overview of balancers' characteristics

Shared characteristics	*Balancers and their membership*	*Contributions to capabilities*	*View on division of labour and interoperability*
• Labelled as 'mediators', 'balancing act' and 'middle ground' • In favour of interorganisational cooperation • Mediate and negotiate among states and organisations alike • Balance the institutionalisation process but do not seek a rapid advancement to accommodate the preferences of others • Atlanticist orientation to diverging degrees	• Multiple members • Can be both original and subsequent members • Generally active in negotiations and in small group activities • Serve as contact points and dialogue partners for other members • Maintain good relations with all member states from both organisations • Use of diplomacy and negotiations to mediate in inter-member state disagreements	• Seek to fill capability gaps equally • Involved in capability development initiatives in both organisations but not very proactive • Balance efforts and capabilities • Low to medium levels of military expenditures • Identified as middle powers in both the EU and NATO • Labelled as 'laggards' • Limitations on the use of force	• Promote interoperability actively • Favour division of labour, where the strengths of both organisations are highlighted and effectively used • Prefer division of labour and interoperability to benefit both organisations equally

(Gehring and Oberthür 2009). In fact, multiple membership is a prerequisite to be categorised as an interorganisational balancer since this gives states the ability to influence decision-making processes about organisations' external relations, the capability to direct policy outcomes and shape decisions over military deployments and mandates. Single membership would lack the required access to important decision-making forums to actually make an impact at the interorganisational level. Balancers utilise their multiple membership to maintain partnerships and minilateral formats to exercise influence, whereby they act as brokers among other member states (cf. Goddard 2009).

The time of accession to the EU and NATO, that is, either as original and founding member or as a subsequent and new addition, is not necessarily decisive (cf. Magliveras 2011). Yet, to serve as a balancer from an early stage, an early accession to an international organisation before the start of interactions with other organisations is beneficial. Being able to mitigate divergences and balance from the earliest moment helps to avoid any competition or rivalry among organisations in the same policy field. Among the four states in this group, only Italy is a founding member of both organisations and can therefore be considered the only original and old member state in this group. Germany is among the creators of the EU and Portugal of the Atlantic Alliance but have equally joined the respective other organisation at a later point in time – West Germany joined NATO in 1955, which was followed by the inclusion of the Federal Republic in 1990, and Portugal joined the EU in 1986. Spain, in contrast, is a subsequent member state because it joined both organisations in the 1980s after its transition to a liberal democracy, and it only gained full membership in NATO in 1995 as a result of the 1986 referendum under a government led by the Spanish Socialist Workers Party.

A shared characteristic of balancers is their Atlanticist orientation in security and defence, although this has been disputed in the case of Germany, which has often been claimed to belong to the Europeanist camp (Miskimmon 2001). While this Atlanticist trace refers primarily to their standpoint on defence policy, it does not ultimately reflect their attitude towards the EU–NATO relationship. Portugal is the most salient example of balancers with an Atlanticist outlook. Due to its geostrategic location on the Atlantic and its long relationship with the US, it has maintained a focus on the Atlantic region for security and defence (Ferreira-Pereira 2007a, 2007b; Robinson 2016). Similarly, Spain and Italy pursue an Atlanticist foreign and security policy orientation and prefer to make use of NATO's capabilities and responsibilities for high intensity military crisis management operations (Portugal 2015; Spain 2013). Germany shows greater ambiguity about whether it demonstrates an Atlanticist or Europeanist orientation. While the Ministry of Foreign Affairs traditionally maintains a European outlook and stresses the importance of developing a European defence capacity, the Ministry of Defence has a tendency towards NATO for security and defence matters (German Officials 3).

Balancers have specific constraints in terms of their defence budgets and the sizes of their armed forces. Most notably, their shared historical experience as former autocratic and fascist regimes have significantly contributed to their middle power status[2] as well as to their overall positioning in the EU and NATO. All four states keep a historical record of dictatorships in the twentieth century: Germany under the Nazi regime (1933–1945), Italy under Mussolini and the era of Italian fascism (1922–1943), Portugal during the Second Republic or also known as *Estada Novo* (1933–1974) and Spain under Franco's dictatorship (1939–1975). This historical experience has strongly shaped balancers' strategic cultures and imprinted their stance on multilateralism in security and defence. For example, two of Germany's guiding principles are 'never again' and 'never alone', and Spain is still hesitant towards greater engagement which is shown by having held a referendum on fully joining NATO (Coates 2000; Iso-Markku 2016; Marrone and Di Camillo 2013; Wurzer 2013). Their middle power status paired with their historical experience and constraints in their foreign and security policy orientation has induced the view of balancers as 'soft powers' and 'civilian powers' (Faleg 2013; Maull 2006; Muniz 2013). What is more, while balancers are generally a homogenous group, they show differences concerning their attitudes and individual positions in the EU and NATO. For example, Germany is considered as Europe's economic powerhouse, whereas the others have suffered heavily from the 2008 economic and financial crisis. Nevertheless, even though Germany has the economic strength, industrial base and technical know-how to develop more sophisticated weaponry and capabilities, it generally demonstrates less willingness than Italy, Portugal and Spain to increase its defence spending and make greater investments (Hyde-Price 2015; Sabatino 2017).

Their level of military capabilities and resources as well as their involvement in security and defence matters has also given balancers the status of 'middle powers' (Dobrescu et al. 2017; Junk and Daase 2013; Marrone and Di Camillo 2013). In this context, some balancers are furthermore labelled as 'laggards', which has been primarily used for Germany but also occasionally for Italy, Portugal and Spain (Mejía 2017; Rodt 2017; Wagner 2005). Balancers are not among those with the most outstanding contributions to military operations or among those actively seeking to launch new missions and operations. But they are constantly and continuously involved in improving interorganisational relations through participation in initiatives, negotiations, trainings and capability development projects (NATO Official 5). Instead of providing leadership, balancers are active in creating and maintaining linkages among member states as well as in the structural developments to combat limited resources and counteract domestic constraints (cf. Kempin 2015).

Use of membership and partnership networks

Balancers are generally in favour of institutionalising the cooperative efforts between the EU and NATO and using their specific position in this relationship as mediators and contact points for other member states. Rooted in their historical experience as former authoritarian regimes in the twentieth century, the foreign, security and defence policies of Germany, Italy, Portugal and Spain all put a strong emphasis on the significance of multilateral organisations through which they seek to take joint actions with their partners and allies. Multilateralism is thus vital for responding effectively to contemporary threats and security challenges (Germany 2006, 2016; Portugal 2015; Spain 2013). Their close attachments to multilateralism and international organisations allow these middle powers to upload their own national interests and preferences to the intergovernmental level, which gives balancers a more vocal and influential position among the powerful member states. A higher degree of institutionalised EU–NATO cooperation fosters multilateralism even further and provides balancers greater leverage on security and defence matters. Membership in international security organisations is also regarded as a legitimising factor for their external action and relations, and their foreign and security policy orientations are deeply embedded in multilateral forums as well as close-knit bilateral and minilateral cooperation frameworks (Barbé and Mestres 2007; Baumann and Hellmann 2001; Cardoso Reis 2013; Faleg 2015; Germany 2016; Italy 2015; Portugal 2015; Spain 2013).

Since balancers are not at the forefront in terms of creating obstacles or initiating arrangements compared to France or the UK, they engage in negotiation processes to make use of their strength as balancing acts. None of the balancers therefore belongs to these fringe groups or troublemakers in regard to either European strategic autonomy, NATO's dominance or interorganisational cooperation. Instead, balancers engage in mediation among member states to alleviate tensions and challenges. Balancers can additionally be regarded as 'support states' (Rodt 2017: 141–142) as well as 'bystanders' (Overhaus 2004: 555). Because of the lack of high level and sophisticated initiatives on the institutional level, with the exception of Germany's idea of the FNC within NATO, especially the behaviour of Southern European states among the balancers has been perceived as rather 'lazy' and 'free-riding' (NATO Official 5).

While states usually make use of their membership in multiple organisations to reduce transaction costs, coordinate their activities and policies and to realise their national interests (see Abbott and Snidal 1998), balancers show signs of equalising their national interests with those of the respective organisations. For example, Germany 'has continued to wrap its domestic and foreign policy within the EU mantle' (Mattox 2011: 122) and has heavily internalised collective security as well as the European foreign, security and defence policy in its domestic context. As this subsection shows, balancers take a specific approach to their membership and partnership networks to mediate among member states in the EU–NATO relationship.

Germany

Germany counts as the most prominent state among balancers whose foreign and security policy and membership in international security organisations is significantly shaped by its historical experiences and national caveats. It has long been claimed to be the 'civilian power' in Europe (Maull 2006) and has imposed itself constitutional and legal limitations concerning the use of military force. Until the ruling by the Federal Constitutional Court on 12 July 1994 (Deutscher Bundestag 2016), Germany was prohibited from participating in military operations excluding humanitarian missions. Yet, the nature of the German Bundeswehr as a so-called *Parlamentsarmee* (parliamentary army) that requires the approval of the Bundestag for each mandate and deployment, has resulted in special rules of engagement for the Bundeswehr based on the 2004 Parliamentary Participation Act. This has significant effects on Germany's engagement in military operations as well as on its foreign and security policy orientation. Traces of an 'anti-militarism' (Baumann and Hellmann 2001: 63; Iso-Markku 2016: 51) and a 'mentality of caution, restraint, and reserve' (Hyde-Price 2015: 601), which have often times hampered Germany's activism in security and defence. The perception of the country's restraint as a decelerating factor as well as the dilemma between its economic growth, and thus the potential for increased defence investments, and the anti-militaristic and restrained attitude towards the use of force have been identified within the EU and among member states (EU Official 4; Romanian Official 1). Within Germany itself, the impact of its national caveat and that it eventually needs to give up its initial misgivings in the security and defence realm have also been acknowledged (German Official 1). Moreover, at the 2014 Munich Security Conference, then German Federal President Joachim Gauck and then Minister of Defence Ursula von der Leyen announced that Germany will take over more responsibilities in international and European security (cf. Gauck 2014; von der Leyen 2014). The traditional rivalry between the Ministry of Defence and the Ministry of Foreign Affairs as well as their different viewpoints have proven to be additional obstacles, which have suspended Germany's efforts in security and defence cooperation (Dyson 2014; Hyde-Price 2015).

To compensate for its national caveats, Germany makes strategic use of its specific assets. Its central geographical location – the so-called *Mittellage* – and its critical size in terms of its physical and economic sizes have both been burdens for Germany's external relations (Fröhlich 2011; Zimmer 1997). It is caught not only geographically but also politically between the East and West as well as between the North and South. Over time, it has made use of this location for the purpose of brokering among member states and international secretariats due to its wide network of bilateral and minilateral relationships. This central position is well suited for its role as a mediator because Germany has always needed to maintain peaceful and stable relations with all of its nine neighbouring countries. This position has been labelled as *Strommitte* ('mid-stream') (German Officials 2), which implies its central location as well as the notion of going with the current. One example of Germany's use of its specific geographical and political location is its mediating efforts between Paris and Washington, two of its closest allies in foreign and security affairs

(Germany 2016). It has an interest in both the transatlantic view and the Gaullist perspective on European security and seeks to keep stable and good relations with both sides. Because Germany does not desire to disappoint any of its partners, it usually approaches them informally before decision-makings to negotiate a common ground as well as to forge a compromise (Kaim and Niedermeier 2011; Meiers 2001; Zyla 2012). This approach has been translated to the level of the EU–NATO interorganisational relationship where Germany prefers a common approach as well as collaboration and cooperation among all partners in terms of EU–NATO relations.

Furthermore, Germany has increasingly become the first point of contact in consultations for other member states when new ideas or initiatives are introduced and when crucial items are added to the agenda. Small and medium-sized member states in both organisations particularly seek to consult and negotiate with Germany in advance (Dutch Official 1; Slovak Official 1). Even more Atlanticist countries, such as Estonia, 'recently [look] more often at (…) Germany for actions' (Estonian Official 1). Consequently, Germany has fostered its role as an increasingly important player in security and defence matters, and its skills as broker and mediator between other states involved in EU–NATO cooperation are highly in demand. Its central position as balancer has thus received wide-spread acceptance and appreciation, which allows Germany to further pursue the key features of this role.

By engaging in informal bilateral and minilateral negotiations, Germany utilises mediation and direct interactions with its closest partners such as France, Italy, Poland, the US and the UK. It therefore acts as linkage point among member states in the EU and NATO. During the early developments of setting up and formalising EU–NATO exchanges, it was stuck between France's preference for European defence autonomy and Britain's perseverance of NATO's primacy. It saw this divide problematic in regard to the interventions in the Balkans and the debates circulating the prime actor to intervene and to become involved. From the early stages of interactions, Germany has been interested in 'reinforcing cooperation between NATO and the European Union' (Overhaus 2004: 556) and institutionalising their relations especially because the UK as well as Greece and Turkey had already consented to further advancements. Therefore, Germany itself saw the development of ESDI as the best option to please France while ultimately keeping the UK interested because NATO would remain a significant player, and also to provide viable options to non-EU NATO member states such as Turkey. Furthermore, throughout the formalisation process, the country demanded higher levels of transparency and complementarity among all actors involved, that is, international secretariats and member states alike, to allow for equal information about negotiations and to find common grounds for consultations (Meiers 2001).

Germany has also been active in bargaining and forging compromises between France and the US, which facilitated EU–NATO cooperation. Under the chancellorship of Helmut Kohl with Klaus Kinkel as Minister for

Foreign Affairs and Volker Rühe as Minister of Defence during the 1990s, the urgent need for compatibility between the EU, ESDI and NATO integrity was made clear. Germany sought to actively pursue the mitigation of tensions between France and the US due to their strong bilateral relationship and the significance of these two states for European and international security (Rees 1996). To proactively mediate, Kinkel took the route of bilateral partnerships to promote this approach. For example, in 1998, Klaus Kinkel and his French counterpart Hubert Védrine drafted a joint call for complementarity between Europe and the US specifically regarding their transatlantic relations, including the area of security and defence (Germany 1998). In addition, to pay justice to its 'culture of compromise' and 'tradition of corporatism' (Wurzer 2013: 35), the German government was furthermore involved in talks with its counterparts from its NATO allies to convince them of the compatibility and complementarity of the EU, the WEU and NATO as well as of the necessity and the advantages of closer cooperation between these actors. This emphasis has been fruitful to reduce the level of mistrust among member states, especially France and the US. For example, in his speech at the 1997 Autumn Summit of the WEU in Paris, Klaus Kinkel (1997) re-emphasised that 'the WEU plays an increasing role as joint between the European Union and NATO'. With this behaviour and these relationships, the country overall aims 'to strike the right balance' (Simón 2017: 76). This demonstrates Germany's balancing act between opposing foreign policy orientations within the Euro-Atlantic security community, such as France and the US, on EU–NATO cooperation and that it has sought to engage on all sides to advance the cooperation process.

As an engaged and networked member state, Germany particularly utilises its bilateral and minilateral relationship such as the Quint and the Friends of Europe groupings. Within these small interest groups, German representatives occasionally invite representatives of other EU and NATO member states to so-called *Kaffeerunden* (coffee meetings) to discuss and negotiate further developments and initiatives as well as to forge compromises and ease tensions on an informal level. In these minilateral negotiation groups, Germany took over the position as broker especially between Atlanticist demands of Britain and the US and Europeanist views expressed by France. For example, during the first stages of initiating and launching a military operation, Germany would first invite its close partners in both the EU and NATO to these *Kaffeerunden* to discuss their preferences and strategic choices for action. Before the issue comes to the decision-making stage, the country seeks to find ways to harmonise diverging interests and preferences. The respective national representative then evaluates the options and seeks to express compromises to comfort its close partners but also to find a way to harmonise the strengths and capabilities of both organisations (German Officials 2). Particularly in these informal meetings, Germany has been able to act as balancer and broker to enhance EU–NATO cooperation and to circumvent political tensions among states.

Italy

Among balancers, Italy is the only original member state of both NATO and the EU though its own path to positioning itself in both organisations has been crucially marked by its domestic developments since the end of the Second World War. Its foreign, security and defence policies are heavily influenced by the domestic political situation and societal context. Domestic politics particularly shape Italy's membership in both the EU and NATO, which has caused 'wavering alignments' with defence partners (Andreatta 2008: 169). These 'blurred lines' have led to lower levels of reliability among its partners in the past, which ultimately forces the government to stay involved as much as feasible (Cladi and Webber 2011: 206). Domestically, it is shaped by the rivalries between socialist and communist parties on the one side and fascist perspectives on the other (Marrone and Di Camillo 2013). Because of these ongoing struggles on the domestic political level, Italy highly values its membership and integration in the Euro-Atlantic security community and emphasises multilateralism in its foreign and security policy orientation (Italy 2015). Over time, Italy has developed characteristics of a balancer that suits its own preferences and national caveats.

Italy has been engaged in the negotiations and debates on European security and defence capacities and capabilities with the primary aim to balance between the often-opposing views of France and the UK. It has made use of its own military capabilities to gain leverage in these negotiations. For example, it followed the UK by deploying troops to Iraq under the coalition of the willing in 2003 and by strengthening its commitment in Afghanistan in 2003, while it concurrently supported the launch of the EU's first autonomous military operation labelled Artemis in the DRC. By supporting and contributing to operations on both sides as well as by engaging in the negotiations on the launch, mandates and troops deployments, it contributed equally to the initiatives to launch military operations by both France and the UK to avoid subsequent consequences that would negatively impact the unity within the EU and NATO as well as their relationship. The country was especially keen to avoid the 'either or' debate and it therefore served as 'a diplomatic and political balancing act' which sought 'to find a "third way, or mediation between the French vision (…) and the UK's pro-Atlantic stance (…)' (Faleg 2013: 64). In the past, primarily during the late 1990s, and in recent occasions, Italy does not seek to attach itself to bigger member states such as France, the UK or the US (Italian Official 1) and alternatively locates itself in the middle ground while negotiating with all sides equally.

In its position as balancer, Italy prefers to maintain relations equally with all allies and partners and does not seek to engage in such informal minilateral cooperative frameworks, which sets itself in contrast to the other balancers who seek close alignments through strong bilateral and minilateral partnerships with other EU and NATO member states. It recognises the need to maintain good relations with the other Mediterranean states and the countries in the Balkans due to the shared neighbourhood, thus also shared security concerns, and occasionally sides with Spain as its partner in Mediterranean security affairs. Italy further allowed itself to enter an asymmetric relationship with the US due to its own middle power status (Marrone and Di Camillo 2013; Schumacher et al. 2016). The country is part of the Friends of Europe group, which includes those allies that promote European security and defence interests within NATO. The main purpose for its engagements and memberships in such informal groupings is that they serve Italy to be part of the club and not left out from key decision-making mechanisms and compromises. Nevertheless, there is no definite close partnership comparable to the Franco–German partnership or the UK–US special relationship. Therefore, as emphasised by one Italian representative, 'at the European level both in the EU and NATO, Italy does not align with or refer to other bigger states'. In general, 'coalition groups should not be based on regional constituency because this would damage the cohesion within both the EU and NATO' (Italian Official 1). The Italian government maintains a 'double loyalty to the EU and the US and firm respect for multilateralism' but often times perceives itself of second-class membership status within NATO (Cladi and Webber 2011: 208). Therefore, it seeks to be engaged in initiatives and projects as much as possible and pursues to maintain good relations with all member states equally. The primary purpose is to avoid 'the feeling of frustration that arises whenever Rome is left out' especially from negotiations among the bigger and more powerful member states (Faleg 2013: 49). As a consequence, Italy uses its formal membership in the EU and NATO to partake in small-scale frameworks and projects which also enable it to act as a balancer and broker due to its balanced approach towards bilateral and minilateral relations.

Portugal and Spain

Both Portugal and Spain's positions within the EU and NATO and their relationship have been influenced by their historical experiences deriving from fascism and isolation as well as their attitudes towards the use of force. While Portugal is an original member in NATO and Spain gained full accession in 1995, they joined the EU together in 1986. Since the beginning of their memberships, they have played active roles in negotiations and debates to advance European security and defence issues. What specifically marks them as balancers is the use of their geographical locations, possession of capabilities and linkages in the Euro-Atlantic security community.

Spain and Portugal make use of their geographical location between the Mediterranean Sea and the Atlantic Ocean to their advantage to maintain relations with key strategic partners. Through this position they have direct links to their most important ally the US, as well as other powerful defence actors such as France and Britain. As Atlantic states they seek to serve as bridges between Europe and North America, which help them to balance between the differing security interests (Cardoso Reis 2013; Ferreira-Pereira 2007b). In the case of Portugal, the country also seeks to act as a broker and mediator within the EU. It pursues to achieve the middle ground between the E3 and particularly between France and Germany. It aims to use this geostrategic position, which makes it also vulnerable to new threats, to avoid any marginalisation in the EU–NATO relationship. By maintaining linkages to both sides of the Atlantic and attaching itself to bigger member states in Europe, such as the E3, it aims to mediate among them. One example of its balancing behaviour is its engagement in debates on procurement. Portugal prefers to purchase and develop new capabilities through either EU or NATO partners, however, with a preference for acquiring capabilities from the US. On one occasion, Portugal opted for German and Dutch submarines, but also acquired new missiles from the US through the NATO procurement process to increase interoperability and to avoid greater divergences among the defence industrial markets in the Euro-Atlantic. Consequently, Portugal tried to support both the EU and NATO and their member states' defence industries by procuring important capabilities through both organisations (Branco 2015; de Melo Palma 2009; Robinson 2016).

One way of vocalising and realising a state's policy preferences and to advance external relations is the use of the Presidency in the CEU. By adding EU–NATO cooperation on the agenda, balancers have successfully made use of their EU Presidencies for the advancement and deepening of EU–NATO cooperation on the one hand, and to find the middle ground among all member states on the other. Three major milestones have been achieved in which the EU Presidencies of Portugal and Germany were decisive. First, after having held the 1996 NATO ministerial meeting, where the Alliance partners in joint action with members of the WEU agreed upon the use of the Alliance's military assets for WEU-led crisis management operations (NATO 1996; Reichard 2006), Germany was once again host to a crucial meeting by the EU heads of states and governments. At the 1999 European Council meeting in Cologne, it was agreed to advance European defence and crisis management capabilities, which were to be beneficial for both the EU and NATO to increase interoperability, cooperation, transparency and mutual consultations between them (European Council 1999).

During its own EU Presidencies in 2000 and 2007, Portugal played a significant role and the outcomes had beneficial implications for the EU–NATO relationship. At the 2000 European Council meeting in Santa Maria da Feira, EU member states decided upon the establishment of ad hoc joint EU–NATO working groups to deepen cooperation on the security issues, capabilities goals, modalities for the EU's access to the Alliance's assets and capabilities and mechanisms for permanent consultations (European Council 2000). What is more, Portugal concurrently held the Presidency in the WEU in which it emphasised the integration of the WEU into the EU's structures.

Portugal also continuously reminded the EU community of its close ties to other Atlantic states. In these debates, the Portuguese geographical location and its Atlanticist foreign and security policy orientation were crucial to maintain a close link between EU and NATO (de Melo Palma 2009; Robinson 2016). During both Presidencies, Portugal was decisive in preparing the meetings and drafting the conclusions, which were filtered according to its policy preferences as well as the common view of all member states on interorganisational cooperation. The decisions taken at the European Council meetings in 1999 and 2000 eventually led to the formulation of the Berlin Plus arrangements, which proved to be a major milestone in the EU–NATO relationship. In addition, during its EU Presidency in 2007 another milestone was achieved, which served to be beneficial for contributing to EU–NATO cooperation and putting the two organisations on a level playing field. Led by France and Germany as well as Portugal as holder of the EU Presidency, EU member states agreed on a set of initiatives for improving European military capabilities and structures including the EDF, MPCC and PESCO. While these initiatives were only officially launched in 2017, they bring an additional input and added value to the EU–NATO relationship (cf. Biscop 2017a, 2017b; Tardy 2021).

Among the balancers, Spain would be considered as the newest multiple member states. It joined both organisations after having transformed into a liberal democracy in 1975 with the end of the Franco era. Yet, due to the outcome of the referendum on NATO membership in 1986, which left it outside the integrated military command structures, it did not fully join the Alliance until 1996. In this situation it was able to participate in working groups and committees, however, it was not involved in NATO's military structures (Arteaga 2013; Serra 1988). Over time, Spain has increasingly perceived its full memberships in both EU and NATO as essential for its foreign, security and defence policy, and 'it feels like a valued partner' in both organisations (Muniz 2013: 90). This value in membership is further demonstrated by its emphasis on solidarity and loyalty as demonstrated not only by its reliability in NATO, particularly in missions and operation, but also by its flexibility and willingness for engagements with different groupings in the Euro-Atlantic (Coletta and García 2013). One of Spain's key assets cannot be counted in material terms or in light of its network of bilateral and minilateral relationships. Instead, its former Minister for Foreign Affairs Javier Solana (1992–1995) was first seconded as NATO Secretary General (1995–1999) and then as the EU's High Representative for the Common Foreign and Security Policy (1999–2009). For the Spanish policy direction, Solana has therefore played a crucial part and contributed to the country's positioning in the EU–NATO relationship and which symbolises its role as balancer (Coates 2000).

Spain's foreign and security policy orientation is also shaped by its domestic political context and the gap between the political elite, the military and the wider public concerning military engagements and the use of force. Due to these divergences, it maintains a balanced approach to the EU and NATO.

Moreover, while it follows a Europeanist approach due to the Union's support of Spain in other policy areas, especially economically and financially, the country shows Atlanticist traits because of its reliance on the US (Arteaga 2013). Similar to Italy, Spain does not seek to be confronted with the 'either or' question and has thus chosen to join the middle ground by balancing its commitments in both organisations. As a middle power in security and defence, Spain is nevertheless regarded among the bigger players in the EU, though because of its peripheral geographical location it sees itself among the second-tier member states in NATO (Muniz 2013). Its geographical position bordering the Mediterranean Sea and caught between France and Portugal makes it a vulnerable state to security threats from the South. Its peripheral place therefore leads to close bilateral cooperation with its neighbours and other Euro-Mediterranean states, particularly with France, Italy, Greece and Portugal, but it also considers the US among its most important allies in defence issues. Spain highly values its bilateral ties as it pursues to strengthen these in order to become a more influential actor on the international stage and especially in international forums (Arteaga 2013; Barbé and Mestres 2007; Coletta and García 2013; Spain 2013).

Contributions to military capabilities, interoperability and division of Labour

Balancers have their own share in the capabilities debate in the EU and NATO as well as their cooperation. Most of these states have been accused of their lack of capabilities commitment and low level of investments, often labelling them as free-riders. Yet, some of the balancers also introduced new initiatives through which they have seeded valuable ideas for fruitful initiatives to overcome burden sharing obstacles since the beginning of the peace dividend. Balancers take an equitable approach to committing their capabilities, resources and troops to the EU and NATO, which has been specifically shaped by their historical experiences, public debates and domestic politics, and the subsequent cautious perspective on the use of force. Their contributions overall signal willingness despite their limited resources to close the gaps between the EU and NATO in a way that is beneficial to both and in which these states can further pursue their balancing act. This subsection explores balancers' input to the development of military capabilities and investments and examines their views on division of labour and their contributions to EU and NATO operations.

As Sperling (2004) and Eilstrup-Sangiovanni (2014) outline, there are several gaps between Europe and North America as well as between the EU and NATO that heavily influence their cooperation, such as in leadership, capabilities and technological investments. Balancers have limited potential to contribute to the leadership gap. Only Germany – alongside France and the UK – 'could make a plausible claim to defence leadership in Europe' (Sperling 2004: 460). External calls and pressures especially from its European partners have become louder, which demand Germany to take the leadership role

(Helwig 2016; Iso-Markku 2016). However, it has frequently been labelled as the 'reluctant hegemon' (Patterson 2011 cited in Junk and Daase 2013: 140) due to its normative foreign policy and approach based on humanitarian and moral principles restricting it from taking over leadership. Germany has been portrayed as a 'sleep-walking giant' because it fails to live up to the expectations brought forward by its partners and allies and to the responsibilities of a major actor in Europe (Hyde-Price 2015). Its internal debates and low defence investments are especially affected by a sense of resolve and restraint accompanied by the missing 'proper institutionalised inter-ministerial "whole of government" approach' (Hyde-Price 2015: 607). Former Federal President Joachim Gauck (2014) and Minister of Defence Ursula von der Leyen (2014) showed signs of a growing sense of responsibility and leadership in security and defence at the 2014 Munich Security Conference. They also raised the point that Germany will need to do more to realise its position in the European security and defence realm, but these promises have so far not materialised. In his speech, Joachim Gauck (2014) stated that

> Germany has long since demonstrated that it acts in an internationally responsible way. But it could – building on its experience in safeguarding human rights and the rule of law – take more resolute steps to preserve and help shape the order based on the European Union, NATO and the United Nations. At the same time, Germany must also be ready to do more to guarantee the security that others have provided it with for decades.

The German government has so far put forward the idea of the FNC in NATO and, in collaboration with Sweden, the idea of pooling and sharing in the EU. To fully develop and consolidate its own position in the European security and defence *directoire* alongside France and the UK, these ideas would require the German government to become accustomed to the leadership role (Glatz and Zapfe 2017). On the institutional level, however, Germany finds itself in a trap since 'other member states tender Germany this leadership role', which is especially the case for small members, yet the country has not asked for such a role (German Officials 1, 2). Germany 'gets pushed to realise this leadership role in CFSP and CSDP' but in the internal debate, policymakers are not convinced that Germany will eventually fulfil these expectations (German Official 1). Against this backdrop, however, it is not willing to take over such a role and prefers to act through minilateral and multilateral forums (Meiers 2001). The external pressures by its partners to take over leadership collides with Germany's key principle of restraint and anti-militarism which therefore explain the country's reticent attitude towards leadership in security and defence.

In the debates on military expenditure, defence investments and capabilities for collective defence and crisis management, most of the balancers have been accused of being 'laggards' and 'free-riders' (Barbé and Mestres 2007;

Eilstrup-Sangiovanni 2014; Hyde-Price 2015; Schumacher et al. 2016; Serra 1988). Spain, for example, lags behind similarly sized and similarly placed member states such as Canada, Italy and Poland in terms of its military budget. The Portuguese armed forces still suffer from the consequences of the 2008 financial and economic crisis. Both Italy and Germany went through a phase of ample restructuring of their armed forces and their military bureaucracies to meet the new challenges, but still remain far from expectations and the political rhetoric of their governments. Consequently, the German Bundeswehr has been labelled as a 'paper army' (De Hoop Scheffer 2016) due to the dire state of its equipment and level of training for high intensity military operations and collective defence scenarios.

As shown in Figure 5.1, Italy records the highest military budget among balancers with 1.7% of its GDP. Portugal ranks second with 1.5% of GDP, while both Germany (1.2%) and Spain (1.2%) make up the most salient laggards (EDA 2016, 2020; NATO 2020; SIPRI 2020). The governments of these states have declared their commitment to the defence pledge of meeting 2% of GDP by 2024 as it was agreed among NATO partners at the 2014 Wales Summit. Allies also agreed to spend at least 20% of their total military expenditures on equipment including research and development by 2024, if they have not already met this target (NATO 2014). Only Italy and Spain have moved closer to this target with 20.94% and 19.31% respectively, and Portugal is situated at the rear end with 10.31% (see Figure 5.2). While Germany is again lagging behind with a share of 13.75% of its total military expenditure allocated to equipment, it spends relatively less on personnel and more on the modernisation of infrastructure compared to the other states in this group. It remains questionable whether the pledges to meet NATO's targets will translate into reality on time. Moreover, for some balancers, NATO's 2% target is an 'over-simplification' and 'just a bar for all states', which does not reflect the real capabilities and commitments of member states (Italian Official 1). While some members might meet this target, not all of their defence expenditure is for the benefit of either the EU or NATO, and therefore rather meaningless

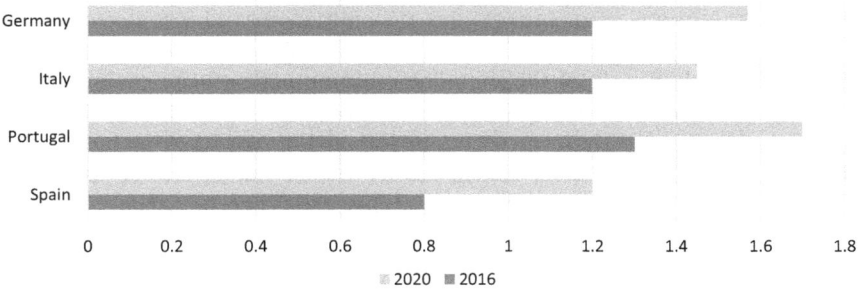

Figure 5.1 Defence expenditure as a share of GDP, 2016 and 2020.

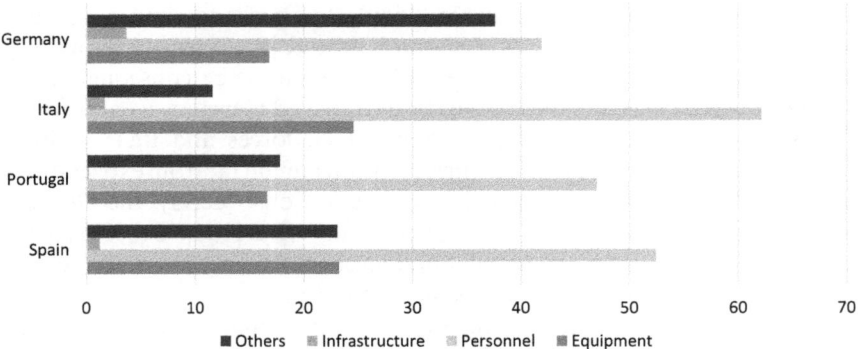

Figure 5.2 Distribution of military expenditure by equipment, personnel, infrastructure and other costs as share of total military expenditure.

for improving the EU–NATO relationship if the capabilities are used solely for national defence purposes.

The level of defence spending signals balancer's middle power status in regard to EU–NATO cooperation. Despite their commitments and recent increases of military expenditures after having agreed to the Alliance's 2% pledge, it becomes evident that balancers have the tendency to focus rather on institutional capacities than on investing in military hardware. As a consequence, balancers have been frequently characterised as free-riders because of their defence budgets that are lower than their financial capabilities. This is particularly targeted at both Italy and Germany, whereas the latter's status as economic giant should translate into higher spendings on security and defence (Hyde-Price 2015; Muniz 2013; Schumacher et al. 2016). Due to their relatively low military expenditures, balancers cannot utilise military power to exert influence, unlike France, Britain or the US. As an alternative, they have to make use of their negotiation and mediation skills instead of their level of ambition and capabilities and collaborate in collective procurement projects. With the peace dividend, increasing financial constraints and decreasing military expenditures of member states, new initiatives and incentives had to be introduced to maintain the level of ambition and capabilities to be able to respond to the challenges of the changing international security environment. Balancers participate in institution-wide defence procurement initiatives, such as DCI in NATO and those projects put forward by the EDA including the CDP. Their engagement and willingness to initiate minilateral cooperation frameworks to minimise the military capability gaps vary, however.

Germany has been the most active member state in maintaining bilateral cooperation such as with France as its most important partner and other neighbouring countries, for example, Poland and the Netherlands. Through the Weimar Triangle, Germany, France and Poland seek to jointly develop military capabilities and trigger new reforms such as of the EU Battlegroups concept. Italy and Spain were invited to join to establish the so-called Weimar Plus cooperative framework. For example, in their Declaration on European Defence, the Weimar Plus group agreed to strengthen efforts on crucial capabilities, including air-to-air refuelling, and to work on the European Air Transport Command (EATC) (France 2012). The latter was finally established in Zaragoza, Spain in 2017 which hosts the European Air Transport Fleet (EATF) (EUISS 2018). Italy is very eager to join the Franco–German core group on capabilities procurement within the EU and also seeks to increase its standing within NATO. It became active in the management of the logistic support-ship procurement programme and the multipurpose patrol vessel procurement programme called *Pattugliatori Polivalenti d'Altura* (Gilli et al. 2015). This shows its first efforts of launching cooperation frameworks in the area of military capability procurement as well as its willingness to expand these initiatives. In contrast, neither Portugal nor Spain have indicated to trigger any joint efforts concerning the modernisation or procurement of their armed forces and capabilities. While they accept invitations to join collaborations, no new initiatives or ideas should be expected to be vocalised any time soon from them (NATO Official 5).

Despite the lacking willingness and limited capacities to become more engaged and take over responsibilities, balancers are well aware of the need to increase interoperability through complementarity, harmonised capability development plans and coordinated trainings as well as the need for a clear division of tasks. They acknowledge the implications of growing functional overlap, which can lead to competition over their limited resources as well as to specialisations of each organisation (cf. Faude 2015). While they do not seek to pursue a clearly defined division of tasks and responsibilities, they see the advantages of having such a division on a case-by-case basis, which would allow for a sustainable and more efficient management of their limited resources. Balancers agree on the benefits of each organisation's comparative advantage, which also triggers the necessity for the EU and NATO to cooperate on both the institutional and the operational levels. Through their participation in military operations, these states also aim to maintain a balanced approach and increase the interoperability between both organisations.

For balancers, a division of labour between the EU and NATO overall 'makes sense' because it allows for the efficient use of scarce resources and particularly sustains the capabilities of every member state's single set of forces (German Officials 3). The armed forces and military assets of European states suffer from severe austerity measures and defence cuts. For Spain, for example, the increasing level of functional overlap between the EU and NATO since the end of the Cold War has initially been perceived as problematic and a division of labour therefore presents a possible solution to avoiding duplication and competition over vital resources and military capabilities (Fojón et al. 2015). Balancers specifically emphasise the need to make use of each organisations' key strengths whereby a division of tasks allows for a more efficient and sustainable management of their armed forces and capabilities.

Both the EU and NATO have different and very specific toolboxes and comparative advantages. Although member states have the ownership of the required capabilities, they provide resources for the use in military operations for both organisations. Balancers such as Germany and Italy emphasise that states should not pose themselves the 'either or' question, but rather the question of how both organisations can make use of their comparative advantages and how the toolboxes of each organisation can contribute to the efficient resolution of conflicts (Italian Official 1; Tettweiler 2015: 36). Consequently, balancers generally agree that the EU and NATO offer these specific toolboxes with unique added values and comparative advantages and that it depends on the type of crisis and conflict to take the decision which organisation is better suited, how more effective coordination mechanisms can be established and how both organisations are best equipped to cooperate on the operational and strategic levels. Balancers further share the opinion that NATO has 'a comparative advantage over the with regard to crisis management operations which require a strong military intervention, while the EU is better suited for civilian or humanitarian operations' (Arteaga 2013: 339). Nevertheless, they often prefer to take actions through the EU because of its much broader toolbox composed of diplomatic, economic, political and military tools and instruments and because the EU has proven to be more successful with its comprehensive civil–military approach (Robinson 2016; Wurzer 2013; Zyla 2012).

While balancers find a division of labour between the EU and NATO meaningful, Germany and Italy have expressed the pressing need to create more synergies, complementarity and interoperability through higher levels of cooperation and the coordination of efforts (German Officials 3, Italian Official 1). For example, the military operations in Afghanistan, where the EU only conducted a civilian mission, as well as in the Western Balkans and the Horn of Africa make illustrative cases. In these instances, the EU's training missions and capacity-building efforts are perceived as great assets to NATO's robustness and military capabilities and seen as significant for sustainable peace and security. Since neither organisation has a complete toolbox for responding effectively and efficiently to international crises, interorganisational interaction is thus inevitable. A division of tasks and responsibilities also helps balancers to serve as brokers in the process of planning military operations. As multiple members they are able to influence and raise their voices in both the PSC and the NAC, while they have the knowledge of each organisation's mandates for conducting military operations at the same time. Accordingly, they engage in discussions among other states to ensure that a division of labour will be negotiated. To broker deals and employ a division of tasks and responsibility between the EU and NATO, balancers utilise their bilateral and minilateral relations and networks, such as the Quint and Friends of Europe groupings. They position themselves between both organisations with the aim to achieve complementarity and cooperation to avoid any competition over resources (Faleg 2013). This brokering behaviour has become visible during the 2014 Ukraine crisis, which involves a number of international actors including the EU, NATO and their member states as well as Russia and the OSCE. Germany, alongside France, has emerged as a key negotiator between Ukraine and Russia. From the beginning, it has also signalled that a concerted approach by the EU and NATO in addition to the OSCE's efforts is crucial to resolve the ongoing crisis. It seeks to make use of the EU's broad toolbox, particularly the diplomatic instruments while considering NATO's deterrence strategy and capabilities if the situation worsens and deems a military response necessary (Pond 2015). This highlights the German culture of restraint as it does not ultimately favour a purely military solution to the crisis, its balancing and brokering behaviour and its preference for a division of labour between the EU and NATO.

There are, however, also diverging voices among balancers on the scope of division of labour. None of these states favours a strict division based on a functional and/or geographical scope between the EU and NATO (Faleg 2013; Tettweiler 2015). One Italian representative expressed his own view on this matter and mentioned that 'a division of labour between the EU and NATO is not good in the future' because it risks to counter attempts to achieve coherence. But he also stated that synergies of their activities and efforts are necessary (Italian Official 1). From the German perspective, a division of tasks on the operational level is meaningful, though it would be vital to take these decisions on a case-by-case basis and that such a division highly depends on the phase of the operation (German Officials 2). One example is the engagement in Bosnia and Herzegovina, where NATO was in charge of the initial entry operation, which includes a rapid response to a crisis, and where the EU took over the operation and was responsible for the conduct of a stabilisation operation. Yet, different views on division of labour exist among those civil servants in Berlin and the civilian and military staff at the EU and NATO permanent representations in Brussels (German Officials 2, 3). This emphasises the difficulty and complexity of finding common grounds among member states on this issue as well as the fact that a strictly defined division of labour between the EU and NATO is not necessarily perceived as beneficial for conducting military operations in shared geographical spaces and operational theatres.

Member states' perspectives and approaches to division of labour between the EU and NATO have further implications on the organisations' interoperability as well as on member states' contributions to multilateral military operations. Generally, the need for interoperability and synergies is widely accepted among balancers due to their lack of military capabilities paired with their emphasis on dialogue, diplomacy and civilian means to crisis management (cf. Italian Official 1; Marrone and Di Camillo 2013). Throughout their memberships, balancers have been active participants and contributors to EU-led and NATO-led military operations (see Appendix C). To date, Italy has contributed to all operations of both NATO and the EU while other states in the group of balancers have participated in the majority of operations, considering some exceptions. Germany contributed to all EU-led military operations and even fills key positions in EUTM Mali and did so similarly in the naval operation EUNAVFOR MED Sophia in the Mediterranean Sea. Its engagement in NATO is of similar record, however, resulting from its abstention from UN Security Council Resolution 1973, it decided against participation in the NATO-led Operation Unified Protector in Libya. Portugal contributed to almost all EU activities with the exception of Operation Althea in Bosnia and Herzegovina as well as in all NATO operations excluding Operation Unified Protector. Similarly, Spain is supportive of multilateral engagements through both organisations. While it contributed to all NATO operations so far, it participated in the majority of EU-led operations with the exceptions of Operation Althea and the newly launched naval operation MED Irini, even though it is the successor of MED Sophia in which Spain had already taken an active part. Although balancers have been participative in almost all military operations, their contributions have often been low which has been justified by their limited resources and national constraints (Fröhlich 2011; Robinson 2016; Zyla 2012).

In terms of participation in EU and NATO operations, balancers show a homogenous picture. In terms of their motivations for participation in collective military operations under these frameworks there is variation among them. One of the prime reasons for Spain, for instance, to partake is its commitment to these organisations, its solidarity as well as the result of forged compromises among its partners (Muniz 2013). In the case of Germany, its main reason to participate equally in international frameworks is its view on creating a balance among its allies and partners and thus to meet the expectation and demands by its closest partners in security and defence, primarily France and the US. In addition, in some of the operational areas it has specific economic interests, which provide a justifiable reason for policymakers and enables Germany to legitimise its participation to its own public. This further justifies its preference for a comprehensive and coordinated approach by both the EU and NATO (Baumann and Hellmann 2001; Junk and Daase 2013; Wurzer 2013). Moreover, both Germany and Italy seek to participate tantamount in EU and NATO operations to strike a balance in their international engagements and follow their balanced principle towards both organisations. Interestingly, however, their contributions to NATO still receive a higher share of assets and capabilities (Eilstrup-Sangiovanni 2014). This further illustrates their political willingness not only to participate in EU and NATO military operations as well as their commitments to multilateral frameworks, but also indicates their balancing approach to cooperation, division of labour and interoperability between the EU and NATO.

Conclusions

This chapter explored the attitudes and role of balancers by focusing on their involvement in the EU–NATO relationship as well as their contributions to cooperation. The main objective of balancers is to mediate and mitigate tensions among other member states as well as between the EU and NATO themselves. By doing so, they act as brokers and mediators and primarily present the middle ground in this interorganisational relationship. What generally identifies Germany, Italy, Portugal and Spain as balancers in EU–NATO cooperation is the scope of their engagement and activities as well as how they use their resources and capabilities. Overall, they have not been very engaged in influencing the formalisation and institutionalisation process of this interorganisational relationship. However, in their positions as brokers and mediators, balancers fill a crucial position which helps to reduce tensions and member state-related challenges to this interorganisational relationship and enables the two organisations to find common grounds. Derived from their historical experiences and shared past of transforming from authoritarian regimes and dictatorships to liberal democracies throughout the twentieth century, balancers' attitude towards military engagement and the use of force is significantly constrained by their domestic political contexts. In fact, these experiences have a crucial impact on their foreign and security policy orientation and their emphasis on multilateral frameworks such as the EU and NATO. Therefore, their involvement in these organisations increased the value of their network of bilateral and minilateral relationships with fellow member states. Their high level of dependency on functioning multilateral frameworks, especially the legitimising factor for external actions in security and defence, further contribute to their ability to act as mediators and brokers. Although balancers' contributions of financial means and capabilities to military operations is limited due their national constraints, they aim to achieve a division of labour between the EU and NATO to make use of each organisation's key strengths and comparative advantages to resolve international crises and conflicts.

Notes

1 The term 'Mittellage' shall not be confused with the negative connotation that circulated during the Bismarckian era, in which Germany's central European location and surrounding by five major powers was perceived as a geopolitical threat, which it sought to counter by a semi-hegemonic strategy. The categorisation and characterisation of Germany as a balancer of interorganisational interaction shall furthermore not be confused with and shall therefore be delimited from Bismarck's balance of power politics.

2 In this case, 'middle power' status refers to balancer's military capabilities in relation to their positioning within NATO and the EU, that is, their location in the centre in terms of their possession of military assets and capabilities available to EU-led and NATO-led military operations and the level of their military expenditures.

References

Abbott, Kenneth W. and Duncan Snidal (1998) 'Why states act through formal international organisations', *The Journal of Conflict Resolution*, 42(1): 3–32.

Algieri, Franco (2011) 'Deutsche Außen- und Sicherheitspolitik im europäischen Kontext: Das abnehmende Strahlen der Integrationsleuchttürme'. *In*: Jäger, Thomas et al. (eds) *Deutsche Außenpolitik*, Wiesbaden: VS Verlag für Sozialwissenschaften, Springer, 126–147.

Andreatta, Filippo (2008) 'Italian Foreign Policy: Domestic politics, international requirements and the European dimension', *European Integration*, 30(1): 169–181.

Arteaga, Felix (2013) 'Spain'. *In*: Biehl, Heiko et al. (eds): *Strategic Cultures in Europe: Security and Defence Policies Across the Continent*, Wiesbaden: Springer VS, 333–342.

Barbé, Esther and Laia Mestres (2007) 'Spain and ESDP'. *In*: Brummer, Klaus (ed) *The South and ESDP: Greece, Italy, Portugal and Spain*, Gütersloh: Bertelsmann, 50–62.

Baumann, Rainer and Gunther Hellmann (2001) 'Germany and the use of force: 'total war', the 'culture of restraint' and the quest for normality', *German Politics*, 10(1): 61–82.

Biscop, Sven (2017a) 'European defence: What's in the CARDs for PESCO? *Egmont Security Policy Brief*, 91: 1–6.

Biscop, Sven (2017b) 'Oratio Pro Pesco', *Egmont Papers*, 91: 1–13.

Branco, Carlos (2015) 'Portugal and the CSDP'. *In*: Fiott, Daniel (ed) *The Common Security and Defence Policy: National Perspectives*, Brussels: Egmont – Royal Institute for International Relations, 83–85.

Cardoso Reis, Bruno (2013) 'Portugal'. *In*: Biehl, Heiko et al. (eds) *Strategic Cultures in Europe: Security and Defence Policies Across the Continent*, Wiesbaden: Springer VS, 281–291.

Cladi, Lorenzo and Mark Webber (2011) 'Italian foreign policy in the post-cold war period: A neoclassical realist approach', *European Security*, 20(2): 205–219.

Coates, Crispin (2000) 'Spanish Defence Policy: Eurocorps and NATO reform', *Mediterranean Politics*, 5(2): 170–189.

Coletta, Daman and David García (2013) 'Willing and able? Spanish statecraft as brokerage'. *In*: Matlary, Janne Haaland and Magnus Petersson (eds) *NATO's European Allies: Military Capability and Political Will*, Basingstoke: Palgrave Macmillan, 178–204.

De Hoop Scheffer, Alexandra (2016) 'Paper Tiger No More', Berlin Policy Journal, September/October issue, https://berlinpolicyjournal.com/paper-tiger-no-more/ (accessed on 28/06/2018).

de Melo Palma, Hugo (2009) 'European by force and by will: Portugal and the European security and defence policy', *EU Diplomacy Papers*, 7: 1–32.

Deutscher Bundestag (2016) Verfassungsrechtliche Grundlage für Auslandseinsätze der Bundeswehr: Überlegungen zur Änderung der verfassungsrechtlichen Praxis, Ausarbeitung No. WD 2 - 3000 - 025/16.

Dobrescu, Madalina et al. (2017) 'Southern Europe: Portugal, Spain, Italy, Malta, Greece, Cyprus'. *In*: Hadfield, Amelia et al. (eds) *Foreign Policies of EU Member States: Continuity and Europeanisation*, Abingdon: Routledge, 83–98.

Dyson, Tom (2014) 'German Defence Policy under the Second Merkel Chancellorship', *German Politics*, 23(4): 460–476.

Eilstrup-Sangiovanni, Mette (2014) 'Europe's defence dilemma', *The International Spectator*, 49(2): 83–116.

European Council (1999) *Conclusions of the Presidency*, Cologne European Council, 3–4 June 1999, www.europarl.europa.eu/summits/kol2_en.htm (accessed on 22/06/2018).

European Council (2000) *Conclusions of the Presidency*, Santa Maria da Feira European Council, 19–20 June 2000, www.europarl.europa.eu/summits/fei1_en.htm (accessed on 22/06/2018).

European Defence Agency (2016) *National Defence Data 2013–2014 and 2015 (est.) of the 27 EDA Member States*, http://eda.europa.eu/docs/default-source/documents/eda-national-defence-data-2013-2014-(2015-est)5397973fa4d264cfa776ff000087ef0f.pdf (accessed on 24/07/2017).

European Defence Agency (2020) *Defence Data 2018–2019: Key Findings and Analysis*, https://eda.europa.eu/publications-and-data/brochures/defence-data-2018-2019 (accessed on 16/03/2021).

European Union Institute for Security Studies (2018) *Yearbook of European Security*, Paris: European Union Institute for Security Studies.

Faleg, Giovanni (2013) 'Italy's "third way" to European defence'. *In*: Santopinto, Federico and Megan Price (eds) *National Visions of EU Defence Policy: Common Denominators and Misunderstandings*, Brussels: CEPS, GRIP and COST, 47–68.

Faleg, Giovanni (2015) 'Ask not what Italy can do for the CSDP'. *In*: Fiott, Daniel (ed) *The Common Security and Defence Policy: National Perspectives*, Brussels: Egmont – Royal Institute for International Relations, 45–46.

Faude, Sebastian (2015) 'Zur Dynamik inter-organisationaler Beziehungen: Wie aus Konkurrenz Arbeitsteilung entsteht', *Politische Vierteljahresschrift*, 49: 294–321.

Ferreira-Pereira, Laura C. (2007a) 'Between Scylla and Charybdis: Assessing Portugal's approach to the common foreign and security policy', *European Integration*, 29(2): 209–228.

Ferreira-Pereira, Laura C. (2007b) 'Portugal and ESDP'. *In*: Brummer, Klaus (ed) *The South and ESDP: Greece, Italy, Portugal and Spain*, Gütersloh: Bertelsmann, 32–49.

Fojón, Enrique et al. (2015) 'Spain and the CSDP'. *In*: Fiott, Daniel (ed) *The Common Security and Defence Policy: National Perspective,* Brussels: Egmont – Royal Institute for International Relations, 49–54.

Fröhlich, Stefan (2011) 'Deutschlands Rolle in der EU und NATO beim Konfliktmanagement in Afghanistan', *Zeitschrift für Außen- und Sicherheitspolitik*, 4(1): 31–43.

Gauck, Joachim (2014) *Germany's Role in the World. Reflections on Responsibility, Norms and Alliances*. Speech Held at 50th Munich Security Conference on 31 January 2014, www.bundespraesident.de/SharedDocs/Reden/EN/JoachimGauck/Reden/2014/140131-Munich-Security-Conference.html (accessed on 28/06/2018).

Gehring, Thomas and Sebastian Oberthür (2009) 'The causal mechanisms of interaction between international institutions', *European Journal of International Relations*, 15(1): 125–156.

Germany (1998) *Gemeinsame deutsch-französische Positionen zu aktuellen Themen der Europapolitik*, Berlin: Government of the Federal Republic of Germany.

Gilli, Andrea et al. (2015) 'The Italian White Paper for international security and defence', *RUSI Journal*, 160(6): 34–41.

Glatz, Rainer L. and Martin Zapfe (2017) 'Ambitious framework nation: Germany in NATO – Bundeswehr capability planning and the "framework nation concept"', *SWP Comments*, 35: 1–8.

Goddard, Stacie E. (2009) 'Brokering change: Networks and entrepreneurs in international politics', *International Theory*, 1(2): 249–281.

Helwig, Niklas (2016) 'Introduction: Germany – rising to the challenge, while maintaining the balance'. *In*: Helwig, Niklas (ed) *Europe's New Political Engine: Germany's Role in the EU's Foreign and Security Policy*, Helsinki: FIIA Report, 15–28.

Hyde-Price, Adrian G.V. (2015) 'The "sleep-walking giant" awakes: Resetting German foreign and security policy', *European Security*, 24(4): 600–616.

Iso-Markku, Tuomas (2016) 'Germany and the EU's security and defence policy: New role, old challenges'. *In*: Helwig, Niklas (ed) *Europe's New Political Engine: Germany's Role in the EU's Foreign and Security Policy*, Helsinki: FIIA Report, 51–68.

Junk, Julian and Christopher Daase (2013) 'Germany'. *In*: Biehl, Heiko et al. (eds) *Strategic Cultures in Europe: Security and Defence Policies Across the Continent*, Wiesbaden: Springer VS, 139–152.

Kaim, Markus and Pia Niedermeier (2011) 'Das Ende the "multilateralen reflexes"? Deutsche NATO- Politik unter neuen nationalen und internationalen Rahmenbedingungen'. *In*: Jäger, Thomas et al. (eds) *Deutsche Außenpolitik*, Wiesbaden: VS Verlag für Sozialwissenschaften, Springer, 105–125.

Kempin, Ronja (2015) 'From reluctance to policy: A new German stance on the CSDP?' *In*: Fiott, Daniel (ed) *The Common Security and Defence Policy: National Perspectives*, Brussels: Egmont – Royal Institute for International Relations, 33–34.

Kinkel, Klaus (1997) *Rede von Bundesminister Dr. Kinkel, Herbsttagung der Versammlung der Westeuropäischen Union,* Speech Held on 3 December 1997 in Paris, www.bundesregierung.de/Content/DE/Bulletin/1990-1999/1997/96-97_Kinkel.html (accessed on 21/06/2018).

Magliveras, Konstantinos D. (2011) 'Membership in international organisations'. *In*: Klabbers, Jan and Asa Wallendahl (eds) *Research Handbook on the Law of International Organisations*, Cheltenham and Northampton: Edward Elgar Publishing, 84–107.

Marrone, Alessandro and Federica Di Camillo (2013): 'Italy'. *In*: Biehl, Heiko et al. (eds) *Strategic Cultures in Europe: Security and Defence Policies Across the Continent*, Wiesbaden: Springer VS, 193–206.

Mattox, Gale A. (2011) 'Germany: From civilian power to international actor'. *In*: Dorman, Andrew M. and Joyce P. Kaufman (eds) *The Future of Transatlantic Relations: Perceptions, Policy and Practice,* Stanford: Stanford University Press, 113–136.

Maull, Hanns W. (2006) 'Zivilmacht Deutschland'. *In*: Hellmann, Gunther et al. (eds) *Handwörterbuch zur deutschen Außenpolitik*, Opladen: VS Verlag, 73–84.

Meiers, Franz-Josef (2001) 'Deutschland: Der dreifache Spagat', *Sicherheit und Frieden*, 19(2): 62–68.

Mejía, Aurora (2017) 'Spain's contribution to Euro-Atlantic security', *Real Instituto Elcano ARI*, 60: 1–7.

Miskimmon, Alistair (2001) Recasting the security bargains: Germany, European security policy and the transatlantic relationship, *German Politics*, 10(1): 83–106.

Muniz, Manuel (2013) 'Spain: The Don Quixote of European defence'. *In*: Santopinto, Federico and Megan Price (eds) *National Visions of EU Defence Policy: Common Denominators and Misunderstanding*, Brussels: CEPS, GRIP and COST, 89–110.

NATO (1996) Final Communiqué of the Ministerial Meeting of the North Atlantic Council in Berlin on 3 June 1996. Press Communiqué M-NAC-1(96)63.

NATO (2014) *Wales Summit Declaration – Issued by the Heads of State and Government Participating in the Meeting of the North Atlantic Council in Wales*, 4–5 September 2014, www.nato.int/cps/ic/natohq/official_texts_112964.htm (accessed on 29/06/2018).

NATO (2020) *Defence Expenditure of NATO Countries (2013–2020)*, www.nato.int/cps/en/natohq/news_178975.htm (accessed on 15/02/2021).

Overhaus, Marco (2004) 'In search of a post-hegemonic order: Germany, NATO and the European security and defence policy', *German Politics*, 13(4): 551–568.

Pond, Elisabeth (2015) 'Germany's real role in the Ukraine crisis: Caught between East and West: Misreading Berlin', *Foreign Affairs*, 94: 2.

Rees, G. Wyn (1996) 'Constructing a European Defence Identity: The Perspective of Britain, France and Germany', *European Foreign Affairs Review*, 1(2): 231–246.

Reichard, Martin (2006) *The EU-NATO Relationship: A Legal and Political Perspective*, Abingdon: Routledge.

Robinson, Steven (2016) 'Still focused on the Atlantic: Accounting for limited Europeanisation of Portuguese foreign policy', *European Security*, 25(1): 134–158.

Rodt, Annemarie Peen (2017) 'Member states policy towards EU military operations'. *In*: Hadfield, Amelia et al. (eds) *Foreign Policies of EU Member States: Continuity and Europeanisation*, Abingdon: Routledge, 131–147.

Sabatino, Ester (2017) 'The Italian White Paper on defence: Common ground with Germany?' *FES International Policy Analysis*, November issue: 1–8.

Schumacher, Tobias et al. (2016) 'Of policy entrepreneurship, bandwagoning and free-riding: EU member states and multilateral cooperation frameworks for Europe's southern neighbourhood', *Global Affairs*, 2(3): 259–272.

Serra, Sr Don Narcis (1988) 'Spain, NATO and Western security', *Adelphi Papers*, 28(229): 3–13.

Simón, Luis (2017) 'France and Germany: The European Union's 'central' member states'. *In*: Hadfield, Amelia et al. (eds) *Foreign Policies of EU Member States: Continuity and Europeanisation*, Abingdon: Routledge, 66–82.

SIPRI (2020) *SIPRI Military Expenditure Data Base 1949–2019*. Stockholm: SIPRI.

Sperling, James (2004) 'Capabilities traps and gaps: Symptom or cause of a troubled transatlantic relationship', *Contemporary Security Policy*, 25(3): 452–478.

Tardy, Thierry (2021) 'For a new NATO-EU bargain', *Egmont Security Policy Brief*, 138: 1–5.

Tettweiler, Falk (2015) 'The CSDP from a German Vantage Point'. *In*: Fiott, Daniel (ed.) *The Common Security and Defence Policy: National Perspectives*, Brussels: Egmont – Royal Institute for International Relations, 35–36.

von der Leyen, Ursula (2014) *Speech at the 50th Munich Security Conference*. Speech held on 31 January 2014, www.securityconference.de/fileadmin/MSC_/2014/Reden/2014-01-31-Speech-MinDef_von_der_Leyen-MuSeCo.pdf (accessed on 28/07/2018).

Wagner, Wolfgang (2005) 'From vanguard to laggard: Germany in European security and defence policy', *German Politics*, 14(4): 455–469.

Wurzer, Christian (2013) 'A German vision of CSDP: "It's taking part that counts"'. *In*: Santopinto, Federico and Megan Price (eds) *National Visions of EU Defence Policy: Common Denominators and Misunderstandings*, Brussels: CEPS/GRIP/COST, 27–46.

Zimmer, Matthias (1997) 'Return of the *Mittellage*? The discourse of the centre in German Foreign Policy', *German Politics*, 6(1): 23–38.

Zyla, Benjamin (2012) 'Deutschlands Schlüsselrolle in den transatlantischen Beziehungen', *Zeitschrift für Außen- und Sicherheitspolitik*, 5(1): 117–135.

6   Neutrals

Austria, Denmark, Finland, Iceland, Malta and Sweden

Neutrals represent a particular group of member states in the EU–NATO interorganisational relationship. These states represent characteristics that in fact occasionally overlap with some commonalities and common attitudes of advocates, blockers and balancers. What makes them primarily distinctive is that they all possess single membership – while two of the states are specific within this group – and their limited resources and capabilities. What is more, neutrals' geostrategic position at the periphery of the Euro-Atlantic security space is another characteristic that disallow them from taking strong advocative or blocking positions. The label 'neutral' should, however, not be confused with militarily neutral states *per se,* although the majority of these states has either been or is still considered to be militarily neutral or non-aligned in the Euro-Atlantic security area. These states pursue specific security and defence interests and objectives in regard to EU–NATO cooperation, although these are relatively limited due to their non-alignment status. They also make selected use of specific political strategies because of their limited resources (Wivel 2005). Subsequently, Austria, Denmark, Finland, Iceland, Malta and Sweden can be labelled as neutrals in EU–NATO relations.

While neutrals generally have a positive attitude towards closer cooperation and enhanced interorganisational interactions between the EU and NATO, they demonstrate fewer clear views on the design, intensity and framework for interorganisational cooperation. With their limited resources, they do not seek to pose any obstacles but acknowledge their own restraints in taking a different position. As a consequence, they show lower levels of active promotion and lower levels of engagement in negotiations and involvement in inter-state tensions of other member states, which makes them look rather indifferent towards interorganisational cooperation. Moreover, neutrals make comparatively low levels of contributions to security organisations and their multilateral operations. This means that they do not have many capacities and resources to actively promote interorganisational cooperation and therefore stand on the sidelines. Key factors for neutrals are also the role of domestic politics, public opinion and the countries' general attitudes in terms of their foreign and security policy orientation as well as cooperation in security and defence. Based on these characteristics and attitudes, some states in the group

DOI: 10.4324/9781003170068-6

of neutrals can also be labelled as boundary cases since they neither actively obstruct or advocate closer EU–NATO cooperation, nor do they take a strong position or engage proactively to enhance this relationship.

Before analysing the characteristics, attitudes and contributions by Austria, Denmark, Finland, Iceland, Malta and Sweden, a remark needs to be made. The existing scholarly literature takes a narrow approach to the military non-alignment and neutrality status of these states in international security organisations. While some countries receive greater attention, primarily Finland, Sweden and Denmark, others have often been neglected or not been moved into the spotlight of academic analyses, which includes specifically Iceland and Malta. The literature nevertheless provides valuable insights that help to further examine the role of these states in the EU–NATO relationship. The following analysis therefore illustrates the role of neutrals and, more specifically, how they have engaged and contributed to the evolution of EU–NATO cooperation. This chapter outlines and describes the shared characteristics that provide the basis of the subsequent examination of neutrals' use and perception of membership as well as their contributions to the military capabilities and operations, interoperability and division of labour between the two organisations.

Shared characteristics of neutrals

The commonalities of neutrals in regard to their membership status, available resources, attitudes and foreign and security policy orientation help to understand their behaviour and engagement in the EU–NATO relationship (see Table 6.1). While these characteristic traits are shared within the group of neutrals, these states also demonstrate some overlaps with advocates, blockers and balancers. The commonality of certain characteristics has emerged from similar historical experiences, political viewpoints and domestic attitudes, such as the general preference for civilian and non-violent means of conflict management and the use of small state strategy. Each state adds individual features, and the extent to which they fulfil the shared characteristics varies according to the issue area.

One key distinctive feature is the single membership status, that is, they are member of either the EU or NATO. In this context, both Malta and Denmark represent special cases, which will be further explored in the following subsections. All of the non-NATO EU member states participate in the PfP programme, which allows them to become involved in collective security activities and NATO-led military operations. Similarly, all of the non-EU NATO members have an FPA facilitating the involvement and contribution to EU civilian and military crisis management operations (NATO 2016; Tardy 2014). Single membership means that their ability to influence decisions and policies and to shape interorganisational interaction is limited because they do not have voice opportunities and thus no decision-making power in those organisations of which they are not a full member (Gehring and Faude 2014).

Table 6.1 Overview of neutrals' characteristics

Shared characteristics	Neutrals and their membership	Contributions to capabilities	View on division of labour and interoperability
• Generally positive towards EU–NATO cooperation • Small or even microstates • Military neutrality or non-alignment or non-allied since the end of the Second World War • Labelled as 'post-neutrals' due to increased engagement	• Single members with partnership agreements • Maintenance of bilateral and minilateral security and defence cooperation including security guarantees outside the EU or NATO • Limited trigger for trouble	• Low level of military budgets and scarce resources • Low contributions to military operations • Participation in EU and NATO rapid response forces (EUBGs and NRF)	• Preference for complementarity • Favour close coordination and exchanges in operations • Favour division of labour to avoid exclusion • See high level of interoperability as vital for their own security and defence

In regard to the timing of accession, the group of neutrals encompasses both original members, such as Iceland and Demark as the founders of NATO, and subsequent members, that is, all the other states whereby Malta was the last one to gain membership.

What combines the states in the group of neutrals is their status as small or even microstates. Whereas Austria, Denmark, Finland and Sweden are regarded as small states, Iceland and Malta are considered to be microstates due to their size in population, economic strength and military power (Dobrescu et al. 2017; Setälä 2005; Wivel 2005). Moreover, with the exception of Austria, all of the neutrals are located on the geographical periphery of the Euro-Atlantic security space. The four Nordics in this group – Denmark, Finland, Iceland and Sweden – make up the northern borders as well as the North-Eastern border in the case of Finland. Common security challenges and interests by the Nordics can be grouped into three categories: (1) maritime security, environment, climate change and natural disasters; (2) cyber security, disinformation and functioning (digital) infrastructures and (3) psychological defence and human security broadly referring to the protection of fundamental rights and freedoms, such as freedom of expression, and the rule of law. They all furthermore express their concerns about the events in Eastern Europe, particularly in Ukraine, and Russia's assertive foreign policy in recent years (Finland 2016; Denmark 2018; Iceland 2015; Sweden 2017). Malta's security interests and threat perceptions, in contrast, are defined by its location in the Mediterranean Sea and it is thus primarily concerned with maritime security as well as terrorism and illegal migration, as it presents the South-Eastern border in Europe (Malta 2017).

In addition to the geographical periphery, neutrals also present the political periphery in both the EU and NATO. They show variance concerning their ability to influence political decisions and shape policies in security and defence. While Denmark has often demonstrated that it seeks closer ties with some of the powerful allies in NATO, especially the UK and the US, in order to play a more active role as a small member state which pictures it as less neutral concerning interorganisational relations, other states among the neutrals often remain on the sidelines. As small and peripheral states, they face specific challenges and differ in their threat perceptions, which diverge from those of middle-sized and larger member states. In regard to their politically peripheral location, which is linked to their status as small states, none of the neutrals has much policy-shaping power and leverage in either the PSC or the NAC. Their low level of resources and military power, or even the non-existence of permanent armed forces in the case of Iceland, impedes neutrals in exerting influence on the policies, proposals and interests, which compete with those of bigger and more powerful members (Cottey 2013; Molis 2006; Setälä 2005; Wivel 2005). Consequently, they find it difficult to shape the policy orientation and external relations of the EU and NATO including their interorganisational relationship.

The historical record of neutrality and military non-alignment, especially during the Second World War and the Cold War, is a key element that delimits neutrals from other member states. This status has been understood and used by neutrals in different ways. For example, Denmark chose neutrality in the beginning of the Second World War due to its geographical location neighbouring Nazi Germany, which later occupied Denmark, and the country's links to the UK. Similarly, Iceland's status as a sovereign kingdom was affected when it entered a personal union with Denmark in the first half of the twentieth century (Petersen 1990). Both Finland and Sweden call themselves 'military non-aligned', while Austria is characterised as 'non-allied', which primarily refers to the alignment with military alliances including NATO (cf. Kammel 2013; Ruffa 2013; Seppo and Forsberg 2013). For some of these states, neutrality is thus deeply rooted in their national approaches to security and defence as well as enshrined in their constitutions. For instance, according to Austria's agreement with the former Soviet Union from 1955, it has committed itself to a policy of neutrality and therefore would not join a military alliance. Similarly, Finland and Sweden keep the option open to join NATO but both agree to make a decision based on the public opinion and the developments of the international security environment (Ilves 2018; Möttölä 2001; Nilsson and Larsbrink 2013; Österreichisches Bundeskanzleramt 1955; Salonius-Pasternak 2018).

With these states' membership in either the EU or NATO, traditional militarily neutral countries have taken positions on the politico-military spectrum and adapted their approach to neutrality and non-alignment.

Accession sparked domestic debates about the continuation and validity of their military neutrality and special status, which has been particularly recorded in Austria, Finland and Iceland (Bailes and Rafnsson 2012; Gärtner 2018; Müller and Maurer 2016). Their position as either militarily neutral, non-aligned or non-allied states has also influenced their categorisation as neutrals in the EU–NATO relationship since they have not positioned themselves in the advocacy camp but have also not actively vetoed any efforts to deepen this relationship. This approach can be translated from their general hesitance towards the use of force as well as their preference for non-violent peacekeeping and civilian crisis management. It is important to note that these member states are not labelled as neutrals because of their general viewpoint on security and defence and their alignment status. Instead, they possess a particular attitude towards EU–NATO relationship in security and defence. Since their accessions to either the EU or NATO, or both organisations in the case of Denmark and Malta, they have been increasingly engaged in the organisations' security and defence policies as well as in the operational activities including crisis management and peacekeeping. As a consequence, Gebhard (2013: 280), Manners and Whitman (2001), Möttölä (2001), Forsberg and Vaahtoranta (2001) and Vaahtoranta and Forsberg (2000) have called them 'post-neutrals' to demonstrate their move away from full military neutrality. A shift towards greater engagement internationally with adapted versions of neutrality has been recorded, such as Austria's 'engaged neutrality' and neutrals' increasing interactions with NATO on the basis of cooperative security and crisis management (Gärtner 2018; Petersson 2018).

One aspect that needs to receive special attention when dealing with neutrals of interorganisational cooperation is the issue of shifting types. Member states in this group have a higher tendency of shifting and embodying boundary cases. For example, one could expect other member states, such as Albania, Croatia, Ireland and Norway, to be categorised in this group because they share some of the characteristics defining states in the group of neutrals, for example, small states with limited military capabilities and resources, less proactive towards promoting closer EU–NATO cooperation and lower levels of active engagement in negotiations. Yet, as it has been indicated by representatives from NATO and some member states, countries like Albania, Croatia and also Norway often attach themselves to one of the advocates – mainly the UK and the US – to support their perspective and engagements in interorganisational cooperation in order to avoid marginalisation, which has not been seen by states in the group of neutrals with the exception of Denmark (Cypriote Officials 2; Italian Official 1; NATO Official 5).

Single membership status and foreign and security policy orientation

There are two key factors shaping neutrals' roles in both international organisations and in interorganisational cooperation: single membership and the status as small states or microstates. With these two features, neutrals are closely attached to multilateralism, and acting through intergovernmental platforms especially in foreign, security and defence affairs is a priority. According to the national security and defence strategies of Iceland and Sweden, for example, these states take a rules-based and comprehensive approach to security and defence and seek to take action primarily through multilateral organisations (Iceland 2015, n.a.; Sweden 2017). Both membership and participation in multilateral organisations such as the EU and NATO thus provide a greater voice for neutral states. Within multilateral organisations, they are able to forge small coalition groups and establish minilateral partnerships with those that share common security threats to upload their interests to the international level. One prime example among neutrals is NORDEFCO which combines the Nordic countries as well as the Baltics on specific occasions. Both the EU and NATO further help to overcome weaknesses and vulnerabilities for small and microstates (Molis 2006; Wivel 2005). This preference for multilateralism can be translated into the preference for institutionalising interorganisational cooperation, which represents a specific form of multilateralism, or even *maxilateralism*.

These states also acknowledge their lack of decision-making power due to their single membership. Formalising EU–NATO cooperation would help to overcome their lack of multiple membership and thus allows them to compensate for their low level of influence (Austria 2010; Finland 2012). Consequently, due to their vulnerabilities and weaknesses emerging from their small state status and their outspoken preference for multilateral action, neutrals prefer and even rely on deepened and formalised interorganisational relations and try to avoid any inequality and marginalisation vis-à-vis multiple member states (Bergquist et al. 2016). However, due to their limited capabilities and resources, they perceive themselves as unable to provide significant contributions to this debate. This has been illustrated by the lack of ideas and direct incentives which help to improve not only the relationship as a whole, but which also provide little to facilitate the formalisation process. Neutrals generally have low profiles in security and defence as well as within international organisations, which has further led to low levels of political courage and little appetite for becoming engaged in shaping interorganisational cooperation.

Each state in the group of neutrals brings forward a certain approach to EU–NATO cooperation as well as an individual foreign and security policy orientation, which includes caveats concerning their memberships. The examination of the motivations and embeddedness of neutrals in bilateral and minilateral cooperation frameworks inside and outside the EU–NATO relationship is an essential aspect that shapes their positions. While states in other types of member states in interorganisational relations often resort to political strategies such as forum-shopping, brokering and hostage-taking (cf. Alter and Meunier 2009; Gehring and Faude 2014; Hofmann 2009), neutrals have limited incentive to do so and therefore prefer to remain less active.

Among neutrals, two states particularly stand out, Denmark and Malta, which will receive greater attention in this analysis.

Finland, Sweden and Iceland

Generally, the Nordic states often consult on foreign, security and defence issues and seek to express a common voice. Concerning the EU–NATO relationship, Finland and Sweden have aligned their policies, with Iceland occasionally joining in, while some differences have still been recorded. In comparison to other neutral and non-aligned states, Finland and Sweden, alongside Denmark, demonstrate cases of less pacifist countries among the neutrals. They maintain conscription, are highly committed to peace operations under the condition of a UN mandate and territorial defence continue to play a vital part of their nationhood that also shape their attitude towards security and defence (Finland 2016; Forsberg 2018; Ruffa 2013; Seppo and Forsberg 2013; Sweden 2017). Finland's non-alignment is rooted in its historical experience with the former Soviet Union, which disallowed it to join the Alliance but did not prevent its accession to the EU in 1995. Although this position does not directly cause any problems for EU–NATO cooperation on the institutional or operational levels, Finland does not seek to make major contributions to closer cooperation (cf. Ojanen 2007, 2008). Sweden, in contrast, sometimes takes an engaging approach by seeking closer cooperation and increasing engagement with NATO. Both Finland and Sweden nevertheless express their commitment to activities in tandem concerning the Alliance due to the high level of alignment of their security interests and positions (Chivvis 2017; Dahl and Järvenpää 2013).

Iceland represents an outlier in the group of neutrals in the EU–NATO interorganisational relationship as well as in comparison to the other Nordics. It epitomises the only state which does not possess standing armed forces and which remains outside armaments collaborations and cooperation efforts. Even though it gained observer status in the WEU, it decided to remain outside the Western European Armaments Group (WEAG) and continued to do so with the WEU's integration into the EU and the establishment of the EDA. This gives Iceland a special status as well as marginal leverage in negotiations and decision-making due to its little resources and thus its negligible contributions and over-reliance on NATO as well as on close partners such as the US (Bailes and Thorhallsson 2006). Moreover, although Iceland signed the FPA with the EU to allow participation in CSDP operations, it indicated that it would seek to negotiate a defence opt-out similar to that of Denmark in case of a possible accession to the EU (Bailes and Rafnsson 2012). This shows that Iceland keeps some general scepticism as well as constraints towards CSDP and the EU's military dimension. But in order not to pose any obstacles, it has tendencies of non-interference and would not veto any advancements and closer cooperation efforts between the EU and NATO.

In regard to formalising EU–NATO cooperation, neutrals such as Sweden and Finland have introduced a limited number of initiatives and ideas to enhance the formalisation process and improve this relationship. Some of these initiatives are of value and relevant for both organisations as well as their relationship because they seek to increase cooperation among their member states. For example, during its EU Presidency, Sweden, was involved in the exchange of letters with then NATO Secretary General George Robertson in 2001. This was directed at formulating provisions for the framework of EU–NATO meetings, which later provided the foundation for the future formalisation of their cooperation (Reichard 2006). In addition, Finland initiated the Northern Dimension in 1999, which is a non-security and non-defence related instrument of cooperation between the EU, Iceland, Norway and Russia. Although it primarily addresses issues such as transportation, health and environment, it also strengthens practical cooperation and exchanges between the EU, its member states and third states, such as Iceland and Norway, which are both members of NATO. In fact, the initiative has also indirectly enhanced the level of trust among these actors and the ability of both Finland and Sweden – the latter joined and strongly supported Finland in this endeavour – to exert some influence in the area of the EU's foreign, security and defence policy (Arter 2000; Haukkala 2003). The Northern Dimension initiative can be seen as a way to indirectly support EU–NATO relations as it fosters cooperation among single and multiple member states, and it also indirectly helped to formalise minilateral partnerships. Although the initiative is targeted at areas outside security and defence, it nevertheless contributes to strengthening cooperation and exchanges, which are beneficial for translating these efforts into enhancing the EU–NATO relationship.

Despite their geographical seclusion from the core of the Euro-Atlantic security community, Finland, Sweden and Iceland engage in bilateral and multilateral frameworks. While both Finland and Sweden rely on their EU membership and initiatives taking place therein, Iceland values its anchor in NATO. As a consequence, Iceland names the US as its main security ally and Finland and Sweden primarily see each other as key security partners (Finland 2016; Iceland n.a.; Sweden 2017). All three member states participate together in minilateral frameworks and especially through NORDEFCO as one of the most well-known minilateral cooperation frameworks within the Euro-Atlantic space. It represents a central part of the overall cooperative endeavours of the Nordic states – Denmark, Finland, Iceland, Norway and Sweden. Closer Nordic cooperation has already been recorded since the end of the Second World War and even aimed at a common Nordic identity based on these countries' attachment to 'Nordicness', albeit to varying degrees (cf. Brommesson 2018; Ojanen and Raunio 2018; Thorhallsson 2018). NORDEFCO was created in 2009 as a merger of previous frameworks and defence structures[1] and seeks to strengthen the defence cooperation among the participating states. It further provides incentives for synergies and armaments collaboration to thwart shortcomings, lacking resources and decreasing budgets. With the strengthening of cooperation through the EU and NATO, NORDEFCO received little attention due to the differing memberships of the Nordic states. Moreover, both Denmark and Iceland have frequently been regarded as outliers because of their peculiarities, that is, Denmark's CSDP opt-out and Iceland's non-existing armed forces (Forsberg 2013; von Voss, Major and Mölling 2013). Yet, regional and minilateral defence cooperation through NORDEFCO, particularly in addition to other cooperation frameworks such as the Nordic Council, 'has been progressively seen as an asset to the enlarged EU and NATO' (Jokela and Iso-Markku 2013: 2). This is because the influence of the Nordic states through either organisation is limited, and for some states such as Sweden, it sometimes even represents the preference over either the EU or NATO. Renewed and enhanced cooperation has been recorded again since the 2010s with the Swedish idea of a Nordic Defence Pact as well as with the signing of the Nordic Declaration on Solidarity in 2011, which is rooted in the new common security concerns in Northern and Eastern Europe.

NORDEFCO highlights an exemplary case of minilateral cooperation which contributes to the EU–NATO relationship, particularly because it consists of single and multiple member states as well as of both militarily neutral and militarily aligned states. The framework helps to formulate collective security and defence interests and preferences and enables closer cooperation among individual states. It furthermore contributes to enhancing collaboration in capabilities and achieving complementarity between the EU and NATO. For example, members in NORDEFCO form the Nordic EU Battlegroup and undertake joint exercises and industrial collaboration to pool and share relevant military capabilities, which has led to a positive impact on joint acquisition and procurement for both organisations.

Denmark

Denmark possesses a special status among the neutrals of the EU–NATO interorganisational relationship, which makes it an outlier among the neutrals of interorganisational interaction. Even though it is considered to be a single member state, Denmark is in fact a multiple member, though not in regard to the military dimension of CSDP. It is among the founding members of NATO and joined the EU in 1973 alongside its close ally, the UK. From the early stages of negotiations on the development of a European defence capacity, Denmark resided with the UK's sceptical view. Domestically, there have also been divisions over Denmark's membership in the European Community, and when the topic of developing CFSP and CSDP emerged, it expressed its deep concerns over the risk of duplicating NATO's efforts (Petersen 1990). Danish scepticism and reluctance towards CFSP and CSDP do therefore not come as a big surprise. However, due to its specific position as *de facto* multiple member, but a single member in security and defence affairs as well as its diverging attitude towards the use of force compared to neutrals, Denmark can also be considered a 'swing state' (Rodt 2017) or boundary case concerning EU–NATO cooperation. What is more, Denmark is one of the exceptional cases among neutrals that has applied political strategies. When EU member states initiated the idea of a European defence capacity, Denmark was not the only country faced with the option to support it while being a member of NATO. It nevertheless chose the turf battle approach by opting out of defence affairs and thereby opted for one organisation at the potential expenses of the other (cf. Hofmann 2009).

In 1991, Denmark held a referendum on its accession to the EU. The majority initially vetoed the accession and specifically the provisions of the Maastricht Treaty. As a result, negotiations between Denmark and the EU yielded in four opt-outs of which one was especially devoted to the EU's aim of developing its own defence policy and capability. Neutrality had already lost its significance with gaining NATO membership, although the country is nevertheless highly committed to international cooperation and multilateralism. But both the public and the political elite perceived that European security would be best achieved through NATO (Wivel 2014). These opt-outs entered into force through the Edinburgh Agreement. Accordingly, Denmark does not participate in or contribute to the planning and conduct of any EU-led military operations. It would also refrain from participating in the development or acquisition of joint EU military capabilities and therefore did not join the EDA or PESCO. In return, it would also not block or prevent any efforts for closer cooperation among other EU member states (Olsen 2007; Olsen and Pilegaard 2005; Rynning 2013).

The defence opt-out has been interpreted differently by the Danish governments succeeding the Edinburgh Agreement. Since the provisions of the agreement are broad and do not mention any precise restrictions, the scope of participation has been widened over time and Denmark has shifted from the traditional 'adaptive foreign policy' to a more proactive stance in European foreign and security policy (Haukkala et al. 2017: 26; Pedersen 2006). From 1992 to 2007, it has applied the defence opt-out nine times, which were primarily addressed at the soft end of the Petersberg Tasks as well as in the run-up of the Council meetings in both Helsinki in 1999 and Lisbon in 2000, which were significant for further developing CSDP (Olsen 2007; Olsen and Pilegaard 2005). The opt-out was primarily regarded as symbolic until 2003 because of the lacking content and capabilities of CSDP. However, with closer cooperation among EU member states and the strengthening of both CFSP and CSDP, Denmark has realised the shortcoming of exclusion. Attempts by Danish prime ministers, such as Anders Fogh Rasmussen and Lars Løkke Rasmussen, have been made to carry out a new referendum with the aim to abolish the defence opt-out and fully integrating Denmark into CSDP, which failed, however (Miles 2014). The opt-out has been perceived as a barrier especially for Danish foreign, security and defence policy and its own international activism (Herolf 2006; Rynning and Rahbek-Clemmensen 2015). According to its national security doctrines, Denmark strives to increase its active engagement and international involvement to achieve peace and security as well as to maintain a high level of interoperability with its European and transatlantic partners (Denmark 2017, 2018). Only with an active role in CSDP and EU-led operations, it would be able to increase its influence and raise its voice internationally. Interestingly, the defence opt-out is not seen as a barrier or obstacle to EU–NATO cooperation since it has been a deliberate choice by the Danish public which could be reversed (EU Official 2).

Both the political elite and the public view Denmark's memberships in the EU and NATO differently and with diverging intentions, which has impacted its policies towards the two organisations and their cooperation. According to the 2000 Eurobarometer Public Opinion Survey on European Defence, Denmark was the only country in which NATO is the first choice with 40% over the EU with 27% (European Commission 2000). In this context, Danish EU membership is set in contrast to its NATO membership and its general foreign, security and defence policy. Accordingly, 'Denmark's approach to the EU's security and defence policy remained one of foot-dragging' (Wivel 2014: 80). Its lack of participation in CSDP paired with its general Euroscepticism has led to lugging activism, although its involvement in NATO has experienced some noteworthy developments. During the Cold War, Denmark has been labelled as a 'repressed' Atlanticist and characterised as a reluctant ally that fell short of incentives and activism (Wivel 2014: 80). With an increase in its level of ambition and changing role in NATO over time, Denmark's position shifted from a 'mainstream' Atlanticist to a 'super Atlanticist' and 'impeccable ally' (Ringsmose and Rynning 2008; Wivel 2014: 80–81). But its new activism and Atlanticist orientation have not been translated into involvement in the EU–NATO relationship and on the contrary, it has remained largely on the sidelines.

Because of its *de facto* multiple membership and its strong attachment to transatlantic security, Denmark can be considered a boundary case. It generally expresses a preference for interorganisational cooperation and stronger ties between the EU and NATO, which are seen as important and essential for its national security. Furthermore, Denmark seeks to preserve US presence in Europe and European security through NATO, while it aims to contribute to the EU's preventive action and civilian efforts to crisis management at the same time (Denmark 2018). The opt-outs from CSDP as well as from cooperation on defence industrial projects and armaments development have therefore posed challenges for Denmark in regard to the EU–NATO relationship. For example, when the EU took over the military command and deployed troops to Bosnia and Herzegovina under Operation Althea, Denmark had to withdraw its troops which were previously under NATO command (Olsen and Pilegaard 2005). While the Danish armed forces were integrated into the already existing command structures on the ground and the troops from its European partners and allies stayed in theatre, Denmark was the only country that was technically forced to withdraw its troops due to the defence opt-out and missing arrangements with the EU. This created a gap in the operation because of the omission of troops and resources. Moreover, the Danish representative is not able to participate in any EU decision-making on defence matters, which prevents access to relevant information. Although Denmark is a general supporter of closer EU–NATO cooperation particularly in terms of dividing tasks and reducing extra costs for individual member states, the defence opt-out excludes Denmark from active participation and contribution to this interorganisational relationship (Larsen 2008; Olsen 2007). As an alternative, Denmark has increased its engagement in bilateral and minilateral cooperation. It occasionally participates in *ad hoc* coalition groups, such as with the US and the UK as its closest allies as well as with Germany. NORDEFCO also plays an increasingly important role which allows to foster cooperation with regional partners that are both members of NATO and the EU, which would be an indirect way to shape the EU's security and defence policy.

Austria and Malta

Two states that keep low profiles in security and defence issues including the EU–NATO relationship are Austria and Malta. Although they are generally in favour of formalising and deepening interorganisational relations, their actual contributions are kept to the minimum. This means that they participate in negotiations and the decision-making processes on establishing and strengthening partnerships with other international actors. However, no notable efforts or involvements have been recorded and their lack of engagement has been rather perceived as having 'no political courage' (NATO Official 5). Moreover, both Austria and Malta prefer not to become more involved than necessary in the external relations of international organisations (Gebhard 2013; Pace 2013). This suggests that they seek to remain on the sidelines and prefer to observe instead of getting involved in shaping EU–NATO cooperation.

With regard to security and defence affairs and the EU–NATO relationship, Malta presents an interesting case among member states. While it joined the EU in 2004, its relations with NATO have been troubled with ups and downs ranging from participation to withdrawing and re-joining the PfP programme. This made the island state a less reliable partner as well as a possible blocker similar to Cyprus. Initially, Malta joined NATO's PfP programme in 1995 but withdrew shortly afterwards in 1996 while it concurrently froze the membership negotiations with the EU under its labour government (Pace 2013). Malta then re-accessed the PfP programme in 2008 after it had already gained full EU membership in 2004 in which it did not negotiate any opt-outs from CFSP or CSDP despite its constitutional neutrality. Furthermore, since joining both the EU and PfP it even attempted to deepen defence cooperation. It subsequently acknowledged that cooperation either with NATO or between the EU and NATO would not clash with its own neutrality (Fiott 2015; Times of Malta 2017). Nevertheless, Malta does not participate in minilateral defence cooperation groups and has opted for non-participation in PESCO, like Denmark.

Yet, single membership means limited capacities to influence the overall decision-making because lobbying for one's own preferences becomes restricted. With the help of bilateral relations in the respective other organisation, such as NATO's PfP programme and the EU's FPAs, this dilemma is sought to be overcome. However, although Malta represents a positive example in which a neutral state does not prevent or obstruct any further efforts towards enhanced EU–NATO cooperation due to its specific national position, it has also not made any contributions to enhancing their relations. In addition, during the time in which it possessed EU membership without any cooperation agreement with NATO, it had in fact been perceived as an obstacle similar to Cyprus because of the wider implications for cooperation under the Berlin Plus arrangements (Pace 2013).

In contrast to Malta, Austria maintains a less troubled relationship with NATO and finds itself in the geographical centre of Europe. Its own non-alignment is rooted in the country's historical experience with the former Soviet Union. After the Second World War, it regained its sovereignty but was restricted by the Allied Powers in regard to its foreign, security and defence policy, which led to the signing of the Declaration of Neutrality in 1955 by the Austrian Parliament that declared the country as a permanently neutral state (Österreichisches Bundeskanzleramt 1955). As a consequence, neutrality disallows Austria to join NATO, but it did not prevent its accession to the EU in 1995. Ever since, this neutrality and non-alignment status have been deeply embedded in Austria's foreign and security policy orientation. It therefore realises its foreign and security policy primarily through the EU, alongside its memberships in the UN and OSCE, but also appreciates its cooperation with NATO and its participation in the PfP programme. Austria also acknowledges the importance of the EU's external partnerships and even expects a future enhancement of EU–NATO cooperation, which it will support as a member in the Euro-Atlantic security community (Austria 2013). Moreover, although its neutrality position does not directly cause any problems for EU–NATO cooperation on the institutional or operational levels and although it generally supports the relationship, Austria does not make major contributions to strengthening this interorganisational relationship (Kammel 2013; Müller and Maurer 2016).

Austria nevertheless brings forward ideas that can be indirectly beneficial for EU–NATO cooperation, such as the creation of the Salzburg Forum in 2003. This is composed of Austria and several Central and Eastern European states including Bulgaria, Croatia, the Czech Republic, Hungary, Poland, Romania, Slovakia and Slovenia. The Salzburg Forum is a minilateral security partnership that enhances exchange, cooperation and trust among its participants. While its main focus is on internal and European-level security, it helps to formulate common interests and preferences, which can be translated to the international as well as to the interorganisational levels (Gebhard 2013; Müller and Maurer 2016). Similar to the Northern Dimension Initiative by Finland, Austria's Salzburg Forum helps to strengthen cooperation among single and multiple member states, particularly between Austria and the Central and Eastern European states with similar threat perceptions and security interests. It indirectly serves to foster EU–NATO cooperation on a member state level and furthermore demonstrates that states in the group of neutrals can make contributions to interorganisational cooperation, although indirectly and unintentionally.

Contributions to military capabilities, operations and division of labour

As single members, neutrals are not affected by the double obligations set by NATO's DCI and the EU's HG, and therefore have a lower risk of duplication. Contributions and military expenditures are voluntary and made by member states on the basis of their political willingness and ability to develop and acquire new weaponry and defence systems (cf. Eilstrup-Sangiovanni 2014; Fiott 2017; Sperling 2004). Meeting one of these capability targets and obligations is nevertheless difficult and even controversial in those states with military neutrality. As small states with historical records of or continued status as militarily neutral and non-aligned states, neutrals are highly aware of their limited resources and less advanced military capabilities. Multilateral frameworks help them to collaborate with bigger and more powerful states to benefit from the assets and capabilities and to reduce their own vulnerability (Molis 2006; Wivel 2005). There are some variances regarding the level of resources and military capabilities among the neutrals in interorganisational relations, however. For example, Denmark has a long track record in military engagement since it is not considered a militarily neutral state, and it pursues a more active foreign and security policy. Its Atlanticist orientation and bilateral ties with the US facilitate the advancement of its military capabilities and drives Denmark to make greater defence investments (Denmark 2018). Similarly, although Sweden seeks to take a leading role in the EU Battlegroups by heading the Nordic Battlegroup and also increases its investments in security and defence, it is conscious about its own constraints and limited resources (Haukkala et al. 2017).

The military expenditures of neutrals do not meet – and are not even close to – NATO's 2% defence pledge (see Figure 6.1). In 2017, Finland was the country with the highest military budget among the neutrals, whereas Iceland takes an exceptional position because it does not possess a standing army and therefore does not record any military expenditure. The defence budgets of neutrals overall vary between 0.6% of GDP in the case of Malta and 1.5% of GDP for Finland (Eurostat 2018; NATO 2020; SIPRI 2020). This locates these countries at the lower end of both EU and NATO member states' military budgets, symbolises their general vulnerability and gives them little leverage in

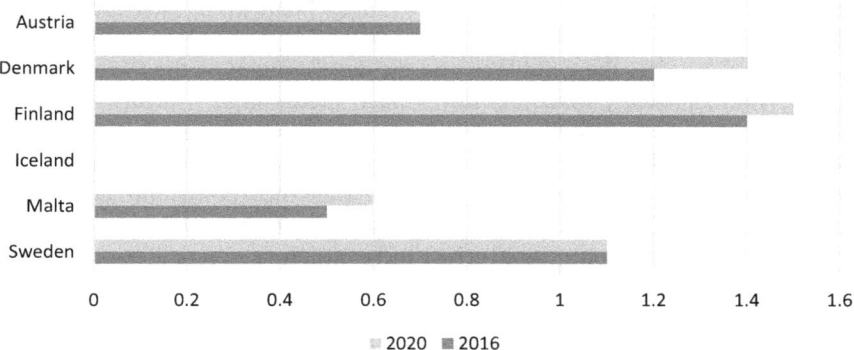

Figure 6.1 Defence expenditure as a share of GDP, 2016 and 2020.

negotiations. With regard to contemporary developments in international and European security, it is interesting to note that especially Northern European – in addition to Eastern European – countries have increased their military budgets. The ongoing crisis in Ukraine and the conflict in the Donbas region as well as Russia's renewed assertive foreign policy behaviour have been named as the main reasons for the rise of their defence expenditures (Jedlaucnik 2015; O'Dwyer 2020). In addition, the distribution of their military expenditures is still highly concentrated on costs for personnel. For example, while Finland follows the rule of thumb of thirds, that is, one third is devoted to each personnel, supplies and procurement, Denmark allocates almost half of its defence budget to personnel costs (45.39%), while barely meeting NATO's target of 20% with 22.35% in 2020 (NATO 2020; Seppo and Forsberg 2013). Despite the military neutrality and non-alignment of the majority of states in the group of neutrals, their defence budgets and distribution of military expenditures are nevertheless guided by either NATO or the EU's principles and targets. Their attempt to meet these targets is reasoned by their European and international solidarity as well as their commitment to shared principles.

Neutrals have often been denounced as 'free-riders' because of their low military expenditures and lack of political willingness to increase their defence capabilities in comparison to other European partners and allies (NATO Official 5). In the debates on burden-sharing in NATO, for example, member states' military budget is the main metric to measure their contributions to the military capabilities debate and part of burden-sharing within the Alliance. Quite frequently, however, the contributions and capabilities in actual terms, such as their indirect contributions in the form of training facilities and joined exercises as well as efforts in crisis management and peace operations including civilian capabilities and humanitarian aid, are often overlooked (cf. Mattelaer 2016). In addition, neutrals have expressed lower levels of political willingness to advance their existing military capabilities and to acquire new ones, which is based on their foreign and security policy orientation and their overall reluctance towards the use of force. Neutrals as small states and microstates still possess some vital resources and important assets. With the transformations after the Cold War and the development of the EU's foreign, security and defence capacities, states have increasingly transformed and specialised their armed forces and defence structures. Some of the neutrals therefore seek to fill niche capabilities and specialised roles. While they might be single member states and it might seem that they contribute only one-sidedly to EU–NATO cooperation, their niche capabilities and assets are key to joint responses to international crises and to enhance practical cooperation.

Malta, for example, has little resources but nevertheless vital ones to offer for both the EU and in circumstances also for NATO. Although its overall defence budget only amounts to 0.6% of its GDP, Malta maintains a key geostrategic position in the Mediterranean Sea with close proximity to North Africa. As Fiott (2015: 94) notes, 'its neutrality and geography appear to move in different directions', but both formulate its foreign and security policy orientation and define its assets especially for crisis management situations. For instance, in spite of its general reluctance to make use of force, it offers a specialisation in nautical and maritime security. Because it was impacted strongly by the Libyan conflict, it responded by contributing financially as well as making use of its special crisis operations command centre and maritime security expertise to allow NATO to conduct Operation Unified Protector and the EU to exercise its border assistance mission EUBAM Libya (Fiott 2015; Pace 2013; Vella 2015). However, while it has contributed to the EU's naval operations with its key assets including maritime command centre and maritime security capabilities, it pulled out of Operation MED Irini in May 2020. It even threatened to veto further operational activities in the area as it is concerned and, above all, feeling left alone to deal with the migration flows crossing the Mediterranean Sea (Scicluna and Emmott 2020). This indicates not only Malta's general willingness to be active and its possession of resources crucial for both the EU and NATO, though to a limited extent, but also that it can in fact utilise these capabilities for leverage and to exert influence.

Over time, most of neutrals' armed forces have specialised primarily in the civilian dimension of CSDP and focused on contributing to the comprehensive approach conducted by both the EU and NATO, combining civilian and military instruments for crisis management. This is above all the preference and focus by militarily neutral, post-neutral or non-aligned states, including Austria, Finland, Iceland, Malta and Sweden (Finland 2012; Iceland n.a.; Malta 2017; Sweden 2017). Austria additionally strives to focus on prevention and specifically on creating a comprehensive security precaution (*umfassende Sicherheitsvorsorge*) (Austria 2010; Kammel 2013). Denmark, in contrast, has specialised in anti-terror capabilities which has been emphasised in the aftermath of the 9/11 attacks as well as its participation in ISAF in Afghanistan and the US-led coalition of the willing in Iraq (Denmark 2016; Rynning 2013).

Finland and Sweden are prime examples that demonstrate their specialisation in civil–military approaches to international crises. For the deployment of troops to crisis situations, both countries first require the legitimacy through a mandate by the UNSC and then discuss civilian solutions and options before taking the decision to deploy troops to either EU-led or NATO-led military operations. Deriving from their historical experiences and neutrality status, they pursue a traditional view on defence and see self-defence as more vital for their own national security than for the solidarity and defence of other states (Dahl and Järvenpää 2013; Ruffa 2013; Seppo and Forsberg 2013). Foremost, Sweden might possess a 'solid military capacity' (Tiilikainen 2006: 54) but sees itself primarily as the guard of norms, values and international law. Within the EU and through the PfP programme, Finland and Sweden make major contributions to the development of civilian instruments and mechanisms. For instance, Finland introduced the idea of the Northern Dimension which was launched in collaboration with Sweden in 2000. The two countries jointly introduced initiatives to strengthen the EU's civilian capabilities and promoted the idea to include the Petersberg Tasks concerning international crisis management in the Amsterdam Treaty (Forsberg and Vaahtoranta 2001; Möttölä 2001). Sweden, however, has often demonstrated its increasing specialisation in aircraft capabilities, which it contributed also to NATO operations. As a consequence, Sweden has even been labelled as a NATO member (Dahl and Järvenpää 2013). This shows that, while neutrals might have smaller defence budgets and lower levels of willingness to use force, they hold other key assets and capabilities, which are required for the conduct of crisis management operations. Because of their preference for multilateral action and despite the single membership status of these states, both the EU and NATO are able to draw on these assets and niche capabilities.

In order to further advance their capabilities and resources, the Nordic countries have collaborated in the development and procurement of military capabilities, especially through the NORDEFCO framework. They have even created formal structures, such as the establishment of NORDAC, to facilitate the collaboration on joint projects. Within these formal structures, they primarily cooperate on logistical coordination for crisis management operations through the Nordic Logistic Concept and in the field of air transport through the Nordica Tactical Air Transport (NORTART). The Nordic states additionally aim to set up joint command and control systems to pool and share their expertise, capabilities and resources to overcome shortages. Yet, the cooperation and coordination among the Nordic countries on capabilities development and acquisition has also proven to be difficult. The projects on the Standard Helicopter Programme and the Viking submarine are the most illustrative examples that highlight the diverging interests and preferences among these states (Jokela and Iso-Markku 2013; von Voss et al. 2013). In contrast to the defence industrial collaboration among the Nordic states, Austria or Malta's participation in such cooperative frameworks is rather shallow. This is reasoned by their neutrality and the continuity of the strong embeddedness of pacifism in their security and defence policies, which ultimately has implications for their (lacking) willingness to advance their military assets and capabilities.

Because of the variances of capabilities, military neutrality, resources and specialisations among neutrals, divergences concerning their views on division of labour have been recorded. Austria and Malta maintain a particular view and take a more distant perspective. Due to their general reluctance regarding the use of force to respond to international crises, they are sceptical about NATO-led military crisis management operations. They consequently have a clear preference for the EU's toolbox which includes diplomatic, economic and political instruments and has a more effective outcome than the military approach taken by NATO in the view of Austria and Malta (Kammel 2013; Pace 2013). Nevertheless, Austria does favour strong cooperation and collaboration between the EU and NATO in crisis management, especially if the use of force is inevitable. In this case, it favours the application of the EU's rich toolbox and civil–military approach in conjuncture with NATO's military capabilities to support equally the core strengths and abilities of both organisations (Austria 2010).

In comparison, Denmark pursues its own specific view on the issue of division of labour between the EU and NATO, in which it follows a pragmatic approach. It prefers a clearly defined division of tasks primarily grounded in its own defence opt-out from CSDP. Accordingly, Denmark favours NATO for undertaking any action in security and defence affairs as well as coalitions of the willing spearheaded by the US for the hard end of the security spectrum. This includes the conduct of military operations, whereas it prefers the EU to take over the civilian dimension (Denmark 2016). For Denmark, 'division of labour means that NATO should be supported in questions of hard security and the EU in questions of soft security' (Rynning 2013: 92). With the intensified debates over European strategic autonomy and sovereignty among EU member states as well as within NATO, specifically with regard to security and defence, Denmark has expressed its lack of support for EU autonomy in hard security and defence matters. But it also does not promote NATO's engagement in the Union's expertise and key areas in civilian crisis management. What is more, Denmark particularly emphasises the need for complementarity and comprehensiveness between the two organisations, ensuring its own place in the Euro-Atlantic security community and the harmonisation of efforts to undermine its own shortcomings due to its CSDP opt-out (cf. Nissen and Larsen 2021). Only a clearly defined division of labour therefore allows Denmark's full participation in NATO-led operations as well as in EU civilian missions, which provides Denmark a greater extent to exert influence in both organisations.

In the cases of Iceland and Sweden, there are some overlaps with the Danish perspective though for different reasons. Iceland shares some of these views since it belongs to the Atlanticist camp and prefers NATO engagement over the EU due to its non-EU membership. It also values the EU's broad toolbox with its comprehensive approach which provides the EU with advantages and key strengths in crisis management operations (Bailes and Rafnsson 2012). Sweden, on the other hand, prefers a clearly defined division of labour because it initially did not fully support the development of the EU's security and defence policy and because it favours taking multilateral action through the UN or with its Nordic cooperation partners. With the shifts in European and international security, the rise of non-traditional and hybrid threats as well as its preference for civilian approaches to crisis management, Sweden supports EU-led actions in which it wants the Union to focus on the civilian dimension of security, while NATO is better equipped to deal with aspects of hard security. This also explains its activism on strengthening the EU's civilian capabilities for crisis management and contributions to NATO despite not being a full member in the Alliance (Raik 2018; Ruffa 2013). Although there is a high level of convergence and similarity between Finland and Sweden, the former maintains a different perspective on division of labour between the EU and NATO. Finland sees the use and engagement of both EU and NATO capabilities in the same theatre as 'natural', however only 'whenever appropriate' (Hopia 2008: 42). These different views among neutrals on the division of tasks and responsibilities between the two organisations in crisis management, as well as the overall diverging viewpoints among all member states, remains a critical aspect for practical EU–NATO cooperation.

As a key approach to facilitating and enhancing EU–NATO cooperation is through contributions and participation in their operations. Because of their limited resources, neutrals have often faced the challenge of limited capabilities available for crisis management operations. Quite often, for example in the case of Malta, financial and logistical contributions have been made instead of troop deployments. Their participation and contributions in EU and NATO operations therefore yield mixed results (see Appendix C). To date, Denmark is the only state among the neutrals that has participated and contributed to all NATO-led operations (Joint Endeavour, SFOR, KFOR, Allied Harmony, Active Endeavour, ISAF, Enduring Freedom HOA, Ocean Shield, Unified Protector, Resolute Support) with the exception of Operation Sea Guardian in the Mediterranean Sea. Because of its CSDP opt-out, it has not been part of any EU-led military operations. Although it could technically contribute to EU military operations, which would imply to join CSDP, this option is not likely due to the previous failed attempts to reverse this opt-out (Miles 2014).

Finland and Sweden indicate that single members are active in the conduct of military operations of both the EU and NATO. In fact, from the early beginnings of their memberships, they have been increasingly participatory with varying motivations. While Sweden seeks to increase its overall influence globally, Finland – and also Iceland – strives for growing peace and stability in Europe's neighbourhood and in geographical areas of interest (Finland 2012; Iceland n.a.; Sweden 2017). This further shows that neither country is averse to closer cooperation and more frequent interactions with the respective organisation of which they are not full members. Finland and Sweden have furthermore aligned their participation in military operations since both have made significant contributions to EU operations (Concordia, Artemis, EUFOR DRC, EUFOR Tchad RCA, Atalanta, MED Sophia, MED Irini) and NATO operations (Joint Endeavour, SFOR, KFOR, ISAF, Resolute Support), whereas Sweden is also among the participants of NATO Operation Unified Protector in Libya. Participating almost equally in multilateral military operations contributes to the interoperability between the EU and NATO and enables these states not only to gain a voice among other member states but also to upload their own security interests. While Iceland shares security threats and interests with Finland and Sweden, it has participated in several NATO operations (Joint Endeavour, KFOR, SFOR, Allied Harmony, ISAF) and also contributed to the EU's Operation Concordia in North Macedonia.

Austria has participated primarily in EU operations where its troops were deployed to the Western Balkans, which also reflects its overall focus on the neighbourhood. With the EU's increasing engagement in crises and conflicts in Africa, a dilemma emerged. While its regional focus is on the EU's direct neighbourhood with particular attention to the Western Balkans, Africa is not among Austria's strategic interests. Moreover, its low contributions and only frequent participation highlight Austria's neutrality status and overall inactivity in the practical side of crisis management (Kammel 2013; Müller and Maurer 2016). In contrast, Malta is the overall outsider in terms of participation in military operations. So far, it has only deployed troops to the EU's maritime security operations in the Gulf of Aden and the Mediterranean Sea (Atalanta, MED Sophia, MED Irini) and its total number of deployed troops in 2010 amount to 0.83% of its overall troop contingent (Pace 2013: 247). Malta's decision to participate and deploy capabilities is derived from the dilemma between its constitutional neutrality and trying to play a more active role in the EU's maritime security as well as pressures from other European states to make contributions to CSDP operations (Fiott 2015).

Overall, the contributions by states in the group of neutrals can be located in the middle to lower end across all member states in the EU and NATO. This shows their general reluctance towards the use of force on the one hand and their limited military capabilities and the focus on civilian solutions on the other hand. This further pushes these states to the sidelines in practical cooperation between the EU and NATO, which is in line by and large with the efforts, viewpoints and foreign and security policy orientations of neutrals in the EU–NATO relationship.

Conclusions

This chapter provided an analysis of the characteristics, attitudes and contributions by neutrals in the EU–NATO interorganisational relationship. The defining factor is their general status as either militarily neutral or non-aligned states as well as their preference for the civilian dimension over the military aspects of security and defence. Moreover, some states in the groups of neutrals face constitutional constraints, such as Austria and Malta, that disallow them to take a more active position.

Neutrals have been characterised as member states with low profiles in security and defence and particularly in regard to the EU–NATO relationship. They also bring forward particular national caveats, primarily their historical record or the continuation of military neutrality and non-alignment. Most of the states among interorganisational neutrals still maintain a high level of reluctance to make use of force and to deploy their troops to international crises and conflicts. Due to the embeddedness of multilateralism in their foreign and security policy orientation, there are signs of greater willingness to act through either the EU or NATO especially in terms of civil–military approaches to conflict management. Closer EU–NATO cooperation would provide room for action that would require the niche capabilities and specialised roles which some of the neutrals have developed over time, such as Malta's focus on maritime security and the civilian tools and instruments by both Finland and Sweden. Moreover, their lack of engagement and contributions to enhancing closer interorganisational cooperation is rooted in their low profiles, limited military capabilities and military neutrality or non-alignment status.

In this regard, Denmark presents a special case as an outlier and a boundary case because it does not share military neutrality with the other states in this group. What is more, Denmark demonstrates comparatively more enthusiasm and activism towards security and defence. Lacking efforts to initiate projects and develop new ideas by all states in the group of neutrals restricts their activism and therefore, neutrals remain overall on the sidelines of the EU–NATO relationship, but nevertheless possess flexible positions and demonstrate their openness to adapt to new circumstances if required.

Note

1 Nordic Armaments Cooperation (NORDAC), Nordic Coordinated Arrangement for Military Peace Support (NORDCAPS) and Nordic Supportive Defence Structures (NORDSUP).

References

Alter, Karen J. and Sophie Meunier (2009) 'The politics of international regime complexity', *Perspectives on Politics, Symposium*, 7(1): 13–24.

Arter, David (2000) 'Small state influence within the EU – The case of Finland's "Northern Dimension Initiative"', *Journal of Common Market Studies*, 38(5): 677–697.

Bailes, Alyson J.K. and Örvar Þ. Rafnsson (2012) 'Iceland and the EU's common security and defence policy: Challenge or opportunity?' *Stjórnmál & Stjórnsysla*, 8(1): 109–131.

Bailes, Alyson J.K. and Baldur Thorhallsson (2006) 'Iceland and the European security and defence policy'. *In*: Bailes, Alyson J.K., Gunilla Herolf and Bengt Sundelius (eds) *The Nordic Countries and the European Security and Defence Policy*, Stockholm: SIPRI, 328–348.

Bergquist, Mats et al. (2016) *The Effects of Finland's Possible NATO Membership: An Assessment*, Helsinki: Ministry of Foreign Affairs.

Brommesson, Douglas (2018) 'Introduction to special section: From Nordic exceptionalism to a third order priority – variations of "Nordicness" in foreign and security policy', *Global Affairs*, 4(4–5): 355–362.

Chivvis, Christopher S. (2017) 'Sweden, Finland and NATO', *GMF Policy Brief*, 24: 1–4.

Cottey, Andrew (2013) 'The European neutrals and NATO: Ambiguous partnership', *Contemporary Security Policy*, 34(3): 446–472.

Dahl, Ann-Sofie and Pauli Järvenpää (2013) 'Sweden, Finland and NATO: Security partners and security providers'. *In*: Dahl, Ann-Sofie and Pauli Järvenpää (eds) *Northern Security and Global Politics: Nordic-Baltic Strategic Influence in a Post-Unipolar World*, Abingdon: Routledge, 124–136.

Dobrescu, Madalina et al. (2017) 'Southern Europe: Portugal, Spain, Italy, Malta, Greece, Cyprus'. *In*: Hadfield, Amelia et al. (eds) *Foreign Policies of EU Member States: Continuity and Europeanisation*, Abingdon: Routledge, 83–98.

Eilstrup-Sangiovanni, Mette (2014) 'Europe's defence dilemma', *The International Spectator*, 49(2): 83–116.

European Commission (2000) *Special Eurobarometer 146: Europe of Defence*, https://data.europa.eu/euodp/data/dataset/S201_54_1_EBS146 (accessed on 05/10/2018).

Eurostat (2018) *Government expenditure on defence*. Last updated on 7 June 2018, https://ec.europa.eu/eurostat/statisticsexplained/index.php/Government_expenditure_on_defence (accessed on 06/09/2018).

Fiott, Daniel (2015) 'Being small, acting tall? Malta and European defence'. *In*: Fiott, Daniel (ed) *The Common Security and Defence Policy: National Perspectives*, Brussels: Egmont – Royal Institute for International Relations, 93–96.

Fiott, Daniel (2017) 'A revolution too far? US defence innovation, Europe and NATO's military-technological gap', *Journal of Strategic Studies*, 40(3): 417–437.

Forsberg, Tuomas (2013) 'The rise of Nordic defence cooperation: A return to regionalism?' *International Affairs*, 89(5): 1161–1181.

Forsberg, Tuomas (2018) 'Finland and NATO: Strategic choices and identity conceptions'. *In*: Cottey, Andrew (ed.) *The European Neutrals and NATO: Non-Alignment, Partnership, Membership?* London: Palgrave Macmillan, 97–127.

Forsberg, Tuomas and Tapani Vaahtoranta (2001) 'Inside the EU, outside NATO: Paradoxes of Finland's and Sweden's post-neutrality', *European Security*, 10(1): 68–93.

Gärtner, Heinz (2018) 'Austria: Engaged neutrality'. *In*: Cottey, Andrew (ed) *The European Neutrals and NATO: Non-alignment, Partnership, Membership?* London: Palgrave Macmillan, 129–149.

Gebhard, Carmen (2013) 'Is small still beautiful? The case of Austria', *Swiss Political Science Review*, 19(3): 279–297.

Gehring, Thomas and Benjamin Faude (2014) 'A theory of emerging order within international complexes: How competition among regulatory international institutions leads to institutional adaptation and division of labour', *Review of International Organisations*, 9(4): 471–498.

Haukkala, Hiski (2003) 'The role of the Northern Dimension in tackling the challenges of a growing EU presence in Northern Europe', *FIIA Occasional Paper Series*, 36: 3–17.

Haukkala, Hiski et al. (2017) 'The Northern European member states'. *In*: Hadfield, Amelia et al. (eds) *Foreign Policies of EU Member States: Continuity and Europeanisation*. Abingdon: Routledge, 23–37.

Herolf, Gunilla (2006) 'The Nordic countries and the EU-NATO relationship: Further comments'. *In*: Bailes, Alyson J.K., Gunilla Herolf and Bengt Sundelius (eds) *Nordic countries and the European Security and Defence Policy*, Stockholm: SIPRI, 67–77.

Hofmann, Stephanie C. (2009) 'Overlapping institutions in the realm of international security: The case of NATO and ESDP', *Perspectives on Politics*, 7(1): 45–51.

Hopia, Henna (2008) *The Finnish Perspective: European Defence – A Way Forward for EU and NATO Defence Cooperation*, Brussels, Helsinki: Centre for European Studies and Suomen Toivo Think Tank.

Ilves, Toomas (2018) We'll Join If It Gets Serious, *l!bera*, Published on 26 January 2018, www.libera.fi/blogs/foreword/?lang=en (accessed on 01/02/2018).

Jedlaucnik, Herwig (2015) *Die Auswirkungen der Ukraine-Krise auf die budgetäre Situation der europäischen Streitkräfte*, Wien: Institut für Strategie und Sicherheitspolitik der Landesverteidigungsakademie, Bundesministerium für Landesverteidigung und Sport.

Jokela, Juha and Tuomas Iso-Markku (2013) 'Nordic defence cooperation: Background, current trends and future prospects?' *NORDIKA Programme/Fondation pour la Recherche Strategique*, 21(13): 1–12.

Kammel, Arnold H. (2013) 'Austria'. *In*: Biehl, Heiko et al. (eds) *Strategic Cultures in Europe: Security and Defence Policies Across the Continent*, Wiesbaden: Springer VS, 19–29.

Larsen, Henrik (2008) 'Denmark and the ESDP opt-out: A new way of doing nothing?' *In*: Archer, Clive (ed.) *New Security Issues in Northern Europe: The Nordic and Baltic States and the ESDP*, Abingdon: Routledge, 78–93.

Manners, Ian and Richard G.Whitman (2001) *The Foreign Policies of European Union Member States*, Manchester: Manchester University Press.

Mattelaer, Alexander (2016) 'US leadership and NATO: Revisiting the principles of NATO burden-sharing', *Parameters*, 46(1): 25–33.

Miles, Lee (2014) 'Not quite a painful choice? Reflecting on Denmark and further European integration'. *In*: Miles, Lee and Anders Wivel (eds) *Denmark and the European Union*, Abingdon: Routledge, 217–227.

Molis, Arūnas (2006) 'The role and interests of small states in developing European security and defence policy', *Baltic Security & Defence Review*, 8: 81–100.

Möttölä, Kari (2001) 'Military cooperation, transatlantic relations and military non-alliance – A conceptual analysis with a focus on the cases of Finland and Sweden', *Österreichische Zeitschrift für Politikwissenschaft (ÖZP)*, 30(4): 393–410.

Müller, Patrick and Heidi Maurer (2016) 'Austrian foreign policy and 20 years of EU membership: Opportunities and constraints', *Österreichische Zeitschrift für Politikwissenschaft (ÖZP)*, 45(2): 1–9.

NATO (2016) *Partnership for Peace Programme.* Last updated on 7 April 2016, www.nato.int/cps/en/natolive/topics_50349.htm (accessed on 16/02/2017).

NATO (2020) *Defence Expenditure of NATO Countries (2013–2020)*, www.nato.int/cps/en/natohq/news_178975.htm (accessed on 15/02/2021).

Nilsson, Sven-Christer and Göran Larsbrink (2013) *Swedish National Security: Challenges and Opportunities Beyond 2014*, Stockholm: The Royal Swedish Academy of War Sciences.

Nissen, Christina and Jessica Larsen (2021): 'European strategic autonomy: From misconceived to useful concept', *DIIS Policy Brief*, 1–4.

O'Dwyer, Gerard (2020) *Nordic Militaries Rekindle Old Alliances, as Russia Warms to the Region, Defence News*, Published on 22 June 2020, www.defensenews.com/smr/transatlantic-partnerships/2020/06/22/nordic-militaries-rekindle-old-alliances-as-russia-warms-to-the-region/ (accessed on 09/03/2021).

Ojanen, Hanna (2007) 'Finland and ESDP'. *In*: Brummer, Klaus (ed) *The North and ESDP*, Gütersloh: Bertelsmann, 34–44.

Ojanen, Hanna (2008) 'Finland and the ESDP: "Obliquely forwards"?' *In*: Archer, Clive (ed) *New Security Issues in Northern Europe: The Nordic and Baltic States and the ESDP*, Abingdon: Routledge, 56–77.

Ojanen, Hanna and Tapio Raunio (2018) 'The varying degrees and meanings of Nordicness in Finnish foreign policy', *Global Affairs*, 4(4–5): 405–418.

Olsen, Gorm Rye (2007) 'Denmark and ESDP'. *In*: Brummer, Klaus (ed) *The North and ESDP*, Gütersloh: Bertelsmann, 22–33.

Olsen, Gorm Rye and Jess Pilegaard (2005) 'The costs of non-Europe? Denmark and the common security and defence policy', *European Security*, 14(3): 339–360.

Österreichisches Bundeskanzleramt (1955) *Bundesverfassung vom 26. Oktober 1955 über die Neutralität Österreichs [Federal Constitutional Law on the Neutrality of Austria]*, www.ris.bka.gv.at/Dokumente/Erv/ERV_1955_211/ERV_1955_211.pdf (accessed on 30/07/2018).

Pace, Roderick (2013) 'Malta'. *In*: Biehl, Heiko et al. (eds) *Strategic Cultures in Europe: Security and Defence Policies Across the Continent*, Wiesbaden: Springer VS, 243–253.

Pedersen, Klaus Carsten (2006) 'Denmark and the European security and defence policy'. *In*: Bailes, Alyson J.K., Gunilla Herolf and Bengt Sundelius (eds) *The Nordic Countries and the European Security and Defence Policy*, Stockholm: SIPRI, 37–49.

Petersen, Nikolaj (1990) 'Denmark's foreign relations in the 1990s', *The Annals of the American Academy of Political and Social Science*, 512: 88–100.

Petersson, Magnus (2018) ' "The allied partner": Sweden and NATO through the realist-idealist lens'. *In*: Cottey, Andrew (ed) *The European Neutrals and NATO: Non-Alignment, Partnership, Membership?* London: Palgrave Macmillan, 73–96.

Raik, Kristi (2018) EU-NATO Boundaries are Becoming More Porous – But Not Disappearing, *l!bera*, Published on 22 January 2018, www.libera.fi/blogs/eu-nato-boundaries-are-becoming-more-porous-but-not-disappearing/?lang=en (accessed on 09/09/2018).

Reichard, Martin (2006) *The EU-NATO Relationship: A Legal and Political Perspective*, Abingdon: Routledge.

Ringsmose, Jens and Sten Rynning (2008) 'The Impeccable Ally? Denmark, NATO, and the Uncertain Future of Top Tier Membership'. *In*: Hvidt, Nanna and Hans Mauritzen (eds) *Danish Foreign Policy Yearbook 2008*, Copenhagen: DIIS, 55–84.

Rodt, Annemarie Peen (2017) 'Member states policy towards EU military operations'. *In*: Hadfield, Amelia et al. (eds) *Foreign Policies of EU Member States: Continuity and Europeanisation*, Abingdon: Routledge, 131–147.

Ruffa, Chiara (2013) 'Sweden'. *In*: Biehl, Heiko et al. (eds) *Strategic Cultures in Europe: Security and Defence Policies Across the Continent*, Wiesbaden: Springer VS, 343–357.

Rynning, Sten (2013) 'Denmark'. *In*: Biehl, Heiko et al. (eds) *Strategic Cultures in Europe: Security and Defence Policies Across the Continent*. Wiesbaden: Springer VS, 85–97.

Rynning, Sten and Jon Rahbek-Clemmensen (2015) 'The absentee: Denmark and ESDP'. *In*: Fiott, Daniel (ed) *The Common Security and Defence Policy: National Perspectives*, Brussels: Egmont – Royal Institute for International Relations, 97–98.

Salonius-Pasternak, Charly (2018) *The Defence of Finland and Sweden: Continuity and Variance in Strategy and Public Opinion, FIIA Briefing Paper, No. 240*, Helsinki: Finnish Institute for International Affairs.

Scicluna, Chris and Robin Emmott (2020) Malta Pulls Out of New EU Libya Sea Patrols in Migration Row, *Reuters,* Published on 8 May 2020, www.reuters.com/article/us-europe-migrants-libya-idUSKBN22K1UT (accessed on 26/02/2021).

Seppo, Antti and Tuomas Forsberg (2013) 'Finland'. *In*: Biehl, Heiko et al. (eds) *Strategic Cultures in Europe: Security and Defence Policies Across the Continent*, Wiesbaden: Springer VS, 99–112.

Setälä, Martti (2005) 'Small states and NATO: Influence and accommodation', *Atlantic Council of Finland Occasional Papers*, 6: 9–36.

SIPRI (2020) *SIPRI Military Expenditure Data Base 1949–2019*. Stockholm: SIPRI.

Sperling, James (2004) 'Capabilities traps and gaps: Symptom or cause of a troubled transatlantic relationship', *Contemporary Security Policy*, 25(3): 452–478.

Tardy, Thierry (2014) 'CSDP: Getting third states on board', *EUISS Brief*, 6: 1–4.

Thorhallsson, Baldur (2018) 'Nordicness as shelter: The case of Iceland', *Global Affairs*, 4(4–5): 377–390.

Tiilikainen, Teija (2006) 'The Nordic countries and the EU-NATO relationship'. In: Bailes, Alyson J.K., Gunilla Herolf and Bengt Sundelius (eds) *Nordic countries and the European Security and Defence Policy*, Stockholm: SIPRI, 50–66.

Times of Malta (2017) 'Malta neutrality "no hurdle" for NATO cooperation', *Times of Malta*, published on 18 May 2017, www.timesofmalta.com/articles/view/20170518/local/maltaneutrality-no-hurdle-for-nato-cooperation.648196 (accessed on 31/07/2018)

Vaahtoranta, Tapani and Tuomas Forsberg (2000) 'Post-neutral or pre-allied? Finnish and Swedish policies on the EU and NATO as security organisations', *NUPI Working Papers*, 29: 3–43.

Vella, Duncan (2015) Malta and the European Union's Common Security and Defence Policy: Challenges and Opportunities, Master's Dissertation, Published Online in University of Malta Library, www.um.edu.mt/library/oar/handle/123456789/10676 (accessed on 30/07/2018).

von Voss, Alicia et al. (2013) 'The state of defence cooperation in Europe', *SWP Working Paper*, 3: 1–14.

Wivel, Anders (2005) 'The security challenge of small EU member states: Interests, identity and the development of the EU as a security actor', *Journal of Common Market Studies*, 43(2): 393–412.

Wivel, Anders (2014) 'A pace-setter out of sync? Danish foreign, security and defence policy and the European Union'. *In*: Miles, Lee and Anders Wivel (eds) *Denmark and the European Union*, Abingdon: Routledge, 80–94.

7   Conclusion and implications

The overall aim of this book was to investigate how member states shape interorganisational cooperation between the EU and NATO. It took a new perspective by capturing how member states contribute to the EU–NATO relationship. This analysis has enhanced the current scholarship on the EU–NATO relationship and the study of interorganisational cooperation among international security organisations by adding the member state perspective and by examining their different positions in shaping the EU–NATO relationship. The focus was first set upon theorising the position and roles of member states in interorganisational interaction, which was based on the current state of the art of the interorganisationalism and organisation studies literatures. This empirical analysis and the development of the typology were driven by the following research question: *Why and how do member states contribute to the (dys-)functionality of the EU-NATO interorganisational relationship?* Moreover, this inquiry was guided by questions on the current state of affairs of EU–NATO cooperation and how member states make use of their minilateral and bilateral relations as well as their capabilities and resources to shape interorganisational cooperation.

Facilitated by the conceptualisation and application of the theoretical framework of interorganisational relations, the typology of member states consisting of four types was developed: advocates, blockers, balancers and neutrals. The set of features of interorganisational interaction and the typology of member states provided the theoretical and conceptual frameworks for the subsequent analysis of the EU–NATO relationship and for the examination of the attitudes, positions and contributions by member states. While every single state can be categorised into one of the types, this categorisation is not fixed, which means that states' positions as well as their affiliations with one of the types are subject to change over time. To understand and examine the diverging attitudes and behaviours towards EU–NATO cooperation in the area of security and defence, a multitude of research methods has been applied. The analysis of official documents included member states' national security and defence strategies, the security and strategic concepts by the EU and NATO and their interorganisational agreements such as the 2002 Joint Declaration on ESDP, 2003 Berlin Plus arrangements and the Security of

DOI: 10.4324/9781003170068-7

Information Agreement as well as the 2016 Joint Declaration and subsequent implementation plans have been vital sources (see Appendix B). In addition, semi-structured interviews with officials and representatives from the EU, NATO and their member states were conducted.

This book has thus far examined the EU–NATO relationship from the perspective of member states by highlighting their differences in attitudes, foreign and security policy orientation, membership and thus their diverging roles in shaping this interorganisational cooperation. This final chapter concludes the findings and reviews the implications for the future of the EU–NATO relationship. First, it summarises the conceptualisation and theoretical findings derived from the framework of interorganisational relations and the typology of member states. Based on the conceptualisations and categorisation, it summarises the empirical findings from the analysis of member states' roles in EU–NATO cooperation. Second, this chapter reflects on the role of member states with a particular focus on the change and continuity of their positions, behaviour and the impact of the domestic political level on their positions. This then enables to draw some generalisable conclusions about the utility of the typology for the analysis of member states in interorganisational cooperation beyond the EU–NATO relationship. Lastly, a number of implications of the findings are drawn for the future relationship between the EU and NATO that take into consideration the recent developments on both the member states and interinstitutional levels. This provides new insights and allows to formulate an outlook for future research in this scholarship.

Member states in the EU–NATO relationship

The main objective of this book was to examine the role of member states in the interorganisational relationship between the EU and NATO. It was primarily guided by a set of questions on the current state of their interactions to identify the obstacles and reasons for the dysfunction of their relationship. This research has been embedded in the wider literature on the EU–NATO relationship since the end of the Cold War in which a number of key themes have been identified: development of an institutional framework, states' use of their membership, capabilities and member state contributes to operations, interoperability and division of labour.

Since the beginning of informal exchanges between the organisations' military staff and between NATO's Secretary General and the EU's High Representative, their relations have made steady progress (Messervy-Whiting 2005). Although both organisations achieved to formulate and sign a number of important and unique agreements since the beginning of their cooperation, including the EU–NATO Declaration on ESDP, the Security of Information Agreement and the Berlin Plus arrangements in 2002 and 2003, there are still several obstacles that disallowed deeper institutionalisation of their relations. One of the obstacles to enhanced cooperation is the capability gap including hardware, technological advancement and investments (Bialos 2005; Fiott 2017; Sperling 2004). These gaps between the two organisations have resulted in an uneven and asymmetric relationship in which member states assume that NATO is the more capable and powerful organisation in terms of security, defence and crisis management, particularly because of the US's military superiority. The EU, in contrast, is often seen as the weaker partner due to the lack of vital military capabilities and the lack of a political will to act, but is nevertheless the preferred option and the choice for European states for comprehensive crisis management because of its wider toolbox. This asymmetry and the differing views on the two organisations have caused some member states to pursue a specific division of labour that warrants interoperability and complementarity. Some member states decide upon a specified division of tasks and responsibilities on a case-by-case basis depending on the type of security threat and crisis situation. So far, there is no clearly defined division of labour between the EU and NATO, which provides greater freedom for both organisations to develop their own capabilities, instruments and policies, but that also risks duplication and further overlaps.

What is more, the analysis of the EU–NATO relationship has revealed that member states pose one of the main constrains to deepening their cooperation. The *Cyprus issue* with the ongoing tensions between Cyprus, Greece and Turkey evidently represents one of the biggest challenges and the prime obstacle to furthering EU–NATO cooperation. However, the examination of member states' behaviours and preferences has shown that the Cyprus issue is not the only challenge that the EU–NATO interorganisational relationship faces. Other states with their national caveats and inter-state disputes as well as national perceptions of EU–NATO cooperation more generally have hampered further enhancement in the past. The most relevant ones to note are France's withdrawal from NATO's military command structures, its fear of US dominance in Europe and the re-emerging focus on European strategic autonomy. This has raised criticism and opposition among other EU and NATO member states, particularly among non-EU NATO member states but also among EU member states (cf. Besch and Scazzieri 2020; Franke and Varma 2019). Military neutrality and non-alignment as well as the disengagement from military alliances such as NATO by Ireland, for example, have also posed a challenge to deepening cooperation. While the majority of European states are overall supportive of the EU–NATO relationship (see Table 7.1), such as the UK, the Baltics and Central and Eastern European states, these have occasionally also hampered the EU to acquire military defence structures and capabilities and thus have automatically created an asymmetric relationship which made achieving cooperation at eye level more difficult. Even though the EU–NATO relationship is evidently progressing since all member states agree that interactions between the two organisations are useful and necessary to meet today's multiple security challenges, the attitudes and positions on the depth and width vary among member states. The overlapping membership and the tensions among some member states therefore significantly influence

Table 7.1 Allocation of states in the typology of member states

Type	Member States
Advocates	Albania, Belgium, Bulgaria, Canada, Croatia, Czech Republic, Estonia, Hungary, Latvia, Lithuania, Luxembourg, Montenegro, the Netherlands, North Macedonia, Norway, Poland, Romania, Slovakia, Slovenia, the UK, the US
Blockers	Cyprus, France, Greece, Ireland, Turkey
Balancers	Germany, Italy, Portugal, Spain
Neutrals	Austria, Denmark, Finland, Iceland, Malta, Sweden

the current state and the future of the EU–NATO relationship. Overall, states take a decisive position in shaping in interorganisational interaction not only because of the need of their agreement but, more importantly, because of their diverging preferences, rationales and attitudes which impact the outcome of cooperation between organisations. The findings of this book highlight the need to consider national characteristics and features, including historical and operational experiences, possession of capabilities, legal constraints, foreign and security policy orientation as well as states' attitudes and approaches according to which they contribute to the design, formalisation and framework cooperation between the EU and NATO.

States such as the UK, the US, the Baltics, BeNeLux and Central and Eastern European countries make up the group of advocates of the EU–NATO relationship. As drivers and promoters of interorganisational cooperation, they are active contributors to both organisations and their exchanges, operations and interoperability. The analysis of their national security documents and the exchanges with national representatives indicated their general support as well as the aspirational view of feasible cooperation. Advocates engage intensively in the formalisation and institutionalisation process and have frequently voiced their supportive view on the EU–NATO relationship to persuade other member states to join them. One key element of advocates is therefore how they utilise their status as multiple members to promote the benefits of the EU–NATO relationship equally in both organisations. Their embeddedness in minilateral networks and coalition groups as well as the maintenance and strengthening of bilateral partnerships has enabled them to convince less enthusiastic members to pose little to no obstacles to further cooperation and exchanges. Among the most prominent advocates are the UK and the Baltics as well as some of the Central and Eastern European states. Britain's bilateral relations with France as its most valued partner in Europe and the historically special relationship with the US as its most important transatlantic ally have proven to be vital for initiating and enhancing EU–NATO cooperation. Examples of the UK's advocative behaviour include the signing of the Franco–British Saint Malo Agreement in 1998, the individual efforts by former NATO Secretary General George

Robertson and the provision of operational headquarters in Northwood to both the EU naval operation EUNAVFOR Atalanta and NATO Operation Ocean Shield. The strong dependence on the US security guarantees through NATO and the EU's comprehensive toolbox have caused the Baltics and Eastern European states to make impeccable contributions to the promotion of enhanced EU–NATO cooperation, which is remarkable considering their status as small states and their limited resources and capabilities.

The analysis of advocates highlights that the motives and strategic interests behind the support for closer EU–NATO cooperation vary across states. While especially some of the smaller states, such as the Baltics and Eastern European countries, are still seeking to foster their place in the Euro-Atlantic security community after having joined as subsequent members, the UK, in contrast, sees this relationship as a necessary and inevitable one to increase its own influence in international politics especially with its own withdrawal from the EU. Despite the different degrees of activism, all states in the group of advocates have made integral contributions to supporting EU–NATO cooperation which have enabled these efforts overall.

In contrast, Cyprus, France, Greece, Ireland and Turkey have been labelled as 'troublemakers' due to their obstructive behaviour. Their external actions, attitudes and sometimes 'schizophrenic' behaviour have posed major obstacles to enhancing the relations between the EU and NATO. While blockers do not completely obstruct the interactions between the two organisations *per se*, their behaviour derived from their national interests and frictions with other member states have slowed down the overall progress of developments. The conflict between Cyprus, Greece and Turkey has been pointed out as the main problem for the institutionalisation process and for the exchange of security information. Unless the Cyprus issue gets resolved and either side stops blocking the other from joining and/or fully participating in the respective other organisation, it will also pose one of the major blockages in the future. However, the analysis has revealed that the Cyprus issue is not the only state-related issue contributing to the dysfunction of the EU–NATO relationship. Additionally, France's strong focus on European strategic autonomy and preference for strengthening the EU's military capacities and capabilities has caused frictions among member states. Its outspoken opposition and fear of US dominance in both Europe and NATO particularly drives its foreign and security orientation towards European autonomy and thus adding further challenges to closer EU–NATO cooperation.

Because blockers have either single or multiple membership, they are selective concerning their participation and contributions of capabilities to military operations when the EU and NATO seek to engage. This is furthermore complicated by the nature of the Berlin Plus arrangements, which provide the practical dimension of cooperation and allow the EU to make use of NATO's military assets and capabilities for EU-led operations. However, one element of these arrangements is the EU–NATO Security of Information Agreement in which Turkey blocks Cyprus from joining the arrangements, and in return, Cyprus has impeded deeper Turkish engagement in European security and defence policies and structures (Acikmese and Triantaphyllou 2012). Furthermore, France's focus on EU defence initiatives outside the formal structures provided by the EU and NATO, such as EI2, indicates its sceptical and cautious approach that has ultimately impacted the EU–NATO relationship. Overall, blockers do not strongly oppose the cooperative efforts in general, instead, they seek to slow down the progress in order to follow their national preferences and not to undermine its security interests.

Choosing a middle way, balancers mediate especially among conflicting member states. Countries such as Germany, Italy, Portugal and Spain have been categorised in the group of balancers because of their involvements in negotiations and coalition groups to mitigate tensions among other member states. Their shared historical past as former authoritarian regimes and dictatorships in the twentieth century has heavily influenced and shaped this approach to security and defence cooperation. With their central geographical location in Europe, status as multiple members, preference for a comprehensive approach to crisis management rooted in their foreign and security policy orientation focusing on multilateralism and civil-military approaches and their middle power status, particularly Germany and Italy are interested in mediating and balancing among other member states equally in both organisations. What is more, Germany's ability to negotiate with some of the more powerful states and the deep embeddedness in bilateral and minilateral relationships demonstrate its vital contribution to the EU–NATO relationship. Germany has become the first point of contact for many small-sized members because it provides a platform for informal exchanges which it utilises to balance among states in both organisations.

The relevance of balancers has received increasing attention whenever a sign of asymmetry and imbalance between the EU and NATO has emerged, which called for brokers and mediators to rebalance the relationship. Balancers have therefore been mostly active in negotiations and consultations regarding the institutional developments of this interorganisational relationship. However, they contribute comparatively little in terms of defence spending, military capabilities and resources. Balancers face high degree of national constraints, either due to their historical past or because of financial reasons, to increase their contributions. Consequently, these states seek to emphasise the comprehensive approach to become actively involved in enhancing further EU–NATO cooperation in which both organisations have their fair share of engagement.

Neutrals are primarily characterised by their minimal degree of engagement in interactions and exchanges between the EU and NATO as well as the neutral view on their relationship. Austria, Denmark, Finland, Iceland, Malta and Sweden have all been identified as primarily neutrals in the EU–NATO interorganisational relationship. As small states located on the geographical periphery of the Euro-Atlantic security space, they have neither the ability nor the willingness to actively promote, block or balance this cooperation.

In addition, their single membership status and limited military capabilities and resources disallow them from taking a more proactive position in the EU–NATO relationship. The outlier in this group is Denmark because it factually possesses a multiple membership status but is constrained in its defence engagements because of its CSDP opt-out, which makes it a *de jure* single member state.

A significant commonality is their historical record or contemporary status of military neutrality and non-alignment. Neutrals' preference for civilian approaches and engagement in the softer spectrum of security and defence tasks is therefore not surprising. While this has caused national constraints on joining a military alliance such as NATO, none of these states seeks to disrupt further cooperation between the two organisations in order not to be left out. As the findings show, Denmark, Finland and Sweden seek to increase their military expenditures and have recently made greater contributions to crisis management operations as well as to developing joint capabilities, such as some of the Finnish–Swedish initiatives and the specialisation in civil–military responses to international crises. Despite the positioning on the sidelines, neutrals are of vital importance for the EU–NATO relationship. They provide niche capabilities which help to improve the comprehensive approach in which both organisations can operate with their expertise and strengths. Nevertheless, due to the many constraints on the domestic political level as well as their national foreign and security positions, none of the neutrals is likely to shift types and make greater contributions to EU–NATO cooperation.

Implications for future EU–NATO cooperation

From the onset, the rationale of this book was to analyse the approaches, attitudes and behaviour of member states towards the EU–NATO relationship. While previous scholarly works have centred their examinations around the interactions on the international bureaucratic and secretariat levels and primarily focused on analyses of practical cooperation in crisis management operations (Duke 2008; Gebhard and Smith 2015; Nováky 2015; Smith 2011; Whitman 2004) or on the institutional dimension and staff-to-staff cooperation (Reichard 2006; Touzovskaia 2006; Varwick and Koops 2009), this research overall argued that member states play an essential role in the evolution of this particular interorganisational relationship. Member states are the key building blocks of both organisations, possess the decision-making power and are driven by specific goals and national caveats. What is more, the findings beg the question about the usefulness of both the analysis and the typology of member states in a broader sense. The aim is therefore to also consider the implications for the future development of the EU–NATO relationship.

Considering member states' foreign and security policy orientation, minilateral and bilateral relations and policy preferences within these two organisations allowed to collect insights about individual states' motives, rationales and perceptions. From a policy perspective, these findings aim to support and facilitate future negotiations and decisions in a way that they provide new knowledge about member states' preferences, perceptions and perspectives concerning cooperation on European security and defence initiatives and projects in the Euro-Atlantic community. The analysis, for example, allows to explain why the UK eventually agreed to the development of the EU's military structures and capabilities and to create CSDP alongside CFSP. Since France and the UK formulated a set of conditions, including that the EU's defence dimension would also be linked closely to NATO's activities and policies, the UK had some degree of influence on the policy designs. Advocating for deeper EU–NATO cooperation would only make sense from the British viewpoint to retain its influence both in European security and transatlantic cooperation (Biscop 1999, 2012). Similarly, looking at the national approach of the US shows its ambiguous approach to European security and burden-sharing, its demand to Europeans to do more while being critical of European strategic autonomy, on the one hand and its support for EU–NATO cooperation to be able to influence European security and defence as a single member on the other hand (cf. Besch and Scazzieri 2020).

As has been argued throughout this book, domestic politics affect a country's foreign, security and defence policies and also its attitude towards interorganisational cooperation between the EU and NATO. Because changes on the domestic level occur, for example, with shifts in government and coalitions as well as through external shocks and developments in the international security environment, member states have the potential to shift from one type to another. They are thus not fixed to a single type. Yet, based on their foreign and security policy orientation and their approaches to security and defence, member states are likely to stay attached to one particular category. Knowing a state's position, and thus its affiliation with the category of member state in interorganisational relations, increases the predictability of a state's response and reaction to policy incentives and to initiatives that are addressed at enhancing EU–NATO cooperation as well as their capabilities and capacities for security and defence more generally.

Overall, the analysis has shown that variances and divergences among members exist which need to be considered by policymakers and analysts alike. Investigating the positions of individual member states and categorising them into the four types enables to identify national caveats and preferences which would provide the necessary information for introducing new initiatives in the future. Knowing a state's position helps to predict its responses and reactions to such new initiatives and would furthermore enable to formulate the future direction of EU–NATO cooperation to incorporate these caveats and to avoid another 'frozen conflict' between the two organisations. More importantly, it has been found that the Cyprus issue and the dispute between Cyprus, Greece and Turkey are not the only political stalemates that need to be overcome, although they are the most intractable and deeply anchored ones. With the involvement of member states in the negotiations, every single state is a potential veto player. Any bilateral tensions and discrepancies can impact the EU–NATO relationship as highlighted, for instance, by the most recent tensions between Turkey and several EU and NATO partners throughout 2019 and 2020 as well as by the unilateral foreign policy approach under the Trump presidency (Dursun-Özkanca 2019; Kaufman 2017). Derived from this analysis, a number of state-related tensions and issues can be predicted that will impact the development of the future EU–NATO relationship.

First of all, with its current nationally driven foreign and security approach within NATO, Turkey under the Erdoğan presidency is expected to act as a troublemaker also in the future. It constantly demonstrates its frustration and disappointment with the lack of integration of non-EU member states, for example in the EDA, and that it is left out from key decisions on European security and defence (Dursun-Özkanca 2019). This frustration and resentment have culminated in the past years and also caused troubles within NATO because of Turkey's foreign policy U-turn. Turkey's rapprochement with Russia, its behaviour in the Mediterranean Sea with regard to Libya and its engagement in the Syrian civil war has been a thorn in the eye of many European NATO allies. Furthermore, while NATO allies argued for a peaceful and negotiated resolution of the conflict between Armenia and Azerbaijan over Nagorno-Karabakh in 2020, Turkey became involved and backed Azerbaijan in this conflict without prior consultations with its allies and partners. In addition, it entered into a naval dispute with France and Greece over the UN arms embargo on Libya in the same year (Got 2020; Pierini 2020). This behaviour indicates that Turkey will also be a decisive state shaping the future of EU–NATO cooperation with its confrontations and tensions with other member states of both organisations.

In contrast to Turkey, France's foreign and security policy orientation has changed towards a more supportive stance on EU–NATO cooperation. Again, it has not vocalised opposition *per se* against their relationship in the past but voiced its concerns and scepticism primarily about US dominance in both Europe and NATO (Perruche 2014). Since re-joining NATO's military command structures in 2009, it has in fact played a more active role within the Alliance, improved its bilateral relationship with the US and introduced and supported crucial security and defence initiatives, such as PESCO and the EI2, that are beneficial for enhancing EU–NATO cooperation. However, France understands European strategic autonomy as 'the ability to decide and to act freely in an interdependent world' (Franke and Varma 2019: 5) and the ability to formulate political goals, creating approaches and implementing ways to realise these goals and, if necessary, with military means. France's ambition and push to realise this understanding of European strategic autonomy is likely to create new tensions within the EU as well as within the wider Euro-Atlantic security community. In this regard, the diverging views and understandings of European strategic autonomy more broadly among EU (and NATO) member states (see Franke and Varma 2019) have the potential for conflicts and misperceptions that can negatively impact future EU–NATO cooperation.

The developments within the EU, including EDF, PESCO and MPCC, are occurring without two of the militarily most powerful member states in the Euro-Atlantic community, the UK and the US. In recent years, both countries encountered many challenges on the domestic level including nationalist and populist governments and Britain's tedious process of withdrawing from the EU. The focus on their domestic political landscapes as well as their geostrategic shifts towards China and the Indo-Pacific region, as outlined in their latest security and defence strategies (UK 2021; US 2021) and thus away from European security, increase concerns over their commitments and investments to enhance EU–NATO cooperation (Besch and Scazzieri 2020; Kaufman 2017). Because the UK and the EU have not (yet) signed a cooperation agreement on foreign, security and defence affairs, it remains to be seen how their future relationship will evolve in this realm and how this will impact Britain's role as the transatlantic bridge in the post-Brexit era.

Besides the 'usual suspects' including Turkey, France, the UK and the US, other domestic issues on the member state level will continue to affect the EU–NATO relationship. For example, Germany's Nord Stream 2 project with Russia has received harsh criticism from the Euro-Atlantic security community. Germany's continuation of the Nord Stream 2 project despite this vocal opposition has created new tensions in the German–US relationship which were sought to improve with the change in the US administration in early 2021. The different perceptions and views on Germany's foreign policy behaviour vis-à-vis Russia as well as the disagreements among EU and NATO member states over how to approach Russia under Vladimir Putin more generally will therefore test the transatlantic relationship (cf. Pagung 2021). This behaviour will furthermore impact Germany's own ability to act as broker and balancer among member states in the EU and NATO. Moreover, the democratic backsliding in several member states, notably in Poland and Hungary, pose additional strains on the internal coherence of both organisations which can have negative effects on their external relations including their own interorganisational relationship (Berschinski 2018).

Taking into account member states' positions and preferences ideally helps to move towards more effective EU–NATO cooperation on both the institutional and operational levels (cf. Aghniashvili 2016). Effective cooperation relies on member states' contributions and support. The typology and the categorisation of each member state provides room for further incentives to allow EU–NATO cooperation to progress and develop in a way that supports all member states and their foreign and security policy orientations. The advantages are manifold. First, this would overcome fragmentation and avoid new frictions among member states concerning shared strategic views on EU–NATO cooperation and combined responses to international threats and challenges. Moreover, this will also lead to greater effectiveness particularly in terms of practical cooperation. In the context of crisis responses, for example, considering member states' positions in the EU–NATO relationship allows the creation of mechanisms to respond especially to hybrid threats that require the toolboxes of both organisations. For instance, the ongoing conflict in Ukraine and the dispute with Russia as well as the subsequent involvement by international security organisations, including the EU and NATO, highlight the necessity of a concerted approach which includes civilian and military components that are to be coordinated effectively (Mälksoo 2018; Pindják 2014).

Interorganisational cooperation and member states: theoretical findings

This research has employed a conceptualisation of interorganisational cooperation to analyse the role of member states in the relationship between the EU and NATO. The framework incorporates a diverse range of theoretical debates, paradigms and viewpoints with roots in the study of regime complexes (Alter and Raustiala 2018; Raustiala and Victor 2004), neoliberalism (Keohane 1982, Krasner 1982), organisational theory, interorganisationalism and interinstitutionalism (Biermann and Koops 2017; Franke 2017; Gehring and Oberthür 2004, 2009; Jönsson 1986, 1993; Lipson 2017) and network analysis (Dorussen and Ward 2008; Hafner-Burton, Kahler and Montgomery 2009; Maoz 2012). It has furthermore reflected on constructivist aspects of international organisations as social actors such as socialisation and learning processes within and between organisations (Checkel 2005; Johnston 2001; Juncos and Pomorska 2006). In addition, it took account of practice approaches to cooperation (Græger 2016, 2017), the role of international bureaucracies and the notion of autonomy of international organisations (Barnett and Finnemore 1999, 2004; Bauer and Ege 2016; Reinalda and Verbeek 1998). With the help of these existing theoretical contributions, a set of key features of interorganisational interaction has been identified and elaborated. These features include the density of network in which the international organisations are located, functional overlap, the level of formalisation of their relations, the frequency of interactions, the level of intensity ranging from absent to minimal, moderate and strong and membership overlap (see Table 2.1). Deriving from these features, key themes have been distilled which then help to examine member states' roles, attitudes and contributions to the EU–NATO relationship. The most salient feature is the issue of membership overlap which is a defining characteristic of EU–NATO cooperation. The use and perception of membership by states has therefore played a central role throughout this analysis. Moreover, member states' embeddedness in bilateral and minilateral partnerships, contributions to EU and NATO operations as well as their standpoints on division of labour and interoperability account for this key feature.

The elaboration of a set of features of interorganisational relations has brought forward a number of strengths and weaknesses drawn from combining different theoretical and conceptual approaches, such as organisation theory, regime complexity, institutionalism and interorganisationalism. While this theoretical eclecticism provides a richness of approaches and viewpoints to understand interorganisational interaction, developing a set of features in this book has still highlighted some shortcomings. First, its application needs to be undertaken more rigorously throughout the different disciplines and each field will need to contribute to the further elaboration of the set of key features as a tool to examine interorganisational relationships. Furthermore, the current framework lacks methodological guidance to assess the intensity, frequency and level of formalisation. For example, it does not yet enable to identify when an interorganisational relationship counts as, for example, moderate or strong. Methodological and analytical tools will therefore need to be developed and tested that identify the threshold levels.

From the onset, this book has argued that member states play a fundamental role in shaping the direction and design of the relationship between the EU and NATO because of their decision-making powers, resources and capabilities. What has been striking, however, is that the role of member states in the study of interorganisational relations has often been overlooked and received little attention in both theoretical and empirical debates. More recently, the focus has shifted towards the growing role of international bureaucracies and secretariats as well as staff-to-staff cooperation (Biermann and Koops 2017; Græger 2016). Yet, states are the foundational building blocks and key providers not only of resources but also the *raison d'être* of international (intergovernmental) organisations. The successes and failures as well as the political directions of international organisations are strongly influenced by member states (Archer 2001). Because of this scarcity of theoretical debates on member states in interorganisational relations, this research has utilised findings from studies on member states in international organisations. For the analysis of the EU and NATO, particularly the distinction between original or old and subsequent or new members as well as between single and multiple members has been most crucial (cf. Gehring and Faude 2014; Koch 2008; Magliveras 2011).

Since this book was interested in examining the role of member states in the EU–NATO relationship, it developed a typology of member states in interorganisational cooperation. Each type is equipped with a specific set of characteristics that describe the attitudes, positions and viewpoints of member states, which help to understand and predict their behaviour towards future initiatives in interorganisational relations. Member states have been categorised into the typology based on a set of selection criteria, which include states' attitudes towards interorganisational interaction and cooperation among international organisations (positive, negative, balanced, indifferent), level of active promotion of closer interorganisational cooperation (absent, low, medium, high), view on division of labour between the international organisations (positive, negative, balanced, indifferent), level of engagement in negotiations (absent, low, medium, high) and material contributions to the international organisations and their operations (absent, low, medium, high). Another key distinguishing factor is a state's approach to foreign and security policy as well as its general political orientation in security and defence. The consideration of states' distinctive characteristics and foreign and security policy orientations helps to further identify bilateral and minilateral relationships among member states that share these orientations and interest particularly in regard to interorganisational relations. Drawn from these criteria, the typology of member states in interorganisational cooperation consists of four types: advocates, blockers, balancers and neutrals (see Table 2.2).

Member states that belong to the group of *advocates* are prominent for promoting interorganisational interaction among other states through bargaining and negotiations. Building ties with other states through bilateral and multilateral partnerships underscores their proactive approach as they make use of their embeddedness in networks and coalition groups to promote their views on interorganisational cooperation. They are also in favour of a clearly defined division of labour to make efficient use of member states' resources as well as to avoid competition and duplication of both organisations. In contrast, *blockers* are defined as the 'troublemakers' because they seek to slow down the process of cooperation. Blockers apply political strategies such as hostage-taking in which they use their own membership against others, and thereby obstruct the division of labour between the organisations as well as the execution of their mandates (cf. Alter and Meunier 2009; Hofmann 2009, 2019). In order to contribute to interorganisational cooperation, *balancers* seek to mediate between the organisations and between other member states to reduce the dividing lines that emerge in interorganisational interactions. Their main aim is to mitigate tensions and broker between states, which they pursue through their multiple membership to build linkages in which they initiate informal negotiations ahead of the decision-making processes. Due to their own limited capabilities, they rely on a division of labour that supports the organisations' comparative advantages and complementarity while also serving their own roles as brokers and balancers. Lastly, *neutrals* are comprised of states that take a neutral standpoint on interorganisational cooperation, that is, they do not take a strong position similar to advocates or blockers. Because of their single membership, limited capabilities and national constraints, these states recognise their restricted abilities to shape interorganisational relations and therefore only make few contributions. This position, however, also induces their dependence on interorganisational cooperation to make use of the joint resources and strengths.

The overall goal of this typology is that it seeks to help making future predictions about the positioning of a specific member state, which is particularly significant when a new policy or initiative is introduced. The ability to foresight potential outcomes based on the location of states in the typology can lead to the identification of states that might seek to obstruct the aspired process. With the help of the typology, similarities and differences can be pointed out, which then enable to formulate new policy ideas and initiatives to the extent that they would receive greater acceptance among all member states. However, member states are not fixed to one of these types and shifts are possible though not frequently. Member states' preference and attitudes towards interorganisational cooperation are determined by their view on the organisations' purposes, national interests, foreign and security policy orientation and historical experiences. Since their positions are not fixed, their affiliations can change over time through the occurrence of external and internal events, such as the onset of new conflicts and crises, change in government and through learning and socialisation with other member states in these international security organisations. Those states that indicate characteristics of more than one type are labelled as boundary cases or 'swing states' (Rodt 2017).

One of the limitations of the typology is therefore that not every member state fits directly into one of the types and cannot be clearly categorised. Shifting across types complicates the overall categorisation of states as well as the predictions of member states' responses to the introduction of new initiatives if their categorisation is not clear due changes on their domestic level. While this research focuses on the analysis and the application of the typology of member states in the EU–NATO relationship, the aim of the typology is also to serve as a point of departure for a more generalisable analytical framework to examine the role of member states in interorganisational cooperation outside this particular relationship. The application requires that overlapping organisations include exchanges and interactions at the member state level to account for member states' influence on interorganisational relations in which their own position plays a significant factor. This means that the typology of member states is limited to those interorganisational relationships that takes place not only on the institutional and inter-bureaucratic levels but that presents more comprehensive interactions with higher scores concerning the degrees of intensity, formality and especially membership overlap.

In addition, the use of typologies is generally difficult where the categorisation relies on information, data and knowledge acquired through third parties, for example, through the conduct of interviews and the examination of secondary literature, in a field that deals with sensitive topics and where access to participants with this knowledge is limited. The analysis of national security and defence strategies has been useful since these provide sources to carve out states' orientations towards the EU and NATO, which also revealed national restraints, attitudes and positions. However, the language of these documents has shown similarities referring to the commonality of wordings and phrasings in official documents. This has added to the difficulty of categorisation because they had to be examined with consideration of the findings from the interviews and the secondary literature. Concerning the specific categorisation of EU and NATO member states into this typology, the adaptability and changing nature of states' foreign and security policy orientations, domestic politics as well as the occurrence of external shocks have posed additional challenges to clearly identify and categorise each state into the typology. Boundary cases, who indicate key characteristics of more than one type, have thus been especially difficult to categorise.

Analysing the role of member states beyond EU–NATO cooperation: applicability and generalisation

One of the greater aims of analysing the roles of member states in the EU–NATO relationship as well as the development of the typology of member states in interorganisational cooperation was to create an analytical framework that contributes more broadly to the study and conceptualisation of the relations between international organisations. Examining the interactions between the EU and NATO and focusing on the particular roles of member states is only one, albeit a very illustrative, case which has been empirically examined in this book. The findings, conceptualisations and, more importantly, the typology seek to be applicable to studies of interorganisational interaction beyond the EU–NATO relationship as well as beyond the area of foreign, security and defence affairs. Yet, only a few examples of interorganisational cooperation exist that meet the criteria outlined by the six features: density of network, functional overlap, formalisation, frequency, intensity and membership overlap.

Concerning the applicability of the typology of member states, however, research has not only been limited but also the number of cases account to just a few. When examining the role of member states and investigating whether particular member states are responsible for promoting or obstructing the cooperative efforts between international organisations, specific positions need to be identified. Most prominently, these are advocates and blockers as well as 'linking-pin' actors connecting different networks and linkages (Jönsson 1986). This would ultimately require a membership overlap to a higher degree between the participating organisations. Without a high level of membership overlap, a state considered to be the advocate would find it difficult to promote interorganisational cooperation if it does not possess the necessary channels to influence the decision-making and policy-shaping processes as well as the required channels of communication through informal networks and minilateral partnerships. The notion of membership overlap is thus a highly explanatory factor. Moreover, a degree of institutional compatibility is necessary so that advocates, blockers, balancers and neutrals have the ability to exert influence and to shape interorganisational interaction.

In the area of foreign, security and defence affairs, a multitude of studies has already been conducted on interorganisational relations. Examples that have received particular attention include the relations between the EU and the UN as well as the relations between the EU with other regional organisations, such as the AU and ASEAN (see Charbonneau 2008; Laatikainen and Smith 2006; Novotny and Portela 2012; Rodt and Okeke 2013). The UN is another particular example that keeps a track record of cooperation with international organisations in the area of peacekeeping and security, including the AU, ASEAN, Economic Community of Western African States (ECOWAS) and NATO because of its reliance on regional organisations, their expertise and resources. Beyond security and defence, the occurrence as well as the study of interorganisational interactions are most prominent in the areas of environmental policy and climate change, energy policy and international trade (Biedenkopf 2017; Franke and Koch 2013; van de Graaf 2017). The theoretical framework of interorganisational relations is thus applicable to examine cooperation between international organisations in a variety of policy fields.

One example where a high degree of membership overlap and some institutional compatibility exist, although limited, mostly occur when the UN cooperates and interacts with regional and sector-specific organisations. Yet, the main actor on the UN side is the UN Secretariat and cooperation takes place primarily on the ambassadorial level. This means that the main representatives from the organisations meet to negotiate and agree on the terms of cooperation, and therefore exclude member states. In some geographical regions, more than one organisation exists that deals with regional and specific policy issues. For instance, there is a very high degree of membership overlap between the AU and ECOWAS and, in fact, all of the ECOWAS members also possess membership in the AU. In recent years, the two organisations have increased their cooperation and even jointly launched the African-led International Support Mission in Mali (AFISMA) (UN 2012). Examples of interorganisational interaction from other policy fields such as trade, energy policy and environmental policy include the interactions between the International Monetary Fund (IMF), World Bank, World Trade Organisation (WTO) and the G20 or the relations between the International Energy Agency (IEA) and the Organisation of the Petroleum-Exporting Countries (OPEC) (Biedenkopf 2017; Freytag and Kirton 2017; van de Graaf 2017).

Outlook and future research

Overall, this book has demonstrated that member states play a crucial part in shaping the relationship between the EU and NATO. There is still more to learn about EU–NATO cooperation due to the evolving process of their relationship. The outcomes of implementing the proposals of the 2016 Joint Declaration and 2018 Implementation Plan remain to be seen. What is more, the changing security environment in Europe and its wider periphery also shape their relationship. New security challenges and threats require adaptation and changes to their capacities and capabilities, which trigger member states to take important decisions on the future security agendas of both organisations. With the emergence of non-traditional and hybrid security threats that demand multi-faceted responses, the EU, NATO and their member states once again need to renegotiate the grand bargain of their division of tasks. The findings of this research consequently guide two strands of future research. The first relates to the EU–NATO relationship and the second addresses the applicability of the typology of member states.

Throughout this book, it was highlighted that there is a greater need for the consideration and inclusion of member states in the study of EU–NATO cooperation. Future research of this particular relationship will therefore need to take into account more intensively the influence by domestic politics on member states' positions within these two organisations, including the change of government and coalitions and the potential shift of foreign and security policy approaches. Particularly the issue of Brexit and the future EU–UK relationship will need to receive greater attention when analysing EU–NATO cooperation, not only on the institutional level but, even more importantly, on the operational level since the UK has been a key provider of military capabilities. Clarifying their relations concerning security and defence issues will be detrimental for identifying avenues for cooperation in European security. Similarly, the renewed commitment to transatlantic security cooperation as well as the revaluation of the EU–US partnership under President Biden sounds promising for both NATO itself and the EU–NATO relationship. Nevertheless, the demands for greater European responsibility and burden-sharing remain high.

In addition, future research will need to consider the progress and improvements on the institutional and interorganisational levels. While scholars interested in EU–NATO cooperation have also shifted their focus towards developments within the organisations in the field of security and defence, special attention has been given to the elaboration of CSDP and the launch of the EU's new instruments such as EDF, MPCC and PESCO. It will be of wider interest to examine the impact of such new tools and mechanisms on the EU–NATO relationship and whether they will lead to greater European autonomy in security and defence or whether they will allow the two organisations to collaborate and cooperate more closely. What is more, with the parallel processes of the EU's Strategic Compass and the negotiations on a new NATO strategic concept based on the NATO 2030 Report (NATO 2020), both organisations are undergoing new adaptation processes. Both seek to broaden their security agendas. For example, NATO aspires to tackle issues such as climate change, human security and pandemics which were traditionally in the realm of the EU's foreign, security and defence policy. Similarly, with the Strategic Compass, the EU strives for a more comprehensive approach to security and defence by also developing and acquiring the necessary instruments and capabilities, including hardware and military capabilities (EU 2021). The adaptation and broadening of security agendas require a debate about the previous lessons learned and, more importantly, the future division of tasks and responsibilities to support each organisation's comparative advantage (Biscop 2021; Tardy 2021).

An additional factor that future research will need to take into account is the role and influence of external actors, including individual states, other international and regional organisations and non-governmental actors involved in the area of security and defence. Individual actors and key states such as Russia as the Eastern neighbour as well as the UN, the AU and the OSCE will have an interest in the development of the EU–NATO relationship and thus need to receive greater attention. The revival and intensification of the interactions between the EU and NATO have emerged with the onset of the Ukraine crisis and the conflict with Russia in 2014. Russia has therefore been seen as one of the triggers for the most recent developments in the EU–NATO relationship. Therefore, Russia cannot be excluded from European security issues and, in fact, it plays a significant role by representing one part of the European security architecture. Russia's new foreign policy direction will thus need to be considered in the future analysis of this special relationship. Likewise, the crises on Europe's southern borders and particularly in the Mediterranean Sea do not only affect the EU and NATO but have also expedited the interests of other international actors in the region, such as the AU. In the past, primarily the EU, but also NATO such as in the Gulf of Aden, has been an active security actor in Africa. Consequently, the occurrence of future crisis situations in the proximity of the Euro-Atlantic security community will determine their interactions with other actors and how these will translate to their own interorganisational relationship.

Avenues for future theoretical research on interorganisational relations and the role of member states will need to move beyond the EU–NATO relationship by applying the typology to cases in other policy areas and in other geographical regions. As mentioned above, this research could include the examination of the UN's relations with regional organisations and regional relationships such as AU–ECOWAS cooperation as well as further elaboration of the interactions between, for instance, the IMF and World Bank and any interactions between international organisations that meet the features of interorganisational relations as outlined in the theoretical framework of this book. By providing an overview of the features of interorganisational cooperation and developing the typology of member states, this book has overall enhanced the scholarship of EU–NATO cooperation. In doing so, it has furthermore contributed to the analysis of interorganisational relations by establishing a conceptual and analytical tool that allows for future studies of interactions between international organisations beyond the EU–NATO relationship.

References

Acikmese, Sinem Akgul and Dimitrios Triantaphyllou (2012) 'The NATO-EU-Turkey trilogy: The impact of the Cyprus conundrum', *Southeast European and Black Sea Studies*, 12(4): 555–573.

Aghniashvili, Tinatin (2016) 'Towards more effective cooperation? The role of states in shaping NATO-EU interaction and cooperation', *Connections: The Quarterly Journal*, 15(4): 67–90.

Alter, Karen J. and Sophie Meunier (2009) 'The politics of international regime complexity', *Perspectives on Politics, Symposium*, 7(1): 13–24.

Alter, Karen J. and Kal Raustiala (2018) 'The rise of international regime complexity', *Annual Review of International Law and Social Science*, 14(1): 329–349.

Archer, Clive (2001) *International Organisations*, 3rd edition, London and New York: Routledge.

Barnett, Michael and Martha Finnemore (1999) 'The politics, power, and pathologies of international organisations', *International Organisation*, 53(4): 699–732.

Barnett, Michael and Martha Finnemore (2004) *Rules for the World: International Organisations in Global Politics*, Ithaca; London: Cornell University Press.

Bauer, Michael W. and Jörn Ege (2016) 'Bureaucratic autonomy of international organisations' secretariats', *Journal of European Public Policy*, 23(7): 1019–1037.

Berschinski, Rob (2018) The Threat Within NATO, *The Atlantic,* Published on 7 April 2018, www.theatlantic.com/international/archive/2018/04/nato-hungary-authoritarianism/557459/ (accessed on 10/04/2021).

Besch, Sophia and Luigi Scazzieri (2020) 'European strategic autonomy and the transatlantic bargain', *CER Policy Brief*, 1–9.

Bialos, Jeffrey P. (2005) 'The United States, Europe and the interoperability gap', *The International Spectator*, 40(2): 53–62.

Biedenkopf, Julia (2017) 'Relations between international organisations in combating climate change'. *In*: Biermann, Rafael and Joachim A. Koops (eds) *Palgrave Handbook of Interorganisational Relations in World Politics,* New York, Basingstoke: Palgrave Macmillan, 649–676.

Biermann, Rafael and Joachim A. Koops (2017) *Palgrave Handbook of Interorganisational Relations in World Politics*, New York, Basingstoke: Palgrave Macmillan.

Biscop, Sven (1999) 'The UK's change of course: A new chance for the ESDI', *European Foreign Affairs Review*, 4(2): 253–268.

Biscop, Sven (2012) 'The UK and European defence: Leading of leaving?' *International Affairs*, 88(6): 1297–1313.

Biscop, Sven (2021) 'EU and NATO strategy: A compass, a concept, and a concordat', *Egmont Security Policy Brief*, 141: 1–8.

Charbonneau, Bruno (2008) 'Dreams of empire: France, Europe, and the new interventionism in Africa', *Modern & Contemporary France*, 16(3): 279–295.

Checkel, Jeffrey R. (2005) 'International institutions and socialisation in Europe: Introduction and framework', *International Organisation*, 59(4): 801–826.

Dorussen, Han and Hugh Ward (2008) 'Intergovernmental organisations and the Kantian Peace: A network perspective', *Journal of Conflict Resolution*, 52(2): 189–212.

Duke, Simon (2008) 'The future of EU–NATO relations: A case of mutual irrelevance through competition?' *Journal of European Integration*, 30(1): 27–43.

Dursun–Özkanca, Oya (2019) *Turkey-West Relations: The Politics of Intra-Alliance Opposition*, Cambridge: Cambridge University Press.

European Union (2021) *Towards a Strategic Compass*, https://eeas.europa.eu/sites/default/files/towards-a-strategic-compass-2021-february.pdf (accessed on 25/03/2021).

Fiott, Daniel (2017) 'A revolution too far? US defence innovation, Europe and NATO's military-technological gap', *Journal of Strategic Studies*, 40(3): 417–437.

Franke, Ulrich (2017) 'Inter-Organisational Relations: Five Theoretical Approaches'. *In*: Renée Marlin-Bennett (ed) *Oxford Research Encyclopedia of International Studies*, New York: International Studies Association and Oxford University Press (online publication).

Franke, Ulrich and Martin Koch (2013) 'Inter-organisational relations as structures of corporate practice', *Journal of International Organizations Studies,* 4(1): 85–103.

Franke, Ulrike and Tara Varma (2019) Independence Play: Europe's Pursuit of Strategic Autonomy, *ECFR Flash Scorecard,* https://ecfr.eu/special/independence_play_europes_pursuit_of_strategic_autonomy/ (accessed on 20/03/2021).

Freytag, Andreas and John J. Kirton (2017) 'Pushed toward partnership: Increasing cooperation between the Bretton Woods Bodies'. *In*: Biermann, Rafael and Joachim A. Koops (eds) *Palgrave Handbook of Inter-Organisational Relations in World Politics*, New York, Basingstoke: Palgrave Macmillan, 569–589.

Gebhard, Carmen and Simon J. Smith (2015) 'The two faces of EU-NATO cooperation: Counter-piracy operations off the Somali coast', *Cooperation and Conflict*, 50(1): 107–127.

Gehring, Thomas and Benjamin Faude (2014) 'A theory of emerging order within international complexes: How competition among regulatory international institutions leads to institutional adaptation and division of labour', *Review of International Organisations*, 9(4): 471–498.

Gehring, Thomas and Sebastian Oberthür (2004) 'Exploring regime interaction: A framework of analysis'. *In*: Underdal, Arild and Oran R. Young (eds) *Regime Consequences: Methodological Challenges and Research Strategies*, Dordrecht: Kluwer, 247–269.

Gehring, Thomas and Sebastian Oberthür (2009) 'The causal mechanisms of interaction between international institutions', *European Journal of International Relations*, 15(1): 125–156.

Got, Antoine (2020) 'Turkey's Crisis With the West: How a New Low in Relations Risks Paralysing NATO', *War on the Rocks,* Published on 19 November 2020, https://warontherocks.com/2020/11/turkeys-crisis-with-the-west-how-a-new-low-in-relations-risks-paralyzing-nato/ (accessed on 23/02/2021).

Græger, Nina (2016) 'European security as practice: EU-NATO communities of practice in the making?' *European Security*, 25(4): 478–501.

Græger, Nina (2017) 'Grasping the everyday and extraordinary in EU-NATO relations: The added value of practice approaches', *European Security*, 26: 3, 340–358.

Hafner-Burton, Emilie M., Miles Kahler and Alexander H. Montgomery (2009) 'Network analysis for international relations', *International Organisation*, 63(3): 559–592.

Hofmann, Stephanie C. (2009) 'Overlapping institutions in the realm of international security: The case of NATO and ESDP', *Perspectives on Politics*, 7(1): 45–51.

Hofmann, Stephanie C. (2019) 'The politics of overlapping organisations: Hostage-taking, forum-shopping and brokering', *Journal of European Public Policy*, 26(6): 883–905.

Johnston, Alastair Iain (2001) 'Treating international institutions as social environments', *International Studies Quarterly*, 45(4): 487–515.

Jönsson, Christer (1986): 'Interorganisation theory and international organisation', *International Studies Quarterly*, 30(1): 39–57.

Jönsson, Christer (1993): 'International organisation and cooperation: An interorganisational perspective', *International Social Science Journal*, 138(4): 463–477.

Juncos, Ana E. and Karolina Pomorska (2006) 'Playing the Brussels game: Strategic socialisation in the CFSP council working groups', *European Integration Online Papers*, 10(11): 1–17.

Kaufman, Joyce P. (2017) 'The US perspective on NATO under Trump: Lessons of the past and prospects for the future', *International Affairs*, 93(2): 251–266.

Keohane, Robert O. (1982) 'The demand for international regimes', *International Organisation*, 36(2): 325–55.

Koch, Martin (2008) *Verselbstständigungsprozesse Internationaler Organisationen*, Wiesbaden: VS Verlag für Sozialwissenschaften.

Krasner, Stephen D. (1982) 'Structural causes and regime consequences: Regimes as intervening variables', *International Organisation*, 36(2): 185–205.

Laatikainen, Katie Verlin and Karen E. Smith (2006) *The European Union at the United Nations: Intersecting Multilateralisms*, Basingstoke: Palgrave Macmillan.

Lipson, Michael (2017) 'Organisation theory and cooperation and conflict among international organisations'. *In*: Biermann, Rafael and Joachim A. Koops (eds) *Palgrave Handbook of Inter-Organisational Relations in World Politics*, New York, Basingstoke: Palgrave Macmillan, 67–96.

Magliveras, Konstantinos D. (2011) 'Membership in international organisations'. *In*: Klabbers, Jan and Asa Wallendahl (eds) *Research Handbook on the Law of International Organisations*, Cheltenham and Northampton: Edward Elgar Publishing, 84–107.

Mälksoo, Maria (2018) 'Countering hybrid warfare as ontological security management: The emerging practices of the EU and NATO', *European Security*, 27(3): 374–392.

Maoz, Zeev (2012) 'How network analysis can inform the study of international relations', *Conflict Management and Peace Science*, 29(3): 247–256.

Messervy-Whiting, Graham (2005) 'The growing EU-NATO relationship: Beyond Berlin', *The International Spectator*, 40(2): 63–73.

NATO (2020) *NATO 2030: United for a New Era. Analysis and Recommendations of the Reflection Group Appointed by the NATO Secretary General*, Published on 25 November 2020, Brussels: NATO.

Nováky, Niklas I.M. (2015) 'Deploying EU military crisis management operations: A collective action perspective', *European Security*, 24(4): 491–508.

Novotny, Daniel and Clara Portela (2012) *EU-ASEAN Relations in the 21st Century: Strategic Partnership in the Making*, Basingstoke: Palgrave Macmillan.

Pagung, Sarah (2021) *Caught in Domestic Politics: German-US Talks on a Nord Stream 2-Deal*, https://dgap.org/en/research/publications/caught-domestic-politics (accessed on 23/03/2021).

Perruche, Jean-Paul (2014) 'From exception to facilitator: What place for France in the EU/NATO partnership in the post-Cold War global world?' *Journal of Transatlantic Studies*, 12(4): 432–442.

Pierini, March (2020) 'How far can Turkey challenge NATO and the EU in 2020?' *Carnegie Europe*, 1–11, https://carnegieeurope.eu/2020/01/29/how-far-can-turkey-challenge-nato-and-eu-in-2020-pub-80912 (accessed on 03/02/2020).

Pindják, Peter (2014) *Deterring Hybrid Warfare: A Chance for NATO and the EU to Work Together?* www.nato.int/docu/review/2014/also-in-2014/deterring–hybrid-warfare/en/index.htm (accessed on 03/11/2018).

Raustiala, Kal and David G. Victor (2004) 'The regime complex for plant genetic resources', *International Organisation*, 58(2): 277–309.

Reichard, Martin (2006) *The EU-NATO Relationship: A Legal and Political Perspective,* Abingdon: Routledge.

Reinalda, Bob and Bertjan Verbeek (1998) *Autonomous Policy Making by International Organisations,* London and New York: Routledge.

Rodt, Annemarie Peen (2017) 'Member states policy towards EU military operations'. *In*: Hadfield, Amelia et al. (eds) *Foreign Policies of EU Member States: Continuity and Europeanisation*, Abingdon: Routledge, 131–147.

Rodt, Annemarie Peen and Jide Martyns Okeke (2013) 'AU-EU "strategic partnership": Strengthening policy convergence and regime efficacy in the African peace and security complex?', *African Security*, 6(3–4): 211–233.

Smith, Simon J. (2011) 'EU-NATO cooperation: A case of institutional fatigue?', *European Security*, 20(2) 243–264.

Sperling, James (2004) 'Capabilities traps and gaps: Symptom or cause of a troubled transatlantic relationship', *Contemporary Security Policy*, 25(3): 452–478.

Tardy, Thierry (2021) 'For a new NATO-EU bargain', *Egmont Security Policy Brief*, 138: 1–5.

Touzovskaia, Natalia (2006) 'EU-NATO relations: How close to "strategic partnership?"' *European Security*, 15(3): 235–258.

United Nations (2012) Security Council Authorises Deployment of African-Led International Support Mission in Mali for Initial Year-Long Period, SC/10870 of 20 December 2012.

van de Graaf, Thijs (2017) 'Organisational interactions in global energy governance'. *In*: Biermann, Rafael and Joachim A. Koops (eds) *Palgrave Handbook of Interorganisational Relations in World Politics*, New York Basingstoke: Palgrave Macmillan, 591–610.

Varwick, Johannes and Joachim A. Koops (2009) 'The European Union and NATO: "shrewd interorganisationalism" in the making?' *In*: Jørgensen, Knud Erik (ed.) *The European Union and International Organisations*, Abingdon: Routledge, 101–130.

Whitman, Richard G. (2004) 'NATO, the EU and ESDP: An emerging division of labour', *Contemporary Security Policy*, 25(3): 430–451.

Appendix A
List of interviews

Title	Description	Date	Location
EU Official 1	EU Official at European External Action Service	14 March 2017	Brussels, Belgium
EU Official 2	EU Official at European External Action Service	22 March 2017	Brussels, Belgium
NATO Official 1	NATO Official at NATO HQ	29 March 2017	Brussels, Belgium
EU Official 3	EU Official at European External Action Service	3 April 2017	Brussels, Belgium
NATO Official 2	NATO Official at NATO HQ	13 April 2017	Brussels, Belgium
Cypriote Official 1	Official at the Cyprus Permanent Representation to the EU	26 April 2017	Brussels, Belgium
French Official 1	Official at the French Delegation to NATO	6 June 2017	Brussels, Belgium
EU Official 4	EU Official at European External Action Service	9 June 2017	Brussels, Belgium
Cypriote Officials 2	Two Officials at the Cyprus Permanent Representation to the EU	9 June 2017	Brussels, Belgium
French Official 2	Official at the French Permanent Representation to the EU	12 June 2017	Brussels, Belgium
German Official 1	Official at the German Permanent Representation to the EU	13 June 2017	Brussels, Belgium
NATO Official 3	NATO Official at NATO HQ	26 June 2017	Brussels, Belgium
German Officials 2	Three Officials at the German Delegation to NATO	28 June 2017	Brussels, Belgium
NATO Officials 4	Two former NATO Officials	20 July 2017	Brussels, Belgium
British Official 1	Official at the British Delegation to NATO	20 July 2017	Brussels, Belgium

Title	Description	Date	Location
German Officials 3	Two Officials at the Federal Ministry of Defence Germany	9 August 2017	Berlin, Germany
Romanian Official 1	Official at the Romanian Delegation to NATO	24 October 2017	Brussels, Belgium
British Officials 2	Two Officials at the British Permanent Representation to the EU	24 October 2017	Brussels, Belgium
Czech Official 1	Official at the Czech Permanent Representation to the EU	25 October 2017	Brussels, Belgium
Slovak Official 1	Official at the Slovak Permanent Representation to the EU	25 October 2017	Brussels, Belgium
Polish Official 1	Official at the Polish Permanent Representation to the EU	26 October 2017	Brussels, Belgium
NATO Official 5	NATO Official at NATO HQ	12 November 2017	Berlin, Germany
Estonian Official 1	Official at the Estonian Permanent Representation to the EU	12 February 2018	Brussels, Belgium
Dutch Official 1	Official at the Dutch Permanent Representation to the EU	13 February 2018	Brussels, Belgium
Italian Official 1	Official at the Italian Delegation to NATO	13 February 2018	Brussels, Belgium
Czech Official 2	Official at the Czech Delegation to NATO	15 February 2018	Brussels, Belgium
Czech Official 3	Official at the Czech Delegation to NATO	15 February 2018	Brussels, Belgium
Estonian Official 2	Official at the Estonian Delegation to NATO	16 February 2018	Brussels, Belgium

Appendix B
List of official documents and strategic security and defence papers

Member state/ international organisation	Year of publication	Title of document	Source
European Union	2003	A Secure Europe in a Better World: European Security Strategy	European Council
European Union	2016	Shared Vision, Common Action: A Stronger Europe – A Global Strategy for the European Union's Foreign and Security Strategy	European External Action Service
European Union/ NATO	2016	Joint Declaration on EU– NATO Cooperation	NATO
NATO	1949	The North Atlantic Treaty (Washington Treaty)	NATO
NATO	1991	The Alliance's New Strategic Concept	NATO
NATO	1999	The Alliance's Strategic Concept	NATO
NATO	2010	Active Engagement, Modern Defence – Strategic Concept for the Defence and Security of the Members of NATO	NATO
NATO	2014	The Wales Declaration on the Transatlantic Bond	NATO
Albania	2004	National Security Strategy	Government of the Republic of Albania
Albania	2012	Military Review	The Centre for Defence Analyses (CDA) of the Albanian Training and Doctrine Command

Member state/ international organisation	*Year of publication*	*Title of document*	*Source*
Austria	2004	Weissbuch 2004: Analyse, Bilanz, Perspektiven	Ministry of Defence
Austria	2008	Weissbuch 2008	Ministry of Defence and Sport
Austria	2010	Weissbuch 2010	Ministry of Defence and Sport
Austria	2012	Weissbuch 2012	Ministry of Defence and Sport
Austria	2013	Austrian Security Strategy: Security in a New Decade – Shaping Security	Federal Chancellery of Austria
Belgium	2000	The Modernisation Plan 2000–2015 of the Belgian Armed Forces	Government of Belgium
Belgium	2016	The Strategic Vision for Defence	Ministry of Defence
Bulgaria	2002	White Paper on Defence	Ministry of Defence
Bulgaria	2010	White Paper on Defence and the Armed Forces of the Republic of Bulgaria	Ministry of National Defence
Canada	2008	Canada First: Defence Strategy	Ministry of National Defence
Canada	2017	Strong, Secure, Engaged: Canada's Defence Policy	Ministry of National Defence
Croatia	2005	Strategic Defence Review	Ministry of Defence
Croatia	2017	National Security Strategy	Ministry of Defence
Cyprus	n.a.	Defence Policy	Online/Website of the Ministry of Defence
Czech Republic	1997	National Defence Strategy of the Czech Republic	Ministry of Defence
Czech Republic	2008	The Military Strategy of the Czech Republic	Ministry of Defence
Czech Republic	2012	The Defence Strategy of the Czech Republic: A Responsible State and a Responsible Ally	Ministry of Defence
Czech Republic	2015	Security Strategy of the Czech Republic	Government of the Czech Republic
Denmark	2009	Danish Defence Agreement 2010–2014	Danish Government

Member state/ international organisation	Year of publication	Title of document	Source
Denmark	2016	Danish Diplomacy and Defence in Times of Change: A Review of Denmark's Foreign and Security Policy	Danish Government
Denmark	2017	A Strong Defence of Denmark: Proposal for new defence agreement 2018–2023	Ministry of Defence (Forsvarsministeret)
Denmark	2018	Foreign and Security Policy Strategy 2019–2020	Danish Government
Denmark	2018	Defence Agreement 2018–2023	Ministry of Defence (Forsvarsministeret)
Estonia	2004	National Security Concept	Government of Estonia
Estonia	2010	National Security Concept	Government of Estonia and Riigikogu (Parliament)
Estonia	2011	National Defence Strategy of Estonia	Ministry of Defence
Finland	2001	Finnish Security and Defence Policy 2001: Report by the Government to Parliament	Government of Finland
Finland	2004	Finnish Security and Defence Policy 2004	Prime Minister's Office
Finland	2010	Security Strategy for Society	Ministry of Defence
Finland	2012	Finnish Security and Defence Policy 2012	Prime Minister's Office
Finland	2016	Government Report on Finnish Foreign and Security Policy	Prime Minister's Office
France	1994	White Paper on Defence	Ministry of Defence
France	2008	The White Paper on Defence and National Security	Ministry of Defence
France	2012	Meeting of the Foreign Affairs Ministers and Ministers of Defence of France, Germany, Italy, Poland and Spain; Paris November 2012	Diplomatie.gouv.fr

Member state/ international organisation	Year of publication	Title of document	Source
France	2013	The White Paper on Defence and National Security: Twelve key points	Ministry of Defence
France	2017	Strategic Review of Defence and National Security: Key Points	Ministry of Defence
Germany	1998	Gemeinsame deutsch-französische Positionen zu aktuellen Themen der Europapolitik	Government of the Federal Republic of Germany
Germany	2003	Defence Policy Guidelines	Ministry of Defence
Germany	2006	White Paper on German Security Policy and the Future of the Bundeswehr	Ministry of Defence
Germany	2016	White Paper on German Security Policy and the Future of the Bundeswehr	Ministry of Defence
Germany	2016	Verfassungsrechtliche Grundlage für Auslandseinsätze der Bundeswehr: Überlegungen zur Änderung der verfassungsrechtlichen Praxis	German Parliament
Greece	1997	White Paper for the Armed Forces	Hellenic Ministry of Defence
Greece	2007	Greek Security Policy in the 21st Century	Thanos Dokos (ed.), Hellenic Foundation for European & Foreign Policy
Hungary	2004	The National Security Strategy of the Republic of Hungary	Government of the Republic of Hungary
Hungary	2012	Hungary's National Security Strategy	Ministry of Foreign Affairs
Iceland	n.a.	Ministry of Foreign Affairs: National Security	Iceland Government Offices; Ministry of Foreign Affairs
Iceland	2015	Parliamentary Resolution on a National Security Policy for Iceland	Icelandic Parliament

Member state/ international organisation	Year of publication	Title of document	Source
Ireland	2007	The White Paper on Defence: Review of Implementation	Department of Defence
Ireland	2015	White Paper on Defence	Department of Defence
Ireland	2016	Strategy Statement 2016–2019	Department of Defence
Italy	2005	The Chief of the Italian Defence Staff Strategic Concept	Ministry of Defence
Italy	2015	White Paper for International Security and Defence	Ministry of Defence
Latvia	2005	The National Security Concept	Ministry of Defence
Latvia	2008	The State Defence Concept	Ministry of Defence
Latvia	2015	The National Security Concept	Ministry of Defence
Latvia	2016	The National Defence Concept	Ministry of Defence
Lithuania	2002	National Security Strategy	Ministry of National Defence
Lithuania	2002	White Paper: Lithuanian Defence Policy	Ministry of National Defence
Lithuania	2017	National Security Strategy	Ministry of National Defence
Lithuania	2017	White Paper: Lithuanian Defence Policy	Ministry of National Defence
Luxembourg	2017	Luxembourg Defence Guidelines for 2025 and Beyond	Ministry of Foreign and European Affairs
Malta	2017	The Armed Forces of Malta: Strategy Paper 2016–2026 – Press Brief	Armed Forces of Malta, Ministry for Home Affairs and National Security
The Netherlands	2000	Summary of the Defence White Paper	Ministry of Defence
The Netherlands	2005	Netherlands Defence Doctrine	Ministry of Defence
The Netherlands	2013	The Dutch Defence Doctrine	Ministry of Defence

Member state/ international organisation	Year of publication	Title of document	Source
The Netherlands	2018	Defence White Paper: Investigating in our people, capabilities and visibility	Ministry of Defence
Norway	2004	Strategic Defence Concept	Ministry of Defence
Norway	2006	Norwegian Defence	Ministry of Defence
Norway	2008	Norwegian Defence	Ministry of Defence
Norway	2013	Norwegian Defence	Ministry of Defence
Poland	2003	National Security Strategy of the Republic of Poland	Ministry of National Defence
Poland	2007	National Security Strategy of the Republic of Poland	Ministry of National Defence
Poland	2014	National Security Strategy of the Republic of Poland	Ministry of National Defence
Poland	2017	The Defence Concept of the Republic of Poland	Ministry of National Defence
Poland	2017	Polish Foreign Policy Strategy 2017–2021	Ministry of Foreign Affairs
Portugal	2015	White Paper for International Security and Defence	Ministry of Defence
Romania	2005	National Security Strategy	Ministry of National Defence
Romania	2005	Military Strategy	Ministry of National Defence
Romania	2006	Foreign Relations and National Security	Romanian Embassy in Belgium
Romania	2007	National Security Strategy	Ministry of National Defence
Romania	2015	National Security Strategy 2015–2019	Ministry of National Defence
Romania	2016	The Military Strategy of Romania	Ministry of National Defence
Romania	2017	EU–NATO: Strategic Partnership	Romanian Delegation to NATO
Slovakia	2001	Security Strategy of the Slovak Republic	Ministry of Defence
Slovakia	2001	Defence Strategy	Ministry of Defence
Slovakia	2005	The Defence Strategy of the Slovak Republic	Ministry of National Defence
Slovakia	2005	Yearbook of Foreign Policy of the Slovak Republic	Ministry of Foreign Affairs

Member state/ international organisation	Year of publication	Title of document	Source
Slovakia	2005	Security Strategy of the Slovak Republic	Ministry of National Defence
Slovakia	2017	Draft Defence Strategy of the Slovak Republic	Unofficial document provided by Slovak Permanent Delegation to the EU
Slovenia	2004	Strategy Defence Review: Comprehensive Summary	Ministry of Defence
Slovenia	2010	Resolution on the National Security Strategy of the Republic of Slovenia	Ministry of Defence
Spain	2000	Defence White Paper	Ministry of Defence
Spain	2012	National Defence Directive 2012: For a Necessary and Responsible Defence	Presidencia del Gobierno (Prime Minister)
Spain	2013	The National Security Strategy: Sharing a Common Project	Presidencia del Gobierno (Prime Minister)
Sweden	1999	Sweden's Security in the 21st Century	Björn von Sydow, Ministry of Defence
Sweden	2004	Our Future Defence: The focus of Swedish defence policy 2005–2007	Ministry of Defence
Sweden	2015	Sweden's Defence Policy 2016–2020	Ministry of Defence
Sweden	2017	National Security Strategy	Prime Minister's Office
Turkey	2000	Defence White Paper	Ministry of Defence
Turkey	2007	Defence White Paper	Ministry of Defence
United Kingdom	1998	Strategic Defence Review	House of Commons Defence Committee, Parliament
United Kingdom	2003	Delivering Security in a Changing World: Defence White Paper	Ministry of Defence
United Kingdom	2008	The future of NATO and European Defence, Ninth Report of Session 2007–2008	House of Commons Defence Committee, Parliament
United Kingdom	2010	A Strong Britain in an Age of Uncertainty: The National Security Strategy	HM Government, Prime Minister of the United Kingdom

Member state/ international organisation	Year of publication	Title of document	Source
United Kingdom	2015	National Security Strategy and Strategic Defence and Security Review: A Secure and Prosperous United Kingdom	HM Government, Prime Minister of the United Kingdom
United Kingdom	2017	The United Kingdom's exit from and new partnership with the European Union	HM Government, Prime Minister of the United Kingdom
United Kingdom	2021	Global Britain in a Competitive Age: Integrated Review of Security, Defence, Development and Foreign Policy	HM Government, Prime Minister of the United Kingdom
United States	1988	National Security Strategy of the United States	President of the United States
United States	1990	National Security Strategy of the United States	President of the United States
United States	1994	National Security Strategy of the United States	President of the United States
United States	2000	National Security Strategy of the United States	President of the United States
United States	2006	National Security Strategy of the United States	President of the United States
United States	2010	National Security Strategy of the United States	President of the United States
United States	2015	National Security Strategy of the United States	President of the United States
United States	2017	National Security Strategy of the United States	President of the United States
United States	2021	Interim National Security Strategic Guidance	President of the United States

Appendix C

Overview of member states' participation and contributions to EU-led and NATO-led military operations

Member state	CSDP operations 2003–2020	NATO operations 2009–2020
Albania	Althea, EUFOR Tchad RCA	SFOR, KFOR, Active Endeavour, ISAF, Resolute Support
Austria	Concordia, Artemis, Althea, EUFOR DRC, EUFOR Tchad RCA, MED Sophia, MED Irini	SFOR, KFOR, ISAF, Resolute Support
Belgium	Concordia, Artemis, EUFOR DRC, EUFOR Tchad RCA, Atalanta	Joint Endeavour, SFOR, KFOR, Allied Harmony, ISAF, Enduring Freedom HOA, Ocean Shield, Unified Protector, Resolute Support
Bulgaria	Concordia, Artemis, Althea, Atalanta, EUFOR Tchad RCA, MED Sophia, MED Irini	SFOR, KFOR, Active Endeavour, ISAF, Unified Protector, Resolute Support, Sea Guardian
Canada	Concordia, Artemis	Joint Endeavour, SFOR, KFOR, Allied Harmony, Active Endeavour, ISAF, Enduring Freedom HOA, Ocean Shield, Unified Protector
Croatia	EUFOR Tchad RCA, Atalanta, MED Sophia, MED Irini	KFOR, Active Endeavour, ISAF, Resolute Support, Sea Guardian
Cyprus	Artemis, EUFOR DRC, EUFOR Tchad RCA, Atalanta, MED Sophia, MED Irini	–
Czech Republic	Concordia, EUFOR DRC, EUFOR Tchad RCA, MED Sophia, MED Irini	SFOR, KFOR, Allied Harmony, ISAF, Resolute Support

Member state	CSDP operations 2003–2020	NATO operations 2009–2020
Denmark	–	Joint Endeavour, SFOR, KFOR, Allied Harmony, Active Endeavour, ISAF, Enduring Freedom HOA, Ocean Shield, Unified Protector, Resolute Support
Estonia	Concordia, Artemis, Althea, Atalanta, EUFOR RCA, MED Sophia, MED Irini	SFOR, KFOR, Active Endeavour, ISAF, Resolute Support
Finland	Concordia, Althea, EUFOR DRC, EUFOR Tchad RCA, EUFOR RCA, Atalanta, MED Sophia, MED Irini	Joint Endeavour, SFOR, KFOR, ISAF, Resolute Support
France	Concordia, Artemis, Althea, EUFOR DRC, EUFOR Tchad RCA, EUFOR RCA, Atalanta, MED Sophia, MED Irini	Joint Endeavour, SFOR, KFOR, Allied Harmony, ISAF, Enduring Freedom HOA, Unified Protector, Sea Guardian
Germany	Concordia, Artemis, Althea, EUFOR DRC, EUFOR Tchad RCA, EUFOR RCA, Atalanta, MED Sophia, MED Irini	Joint Endeavour, SFOR, KFOR, Allied Harmony, Active Endeavour, ISAF, Enduring Freedom HOA, Ocean Shield, Resolute Support, Sea Guardian
Greece	Concordia, Artemis, Althea, EUFOR DRC, EUFOR Tchad RCA, Atalanta, MED Sophia, MED Irini	Joint Endeavour, SFOR, KFOR, Allied Harmony, Active Endeavour, ISAF, Enduring Freedom HAO, Ocean Shield, Unified Protector, Resolute Support, Sea Guardian
Hungary	Concordia, Artemis, Althea, EUFOR DRC, EUFOR Tchad RCA, Atalanta, MED Sophia, MED Irini	SFOR, KFOR, Allied Harmony, ISAF, Resolute Support
Iceland	Concordia	Joint Endeavour, SFOR, KFOR, Allied Harmony, ISAF, (Resolute Support)
Ireland	Artemis, Althea, EUFOR DRC, EUFOR Tchad RCA, Atalanta, MED Sophia, MED Irini	SFOR, KFOR, ISAF, (Resolute Support)
Italy	Concordia, Artemis, Althea, EUFOR DRC, EUFOR Tchad RCA, EUFOR RCA, Atalanta, MED Sophia, MED Irini	Joint Endeavour, SFOR, KFOR, Allied Harmony, Active Endeavour, ISAF, Enduring Freedom HOA, Ocean Shield, Unified Protector, Resolute Support, Sea Guardian
Latvia	Concordia, Althea, EUFOR RCA, MED Sophia, MED Irini	SFOR, KFOR, ISAF, Resolute Support

Member state	CSDP operations 2003–2020	NATO operations 2009–2020
Lithuania	Concordia, Althea, EUFOR DRC, EUFOR Tchad RCA, MED Sophia, MED Irini	SFOR, KFOR, ISAF, Resolute Support
Luxembourg	Concordia, Althea, EUFOR DRC, EUFOR Tchad RCA, Atalanta, MED Sophia, MED Irini	Joint Endeavour, SFOR, KFOR, Allied Harmony, ISAF, Resolute Support
Malta	Atalanta, MED Sophia, (MED Irini)	(Unified Protector)
Netherlands	Concordia, Artemis, Althea, EUFOR DRC, EUFOR Tchad RCA, EUFOR RCA, Atalanta, MED Sophia, MED Irini	Joint Endeavour, SFOR, KFOR, Allied Harmony, ISAF, Enduring Freedom HAO, Ocean Shield, Unified Protector, Resolute Support
Norway	Concordia, Atalanta	Joint Endeavour, SFOR, KFOR, Allied Harmony, Active Endeavour, ISAF, Ocean Shield, Unified Protector, Resolute Support
Poland	Concordia, Althea, EUFOR DRC, EUFOR Tchad RCA, EUFOR RCA, Atalanta, MED Sophia, MED Irini	SFOR, KFOR, Allied Harmony, Active Endeavour, ISAF, Resolute Support
Portugal	Concordia, Artemis, Althea, EUFOR DRC, EUFOR Tchad RCA, EUFOR RCA, Atalanta, MED Sophia, MED Irini	Joint Endeavour, SFOR, KFOR, Allied Harmony, Active Endeavour, ISAF, Enduring Freedom HOA, Ocean Shield, Resolute Support, Sea Guardian
Romania	Concordia, Artemis, Althea, EUFOR DRC, EUFOR Tchad RCA, EUFOR RCA, Atalanta, MED Sophia, MED Irini	SFOR, KFOR, ISAF, Unified Protector, Resolute Support, Sea Guardian
Slovakia	Concordia, Althea, EUFOR DRC, EUFOR Tchad RCA, MED Sophia	SFOR, KFOR, ISAF, Resolute Support
Slovenia	Concordia, Althea, EUFOR DRC, EUFOR Tchad RCA, Atalanta, MED Sophia, MED Irini	SFOR, KFOR, ISAF, Resolute Support
Spain	Concordia, Artemis, Althea, EUFOR DRC, EUFOR Tchad RCA, EUFOR RCA, Atalanta, MED Sophia	Joint Endeavour, SFOR, KFOR, Allied Harmony, Active Endeavour, ISAF, Enduring Freedom HOA, Ocean Shield, Unified Protector, Resolute Support, Sea Guardian
Sweden	Concordia, Artemis, EUFOR DRC, EUFOR Tchad RCA, Atalanta, MED Sophia, MED Irini	Joint Endeavour, SFOR, KFOR, ISAF, Unified Protector, Resolute Support

Member state	CSDP operations 2003–2020	NATO operations 2009–2020
Turkey	Concordia, Althea, EUFOR DRC	Joint Endeavour, SFOR, KFOR, Allied Harmony, Active Endeavour, ISAF, Enduring Freedom HOA, Ocean Shield, Unified Protector, Resolute Support, Sea Guardian
United Kingdom	Concordia, Artemis, Althea, EUFOR DRC, EUFOR Tchad RCA, Atalanta, MED Sophia	Joint Endeavour, SFOR, KFOR, Allied Harmony, Active Endeavour, ISAF, Enduring Freedom HOA, Ocean Shield, Unified Protector, Resolute Support, Sea Guardian
United States	–	Joint Endeavour, SFOR, KFOR, Allied Harmony, Active Endeavour, ISAF, Enduring Freedom HOA, Ocean Shield, Unified Protector, Resolute Support, Sea Guardian

Index

Lightning Source UK Ltd.
Milton Keynes UK
UKHW021957110422
401434UK00003B/44